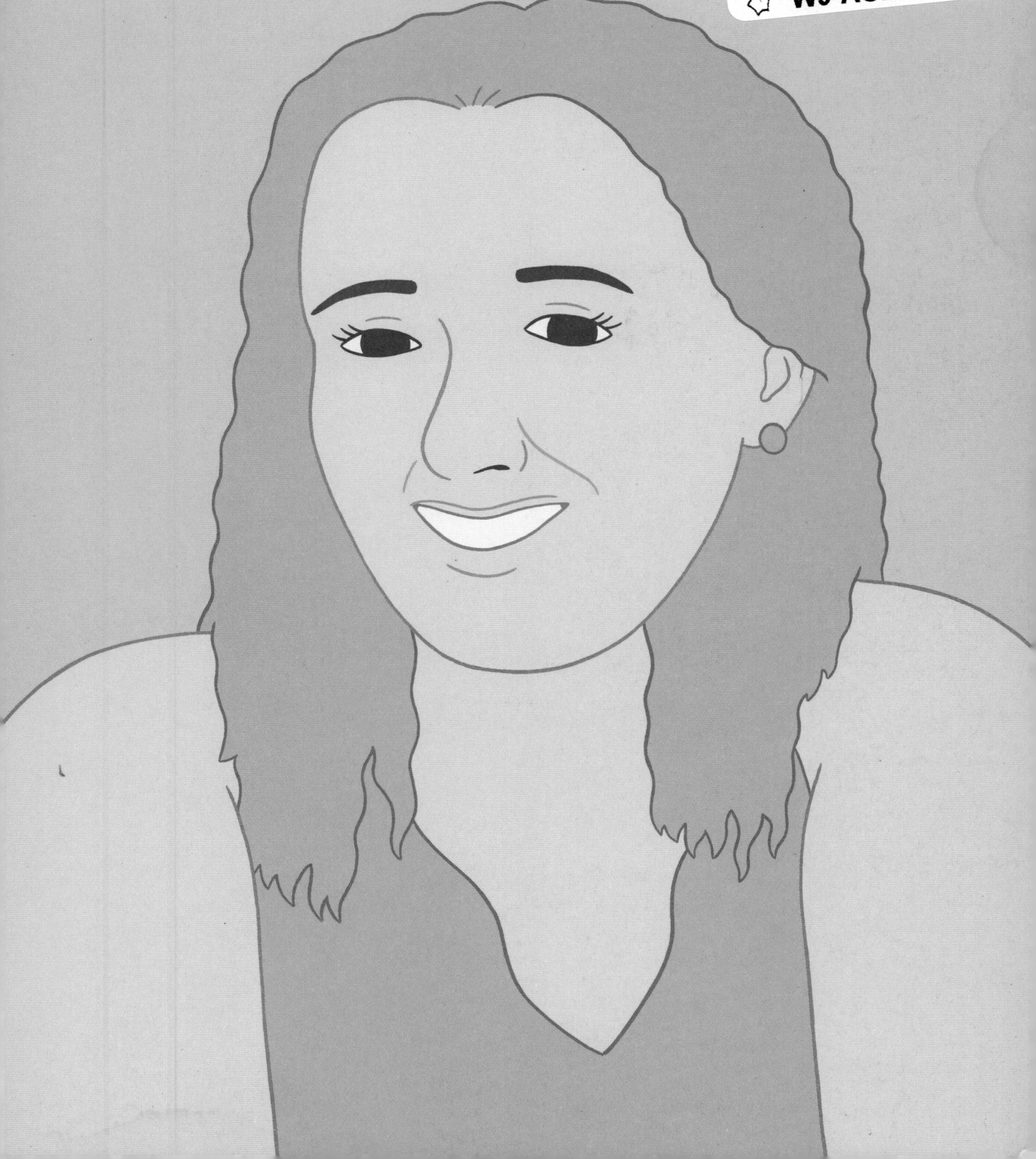

DRAWNANDQUARTERLY.COM

FIRST EDITION: JANUARY 2016. SECOND PRINTING: JANUARY 2017.
THIRD PRINTING: OCTOBER 2018. PRINTED IN CHINA.

10 9 8 7 6 5 4 3

LIBRARY AND ARCHIVES CANADA CATALOGUING IN PUBLICATION
DRNASO, NICK, AUTHOR, ILLUSTRATOR
        BEVERLY/NICK DRNASO.
ISBN 978-1-77046-225-0 (PAPERBACK)
        1. TEENAGERS - COMIC BOOKS, STRIPS, ETC.
        2. SUBURBS - COMIC BOOKS. STRIPS, ETC.
        3. GRAPHIC NOVELS. I. TITLE.
PN6727. D76B48 2016   741.5'973   C2015-904931-8

PUBLISHED IN THE USA BY DRAWN & QUARTERLY,
A CLIENT PUBLISHER OF FARRAR, STRAUS AND GIROUX; ORDERS: 888-330-8477.
PUBLISHED IN CANADA BY DRAWN & QUARTERLY,
A CLIENT PUBLISHER OF RAINCOAST BOOKS; ORDERS: 800-663-5714.
PUBLISHED IN THE UNITED KINGDOM BY DRAWN & QUARTERLY,
A CLIENT PUBLISHER OF PUBLISHERS GROUP UK; ORDERS: INFO@PGUK.CO.UK.

LOVE & THANKS: SARAH LEITTEN, IVAN BRUNETTI, CHUCK FORSMAN, RANDY,
CHRIS WARE, CHRIS OLIVEROS, THE NUDD FAMILY, ONSMITH, JUSTIN WITTE,
TRACY HURREN, ANDREW POCIUS, AND CHRIS & MARILYN DRNASO.

Beverly

BY NICK DRNASO
DRAWN & QUARTERLY

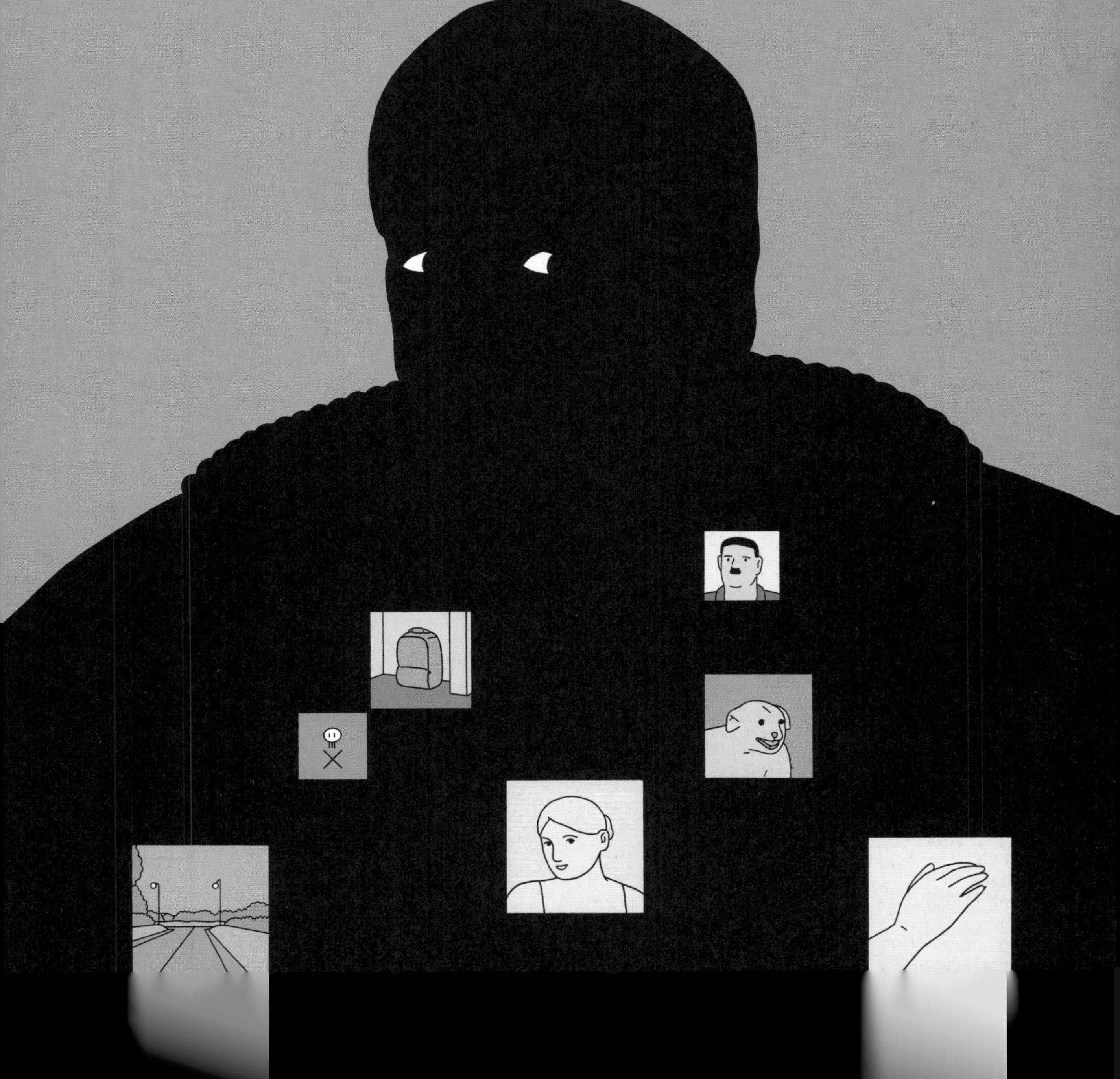

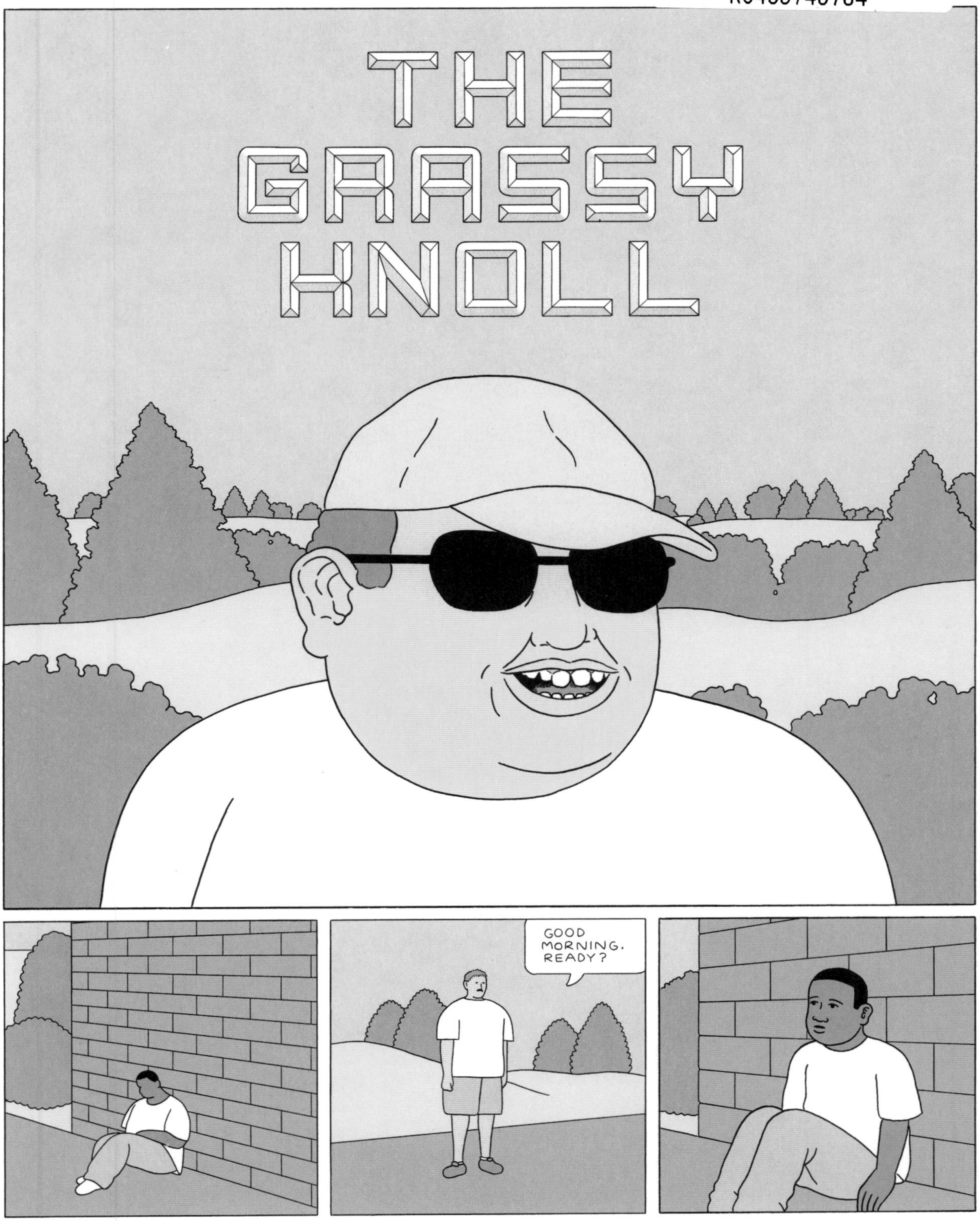
THE GRASSY KNOLL
GOOD MORNING. READY?

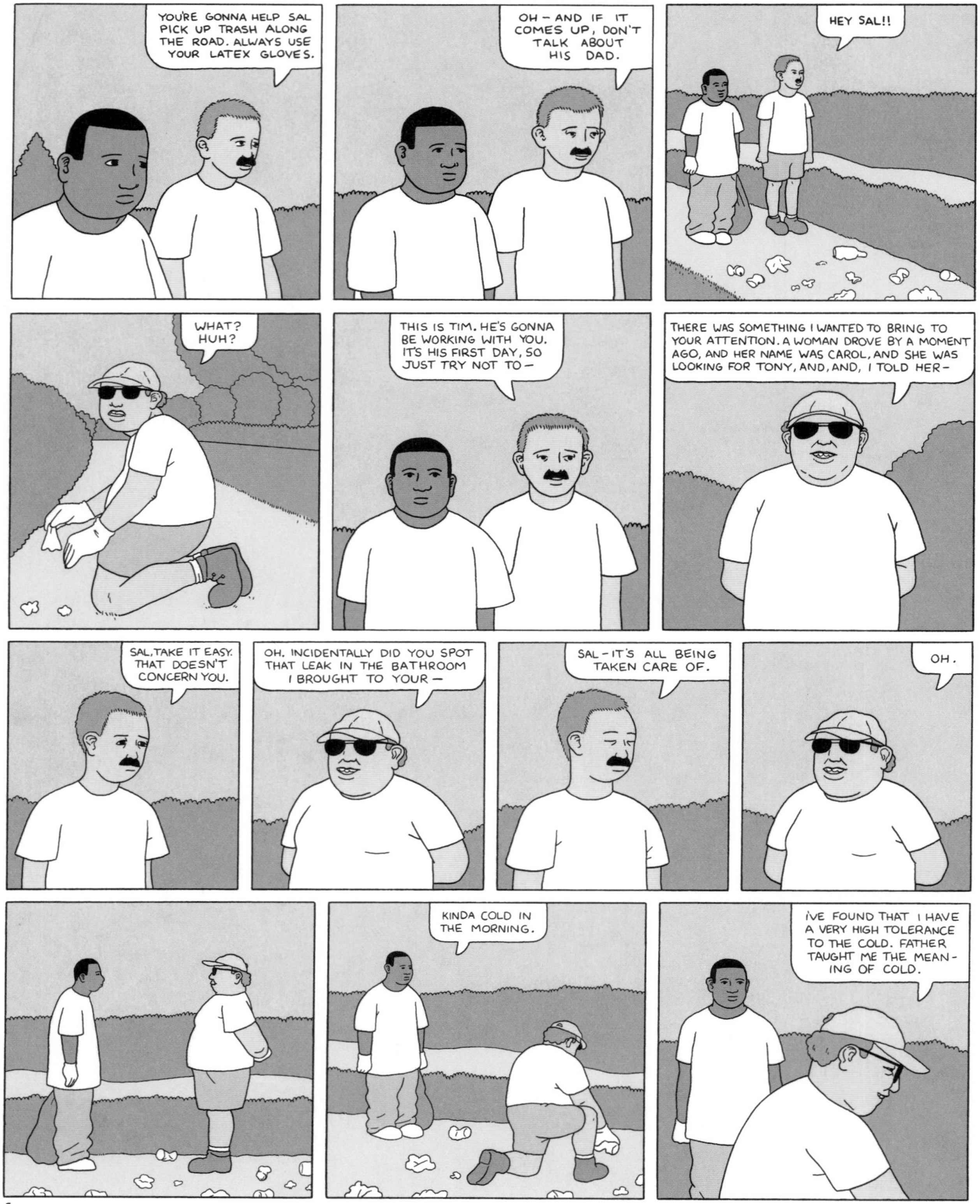
YOU'RE GONNA HELP SAL PICK UP TRASH ALONG THE ROAD. ALWAYS USE YOUR LATEX GLOVES.
OH – AND IF IT COMES UP, DON'T TALK ABOUT HIS DAD.
HEY SAL!!
WHAT? HUH?
THIS IS TIM. HE'S GONNA BE WORKING WITH YOU. IT'S HIS FIRST DAY, SO JUST TRY NOT TO –
THERE WAS SOMETHING I WANTED TO BRING TO YOUR ATTENTION. A WOMAN DROVE BY A MOMENT AGO, AND HER NAME WAS CAROL, AND SHE WAS LOOKING FOR TONY, AND, AND, I TOLD HER –
SAL, TAKE IT EASY. THAT DOESN'T CONCERN YOU.
OH. INCIDENTALLY DID YOU SPOT THAT LEAK IN THE BATHROOM I BROUGHT TO YOUR –
SAL – IT'S ALL BEING TAKEN CARE OF.
OH.
KINDA COLD IN THE MORNING.
I'VE FOUND THAT I HAVE A VERY HIGH TOLERANCE TO THE COLD. FATHER TAUGHT ME THE MEANING OF COLD.

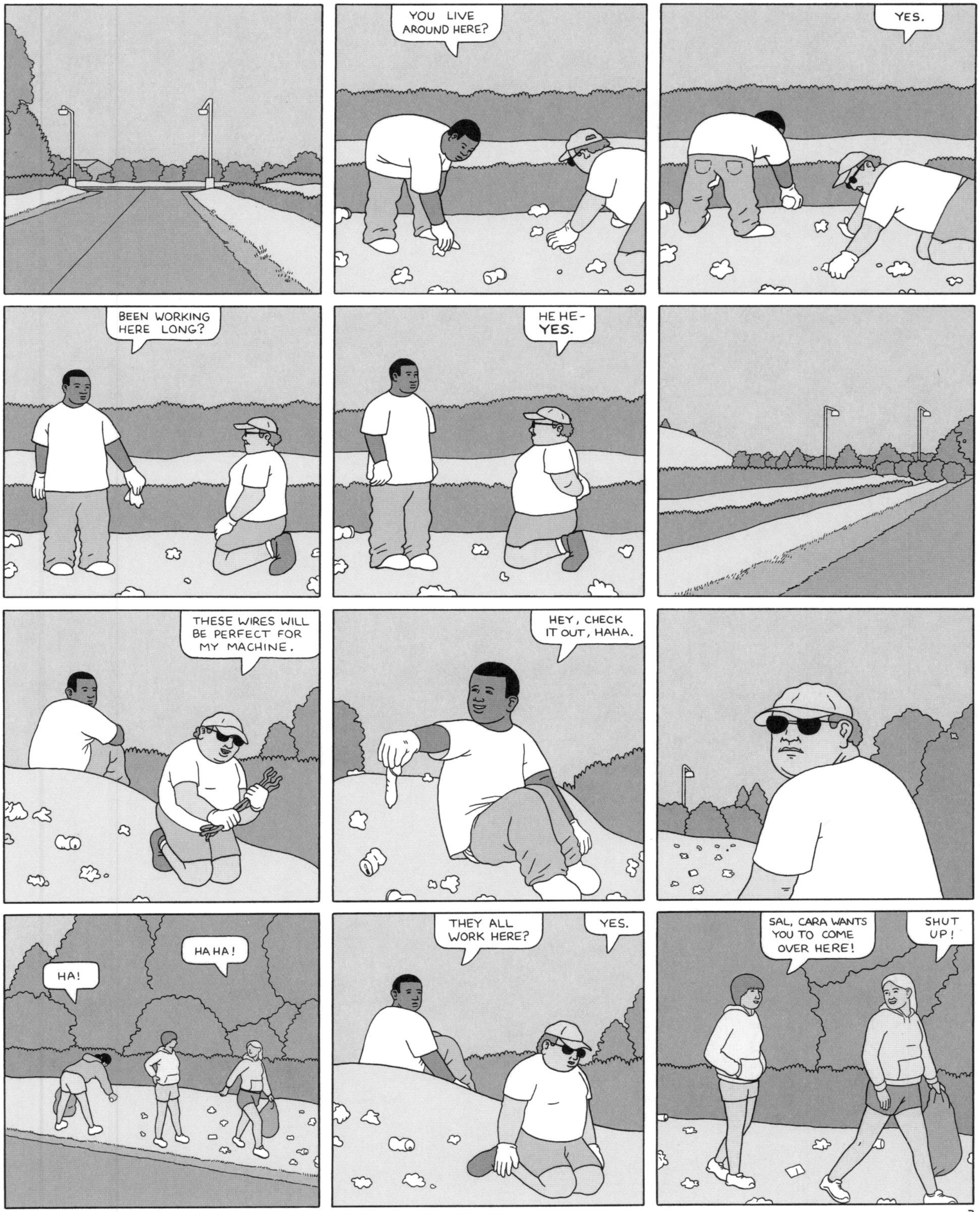
YOU LIVE AROUND HERE?
YES.
BEEN WORKING HERE LONG?
HE HE- YES.
THESE WIRES WILL BE PERFECT FOR MY MACHINE.
HEY, CHECK IT OUT, HAHA.
HA!
HA HA!
THEY ALL WORK HERE?
YES.
SAL, CARA WANTS YOU TO COME OVER HERE!
SHUT UP!

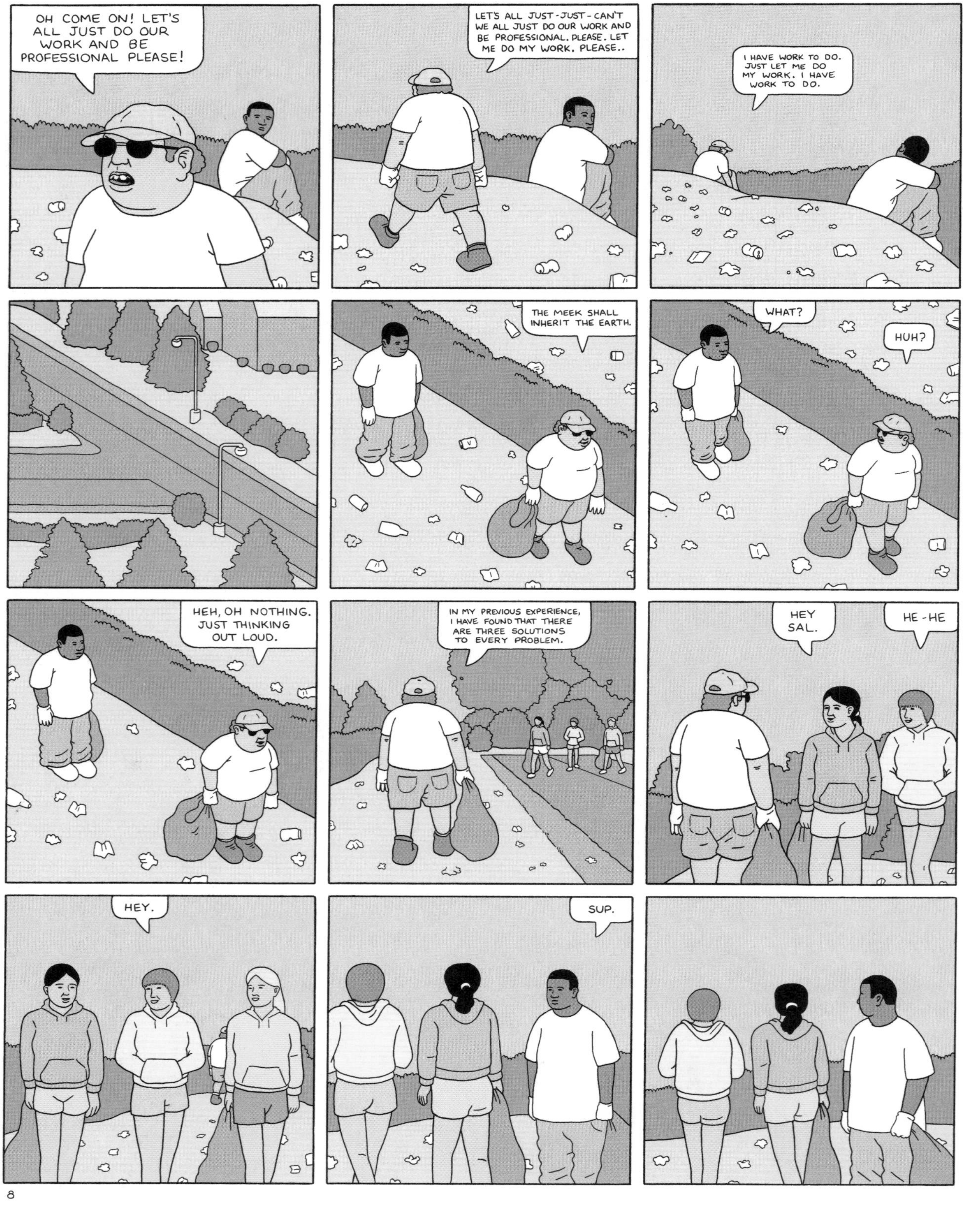
OH COME ON! LET'S ALL JUST DO OUR WORK AND BE PROFESSIONAL PLEASE!
LET'S ALL JUST-JUST-CAN'T WE ALL JUST DO OUR WORK AND BE PROFESSIONAL. PLEASE. LET ME DO MY WORK. PLEASE..
I HAVE WORK TO DO. JUST LET ME DO MY WORK. I HAVE WORK TO DO.
THE MEEK SHALL INHERIT THE EARTH.
WHAT?
HUH?
HEH, OH NOTHING. JUST THINKING OUT LOUD.
IN MY PREVIOUS EXPERIENCE, I HAVE FOUND THAT THERE ARE THREE SOLUTIONS TO EVERY PROBLEM.
HEY SAL.
HE-HE
HEY.
SUP.

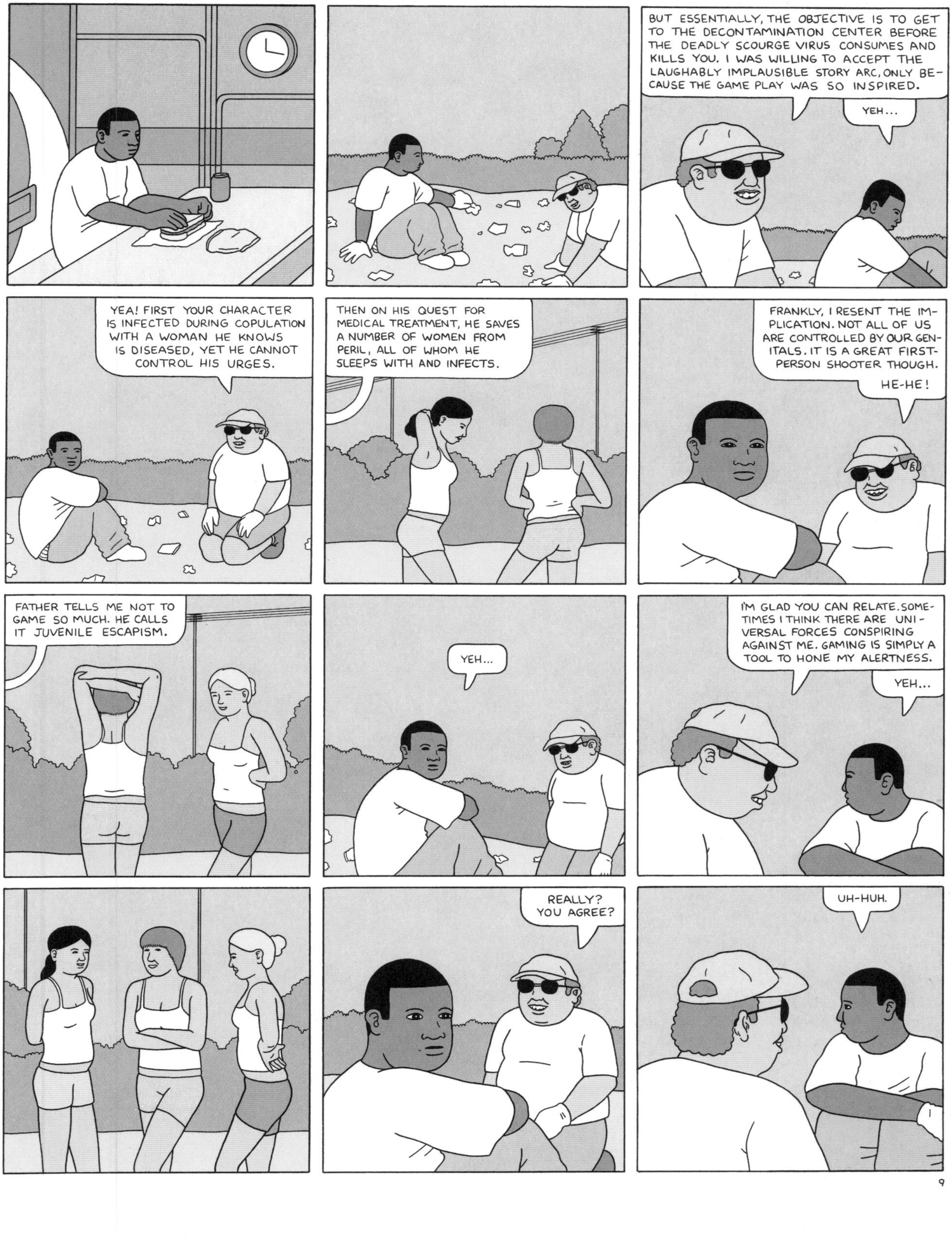
BUT ESSENTIALLY, THE OBJECTIVE IS TO GET TO THE DECONTAMINATION CENTER BEFORE THE DEADLY SCOURGE VIRUS CONSUMES AND KILLS YOU. I WAS WILLING TO ACCEPT THE LAUGHABLY IMPLAUSIBLE STORY ARC, ONLY BECAUSE THE GAME PLAY WAS SO INSPIRED.
YEH...
YEA! FIRST YOUR CHARACTER IS INFECTED DURING COPULATION WITH A WOMAN HE KNOWS IS DISEASED, YET HE CANNOT CONTROL HIS URGES.
THEN ON HIS QUEST FOR MEDICAL TREATMENT, HE SAVES A NUMBER OF WOMEN FROM PERIL, ALL OF WHOM HE SLEEPS WITH AND INFECTS.
FRANKLY, I RESENT THE IMPLICATION. NOT ALL OF US ARE CONTROLLED BY OUR GENITALS. IT IS A GREAT FIRST-PERSON SHOOTER THOUGH.
HE-HE!
FATHER TELLS ME NOT TO GAME SO MUCH. HE CALLS IT JUVENILE ESCAPISM.
YEH...
I'M GLAD YOU CAN RELATE. SOMETIMES I THINK THERE ARE UNIVERSAL FORCES CONSPIRING AGAINST ME. GAMING IS SIMPLY A TOOL TO HONE MY ALERTNESS.
YEH...
REALLY? YOU AGREE?
UH-HUH.

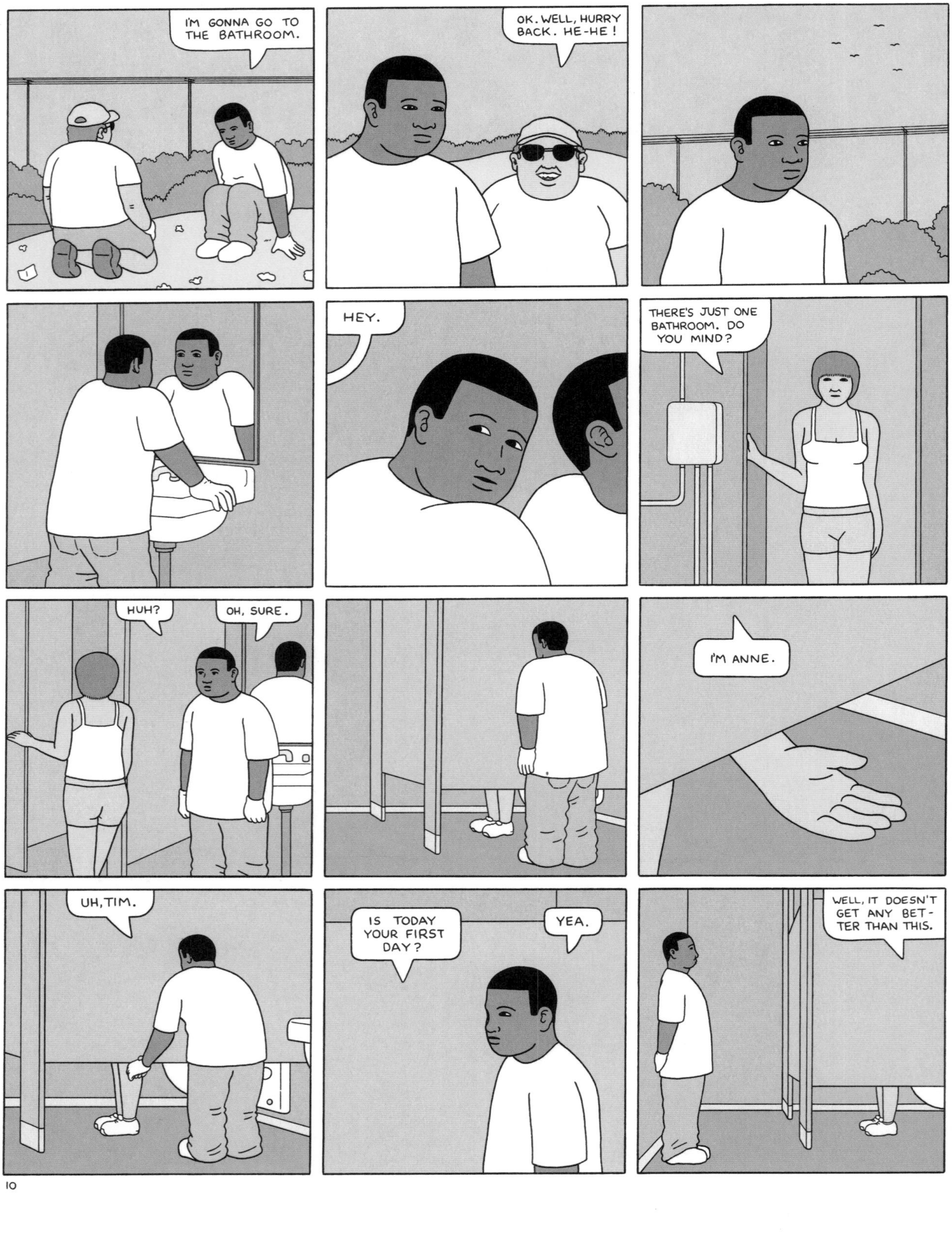
I'M GONNA GO TO THE BATHROOM.
OK. WELL, HURRY BACK. HE-HE!
HEY.
THERE'S JUST ONE BATHROOM. DO YOU MIND?
HUH?
OH, SURE.
I'M ANNE.
UH, TIM.
IS TODAY YOUR FIRST DAY?
YEA.
WELL, IT DOESN'T GET ANY BETTER THAN THIS.

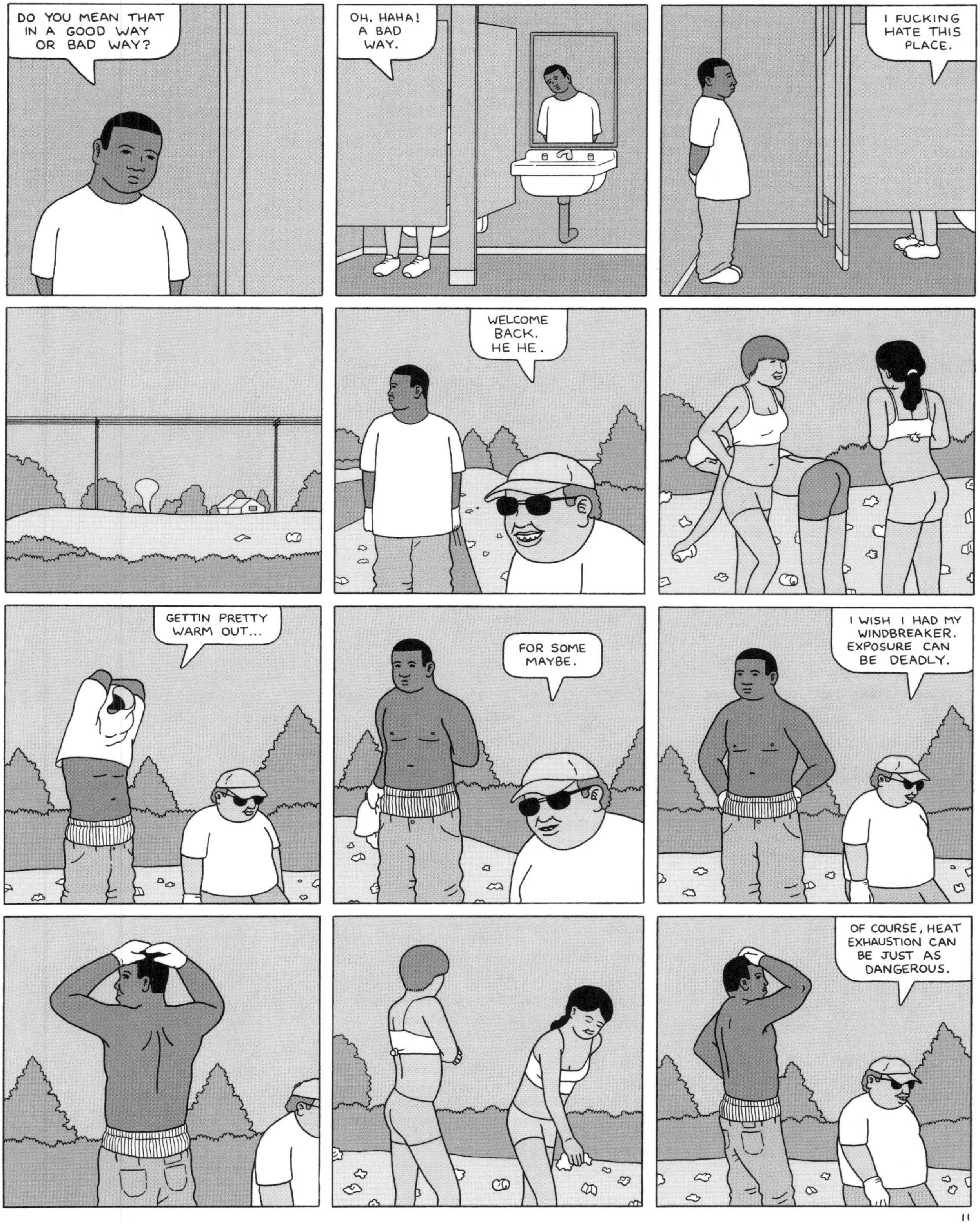
DO YOU MEAN THAT IN A GOOD WAY OR BAD WAY?
OH. HAHA! A BAD WAY.
I FUCKING HATE THIS PLACE.
WELCOME BACK. HE HE.
GETTIN PRETTY WARM OUT...
FOR SOME MAYBE.
I WISH I HAD MY WINDBREAKER. EXPOSURE CAN BE DEADLY.
OF COURSE, HEAT EXHAUSTION CAN BE JUST AS DANGEROUS.

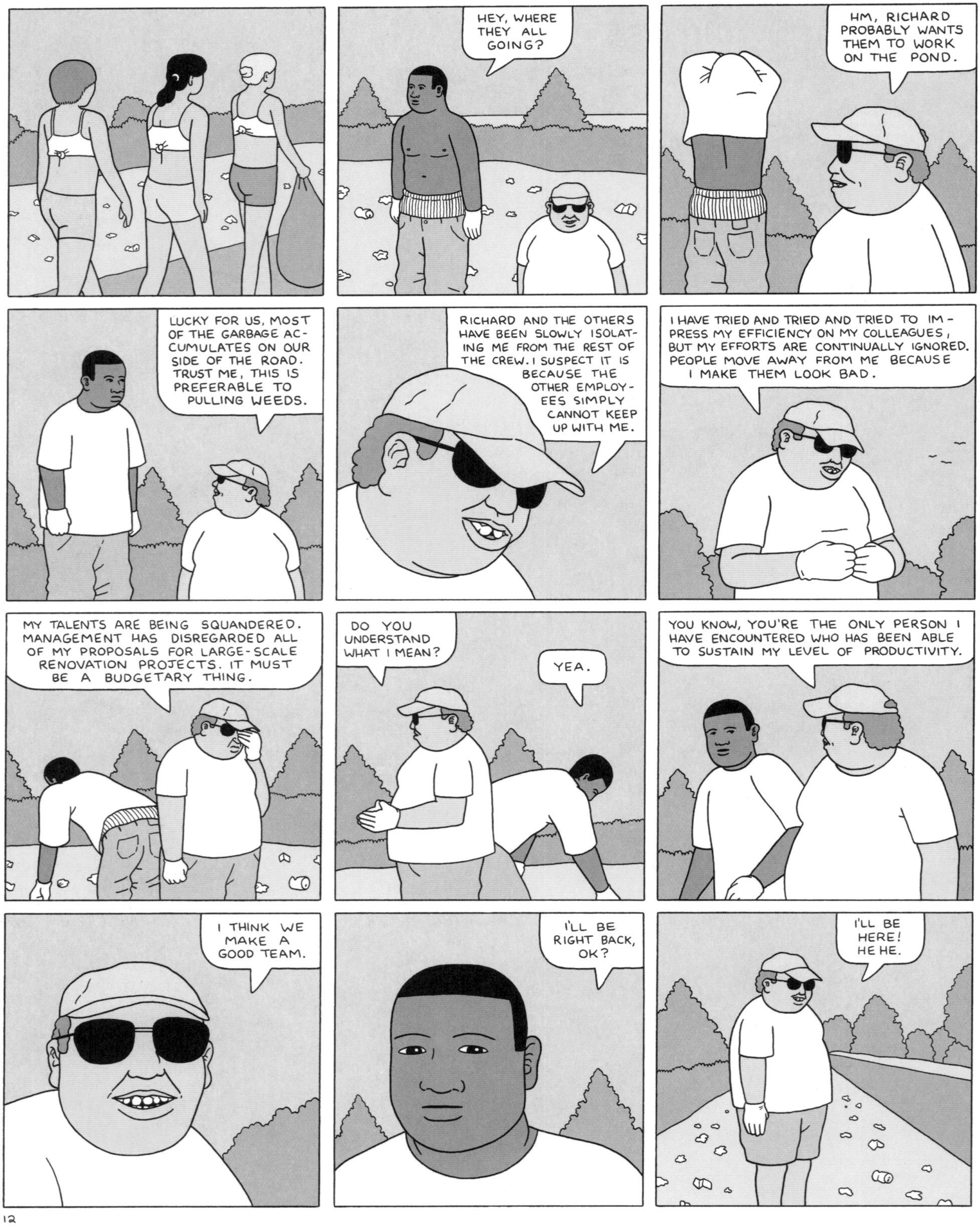
HEY, WHERE THEY ALL GOING?
HM, RICHARD PROBABLY WANTS THEM TO WORK ON THE POND.
LUCKY FOR US, MOST OF THE GARBAGE AC-CUMULATES ON OUR SIDE OF THE ROAD. TRUST ME, THIS IS PREFERABLE TO PULLING WEEDS.
RICHARD AND THE OTHERS HAVE BEEN SLOWLY ISOLAT-ING ME FROM THE REST OF THE CREW. I SUSPECT IT IS BECAUSE THE OTHER EMPLOY-EES SIMPLY CANNOT KEEP UP WITH ME.
I HAVE TRIED AND TRIED AND TRIED TO IM-PRESS MY EFFICIENCY ON MY COLLEAGUES, BUT MY EFFORTS ARE CONTINUALLY IGNORED. PEOPLE MOVE AWAY FROM ME BECAUSE I MAKE THEM LOOK BAD.
MY TALENTS ARE BEING SQUANDERED. MANAGEMENT HAS DISREGARDED ALL OF MY PROPOSALS FOR LARGE-SCALE RENOVATION PROJECTS. IT MUST BE A BUDGETARY THING.
DO YOU UNDERSTAND WHAT I MEAN?
YEA.
YOU KNOW, YOU'RE THE ONLY PERSON I HAVE ENCOUNTERED WHO HAS BEEN ABLE TO SUSTAIN MY LEVEL OF PRODUCTIVITY.
I THINK WE MAKE A GOOD TEAM.
I'LL BE RIGHT BACK, OK?
I'LL BE HERE! HE HE.

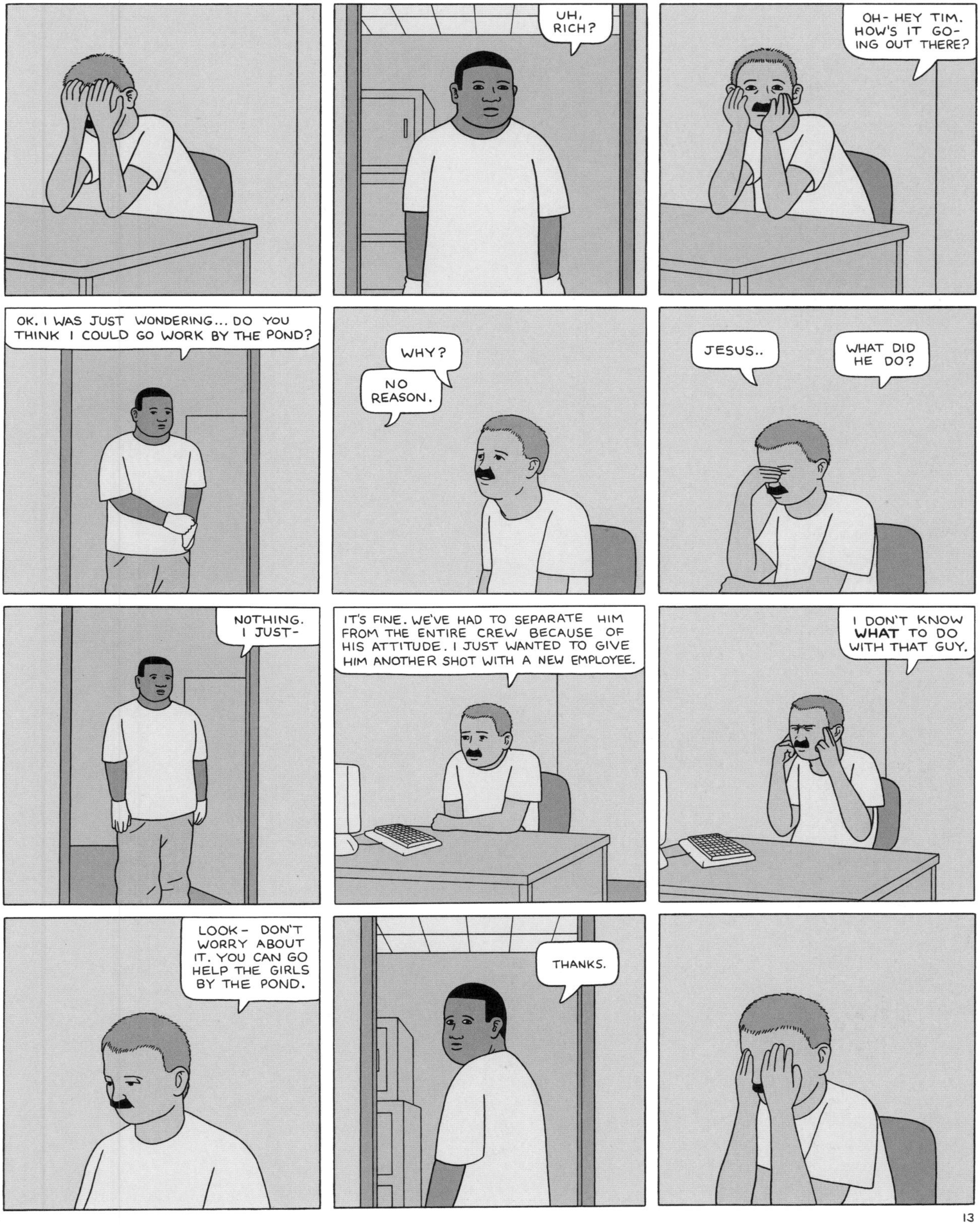
UH, RICH?
OH- HEY TIM. HOW'S IT GOING OUT THERE?
OK. I WAS JUST WONDERING... DO YOU THINK I COULD GO WORK BY THE POND?
WHY?
NO REASON.
JESUS..
WHAT DID HE DO?
NOTHING. I JUST-
IT'S FINE. WE'VE HAD TO SEPARATE HIM FROM THE ENTIRE CREW BECAUSE OF HIS ATTITUDE. I JUST WANTED TO GIVE HIM ANOTHER SHOT WITH A NEW EMPLOYEE.
I DON'T KNOW **WHAT** TO DO WITH THAT GUY.
LOOK- DON'T WORRY ABOUT IT. YOU CAN GO HELP THE GIRLS BY THE POND.
THANKS.

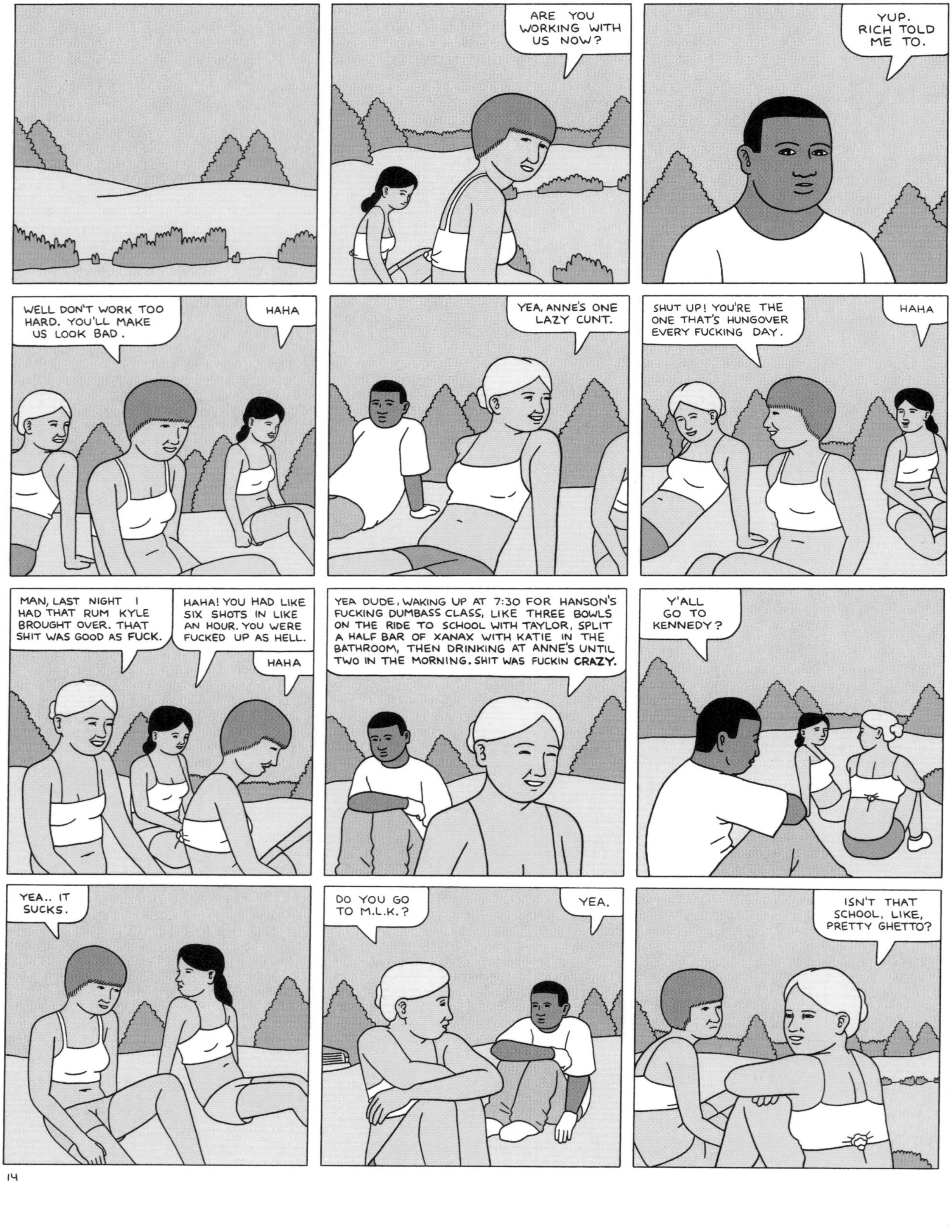
ARE YOU WORKING WITH US NOW?
YUP. RICH TOLD ME TO.
WELL DON'T WORK TOO HARD. YOU'LL MAKE US LOOK BAD.
HAHA
YEA, ANNE'S ONE LAZY CUNT.
SHUT UP! YOU'RE THE ONE THAT'S HUNGOVER EVERY FUCKING DAY.
HAHA
MAN, LAST NIGHT I HAD THAT RUM KYLE BROUGHT OVER. THAT SHIT WAS GOOD AS FUCK.
HAHA! YOU HAD LIKE SIX SHOTS IN LIKE AN HOUR. YOU WERE FUCKED UP AS HELL.
HAHA
YEA DUDE, WAKING UP AT 7:30 FOR HANSON'S FUCKING DUMBASS CLASS, LIKE THREE BOWLS ON THE RIDE TO SCHOOL WITH TAYLOR, SPLIT A HALF BAR OF XANAX WITH KATIE IN THE BATHROOM, THEN DRINKING AT ANNE'S UNTIL TWO IN THE MORNING. SHIT WAS FUCKIN CRAZY.
Y'ALL GO TO KENNEDY?
YEA.. IT SUCKS.
DO YOU GO TO M.L.K.?
YEA.
ISN'T THAT SCHOOL, LIKE, PRETTY GHETTO?

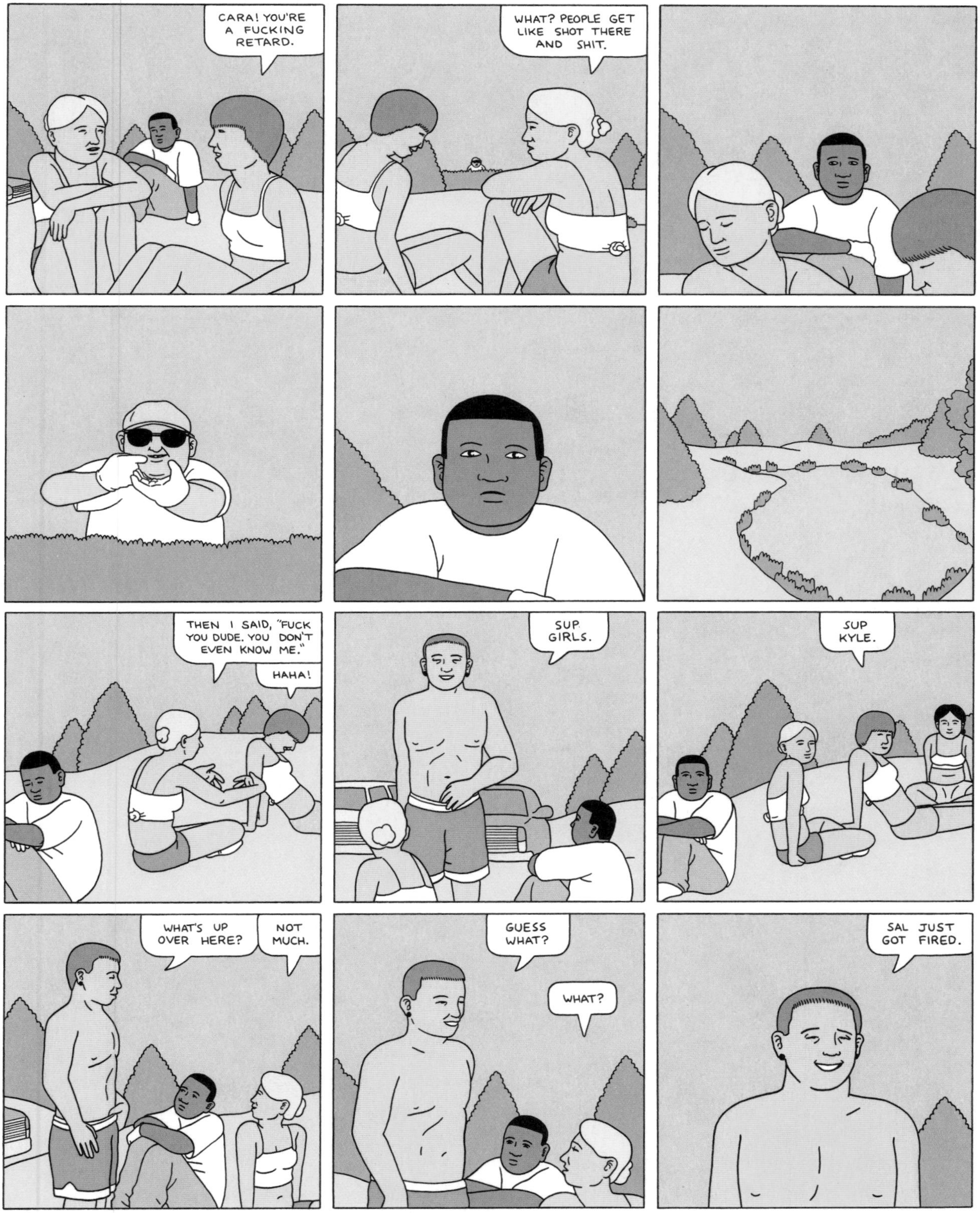
CARA! YOU'RE A FUCKING RETARD.
WHAT? PEOPLE GET LIKE SHOT THERE AND SHIT.
THEN I SAID, "FUCK YOU DUDE. YOU DON'T EVEN KNOW ME."
HAHA!
SUP GIRLS.
SUP KYLE.
WHAT'S UP OVER HERE?
NOT MUCH.
GUESS WHAT?
WHAT?
SAL JUST GOT FIRED.

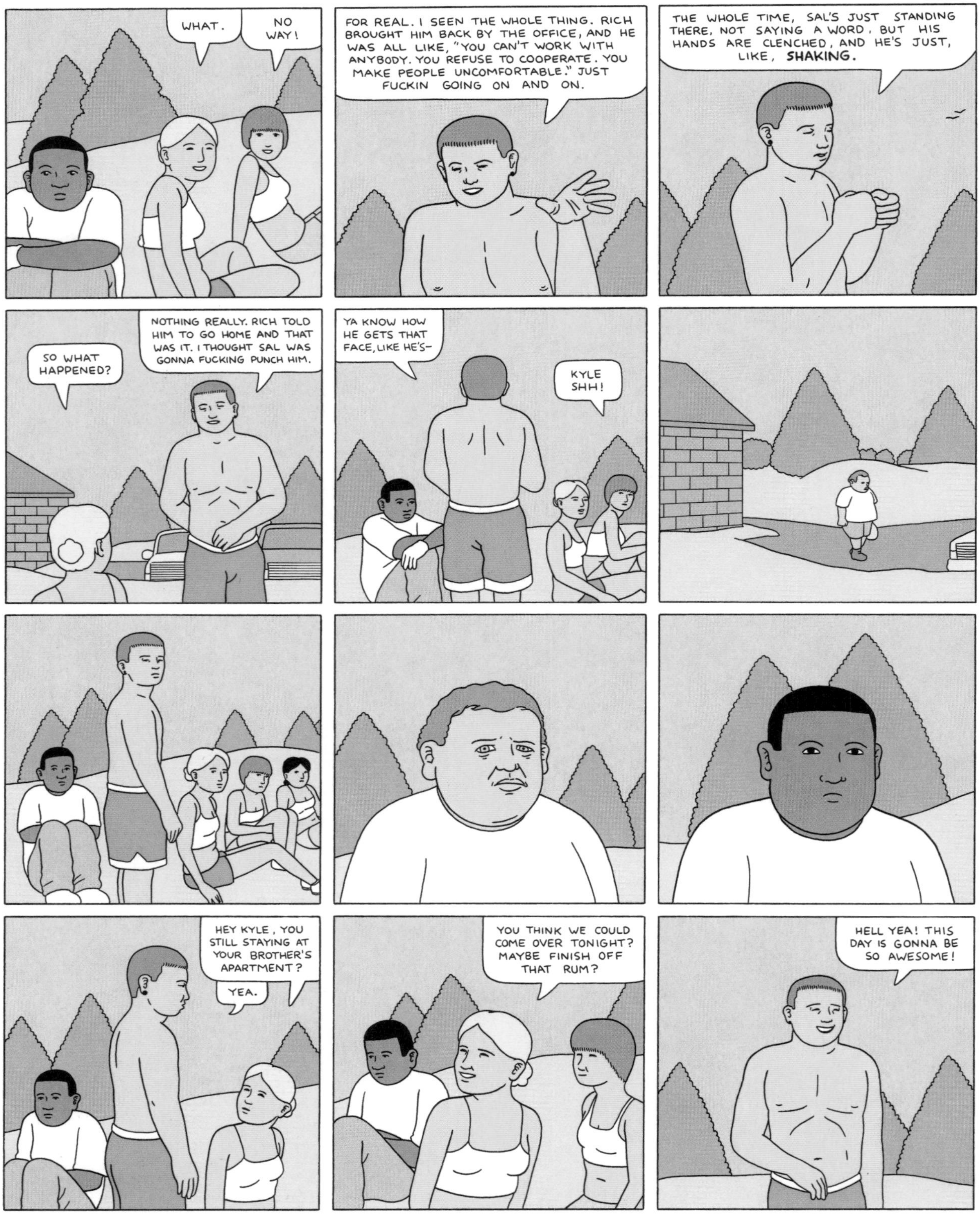
WHAT.
NO WAY!
FOR REAL. I SEEN THE WHOLE THING. RICH BROUGHT HIM BACK BY THE OFFICE, AND HE WAS ALL LIKE, "YOU CAN'T WORK WITH ANYBODY. YOU REFUSE TO COOPERATE. YOU MAKE PEOPLE UNCOMFORTABLE." JUST FUCKIN GOING ON AND ON.
THE WHOLE TIME, SAL'S JUST STANDING THERE, NOT SAYING A WORD, BUT HIS HANDS ARE CLENCHED, AND HE'S JUST, LIKE, **SHAKING.**
SO WHAT HAPPENED?
NOTHING REALLY. RICH TOLD HIM TO GO HOME AND THAT WAS IT. I THOUGHT SAL WAS GONNA FUCKING PUNCH HIM.
YA KNOW HOW HE GETS THAT FACE, LIKE HE'S—
KYLE SHH!
HEY KYLE, YOU STILL STAYING AT YOUR BROTHER'S APARTMENT?
YEA.
YOU THINK WE COULD COME OVER TONIGHT? MAYBE FINISH OFF THAT RUM?
HELL YEA! THIS DAY IS GONNA BE SO AWESOME!

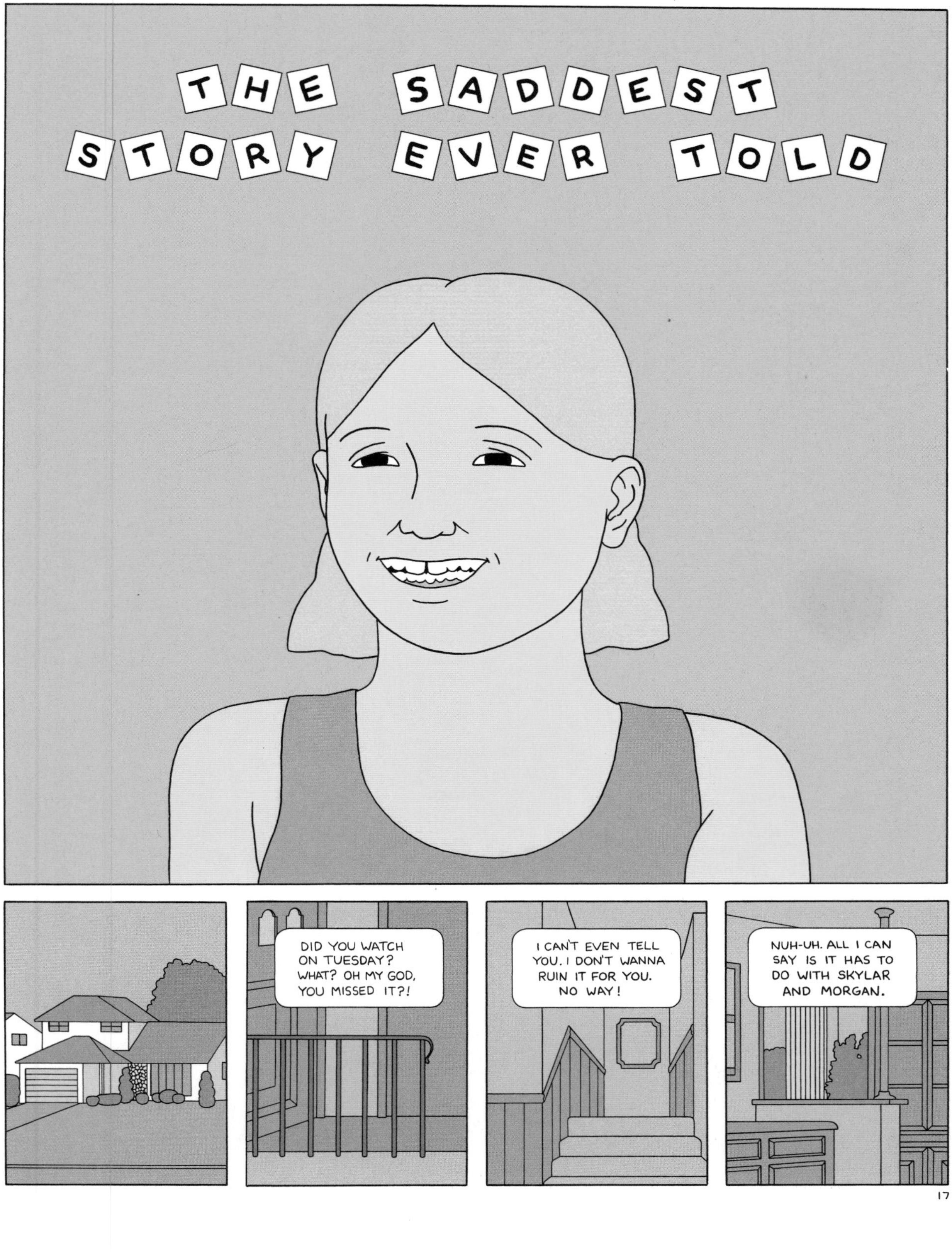
THE SADDEST STORY EVER TOLD
DID YOU WATCH ON TUESDAY? WHAT? OH MY GOD, YOU MISSED IT?!
I CAN'T EVEN TELL YOU. I DON'T WANNA RUIN IT FOR YOU. NO WAY!
NUH-UH. ALL I CAN SAY IS IT HAS TO DO WITH SKYLAR AND MORGAN.

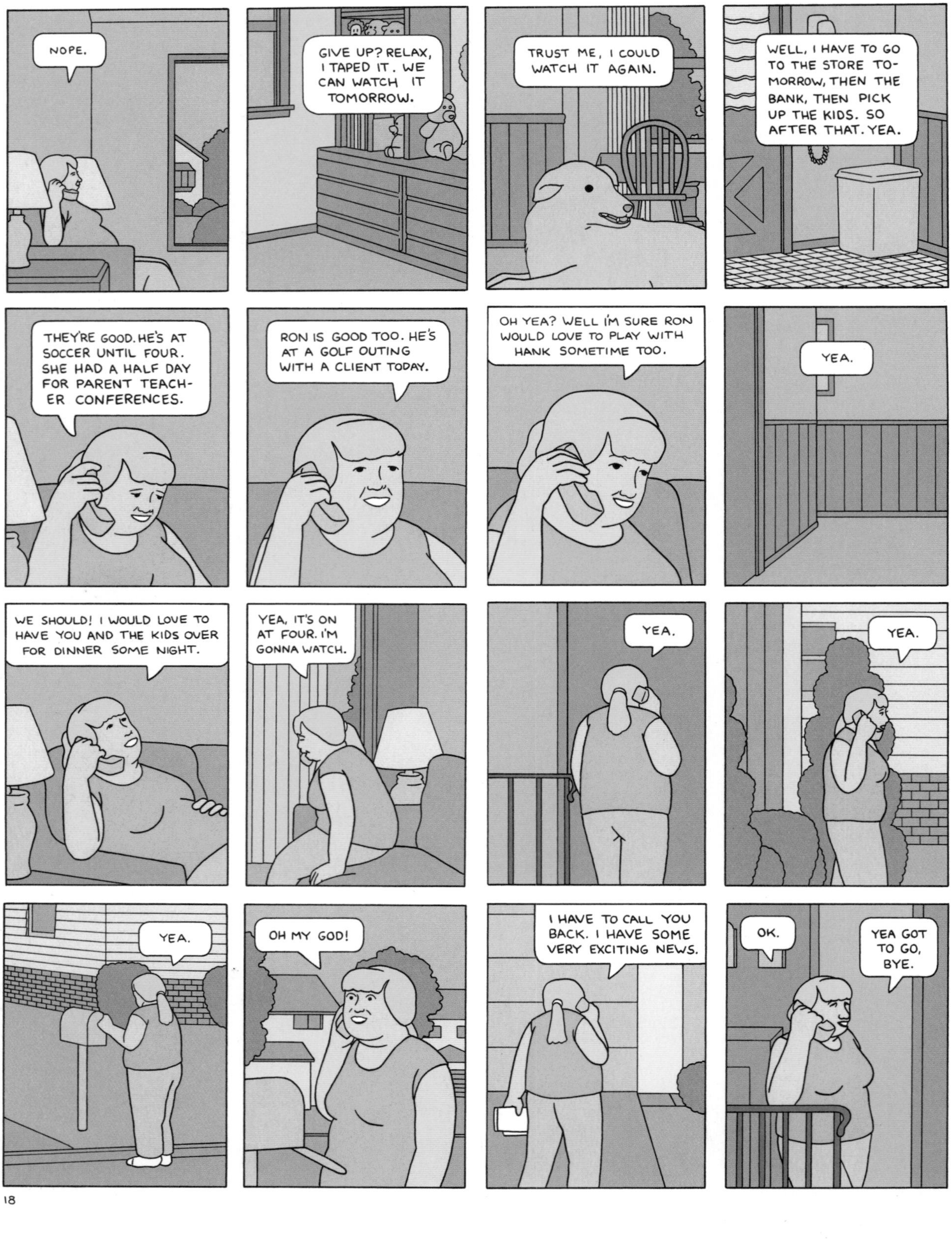
NOPE.
GIVE UP? RELAX, I TAPED IT. WE CAN WATCH IT TOMORROW.
TRUST ME, I COULD WATCH IT AGAIN.
WELL, I HAVE TO GO TO THE STORE TO-MORROW, THEN THE BANK, THEN PICK UP THE KIDS. SO AFTER THAT. YEA.
THEY'RE GOOD. HE'S AT SOCCER UNTIL FOUR. SHE HAD A HALF DAY FOR PARENT TEACH-ER CONFERENCES.
RON IS GOOD TOO. HE'S AT A GOLF OUTING WITH A CLIENT TODAY.
OH YEA? WELL I'M SURE RON WOULD LOVE TO PLAY WITH HANK SOMETIME TOO.
YEA.
WE SHOULD! I WOULD LOVE TO HAVE YOU AND THE KIDS OVER FOR DINNER SOME NIGHT.
YEA, IT'S ON AT FOUR. I'M GONNA WATCH.
YEA.
YEA.
YEA.
OH MY GOD!
I HAVE TO CALL YOU BACK. I HAVE SOME VERY EXCITING NEWS.
OK.
YEA GOT TO GO, BYE.

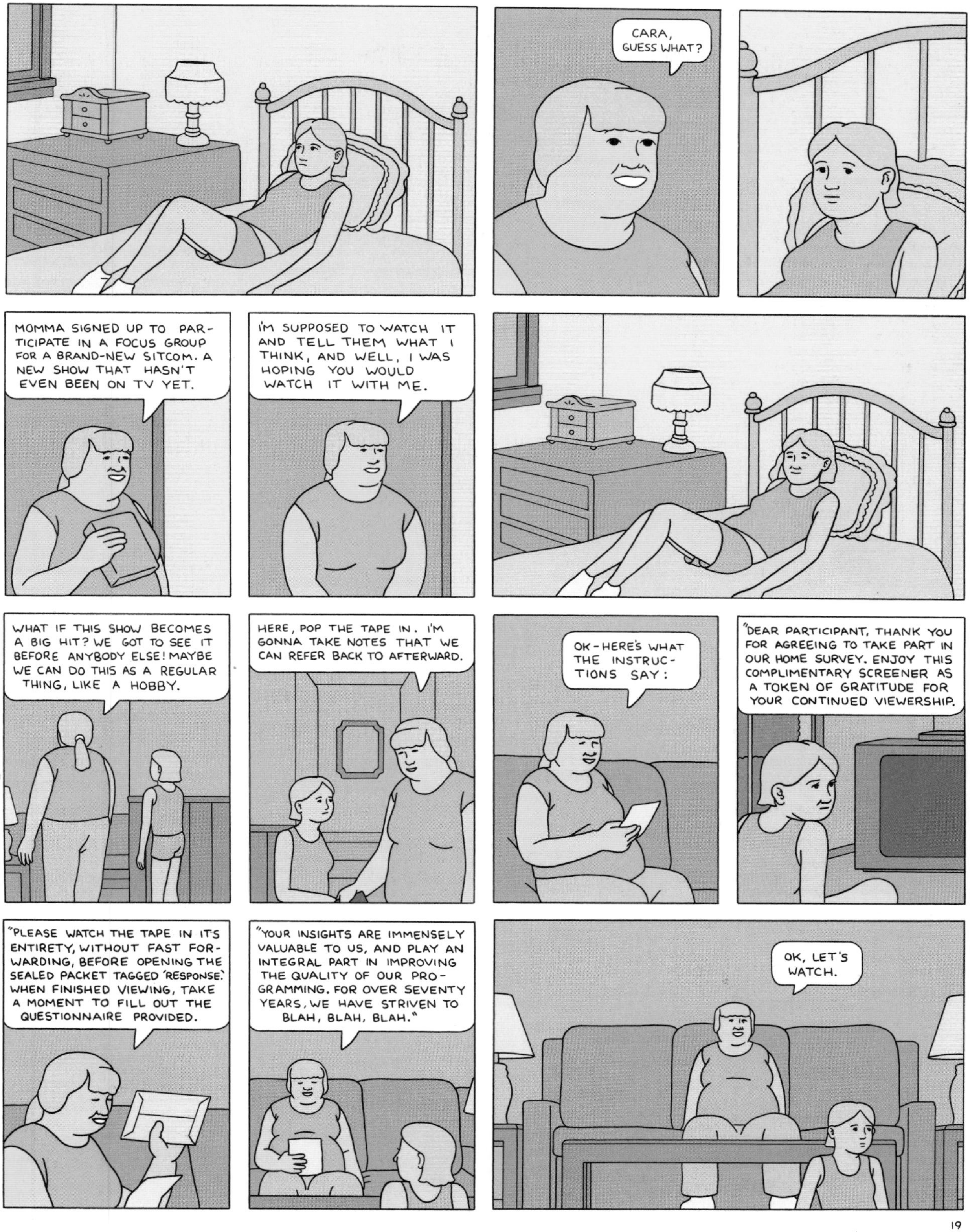
CARA, GUESS WHAT?
MOMMA SIGNED UP TO PARTICIPATE IN A FOCUS GROUP FOR A BRAND-NEW SITCOM. A NEW SHOW THAT HASN'T EVEN BEEN ON TV YET.
I'M SUPPOSED TO WATCH IT AND TELL THEM WHAT I THINK, AND WELL, I WAS HOPING YOU WOULD WATCH IT WITH ME.
WHAT IF THIS SHOW BECOMES A BIG HIT? WE GOT TO SEE IT BEFORE ANYBODY ELSE! MAYBE WE CAN DO THIS AS A REGULAR THING, LIKE A HOBBY.
HERE, POP THE TAPE IN. I'M GONNA TAKE NOTES THAT WE CAN REFER BACK TO AFTERWARD.
OK-HERE'S WHAT THE INSTRUCTIONS SAY:
"DEAR PARTICIPANT, THANK YOU FOR AGREEING TO TAKE PART IN OUR HOME SURVEY. ENJOY THIS COMPLIMENTARY SCREENER AS A TOKEN OF GRATITUDE FOR YOUR CONTINUED VIEWERSHIP.
"PLEASE WATCH THE TAPE IN ITS ENTIRETY, WITHOUT FAST FORWARDING, BEFORE OPENING THE SEALED PACKET TAGGED 'RESPONSE.' WHEN FINISHED VIEWING, TAKE A MOMENT TO FILL OUT THE QUESTIONNAIRE PROVIDED.
"YOUR INSIGHTS ARE IMMENSELY VALUABLE TO US, AND PLAY AN INTEGRAL PART IN IMPROVING THE QUALITY OF OUR PROGRAMMING. FOR OVER SEVENTY YEARS, WE HAVE STRIVEN TO BLAH, BLAH, BLAH."
OK, LET'S WATCH.

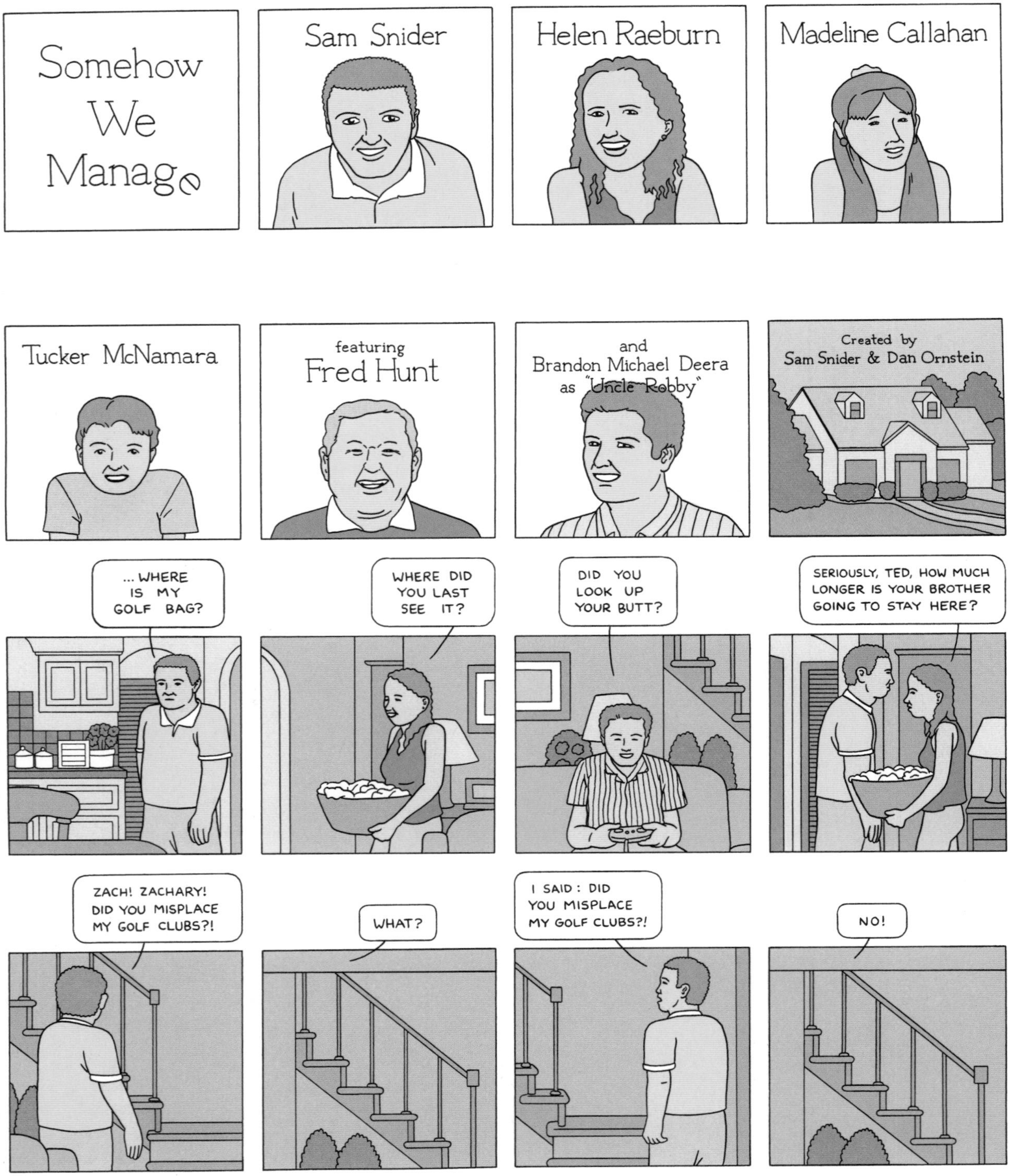

Somehow We Manage
Sam Snider
Helen Raeburn
Madeline Callahan
Tucker McNamara
featuring Fred Hunt
and Brandon Michael Deera as "Uncle Robby"
Created by Sam Snider & Dan Ornstein
... WHERE IS MY GOLF BAG?
WHERE DID YOU LAST SEE IT?
DID YOU LOOK UP YOUR BUTT?
SERIOUSLY, TED, HOW MUCH LONGER IS YOUR BROTHER GOING TO STAY HERE?
ZACH! ZACHARY! DID YOU MISPLACE MY GOLF CLUBS?!
WHAT?
I SAID: DID YOU MISPLACE MY GOLF CLUBS?!
NO!

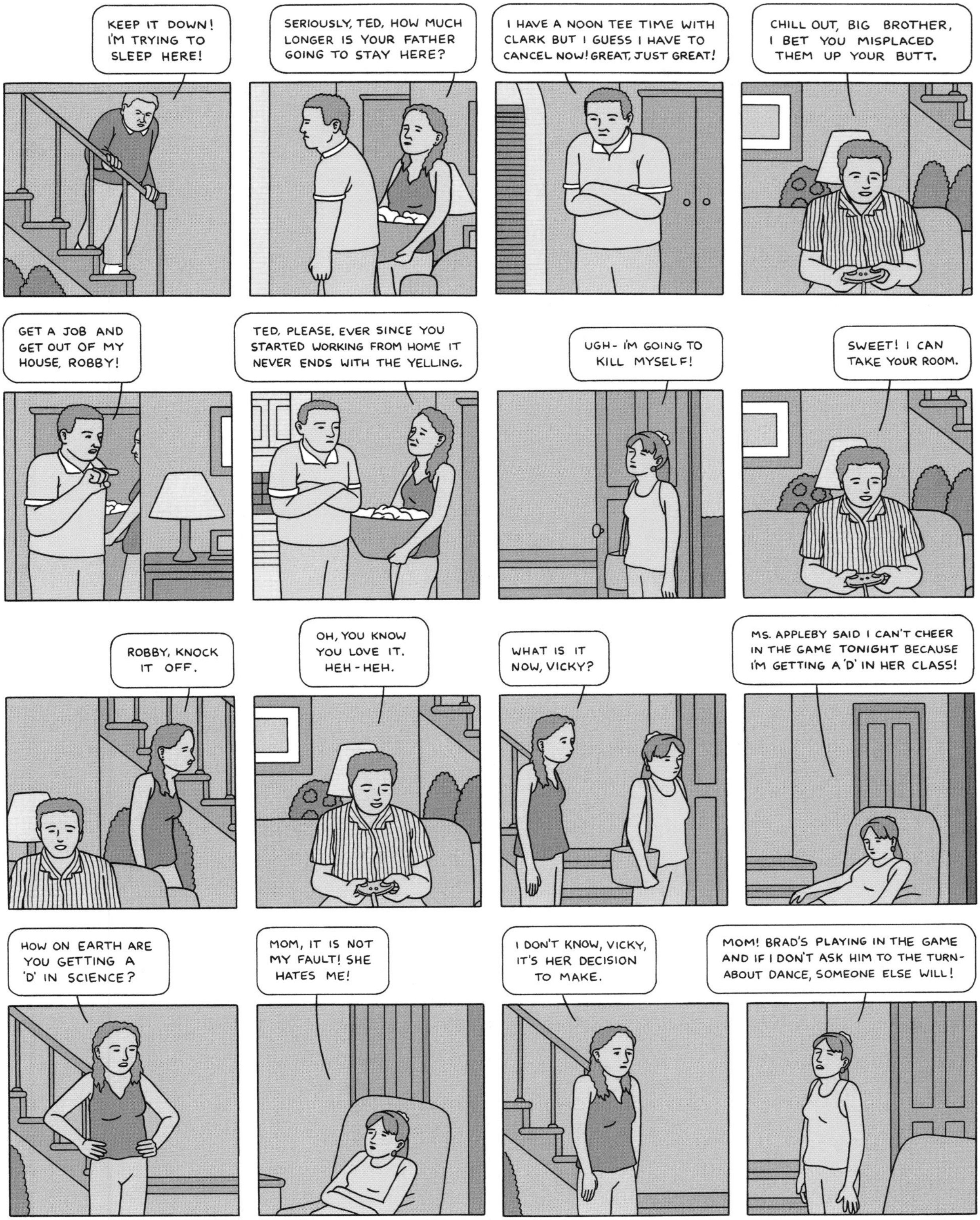
KEEP IT DOWN! I'M TRYING TO SLEEP HERE!
SERIOUSLY, TED, HOW MUCH LONGER IS YOUR FATHER GOING TO STAY HERE?
I HAVE A NOON TEE TIME WITH CLARK BUT I GUESS I HAVE TO CANCEL NOW! GREAT, JUST GREAT!
CHILL OUT, BIG BROTHER, I BET YOU MISPLACED THEM UP YOUR BUTT.
GET A JOB AND GET OUT OF MY HOUSE, ROBBY!
TED, PLEASE. EVER SINCE YOU STARTED WORKING FROM HOME IT NEVER ENDS WITH THE YELLING.
UGH- I'M GOING TO KILL MYSELF!
SWEET! I CAN TAKE YOUR ROOM.
ROBBY, KNOCK IT OFF.
OH, YOU KNOW YOU LOVE IT. HEH-HEH.
WHAT IS IT NOW, VICKY?
MS. APPLEBY SAID I CAN'T CHEER IN THE GAME TONIGHT BECAUSE I'M GETTING A 'D' IN HER CLASS!
HOW ON EARTH ARE YOU GETTING A 'D' IN SCIENCE?
MOM, IT IS NOT MY FAULT! SHE HATES ME!
I DON'T KNOW, VICKY, IT'S HER DECISION TO MAKE.
MOM! BRAD'S PLAYING IN THE GAME AND IF I DON'T ASK HIM TO THE TURN-ABOUT DANCE, SOMEONE ELSE WILL!

YOU CAN STILL GO TO THE GAME EVEN IF YOU'RE NOT CHEERING THOUGH.

THERE'S A BIG TEST ON MONDAY AND SHE SAID THE ONLY WAY I CAN PASS IS IF I STUDY ALL WEEKEND.

WELL, VICKY, YOUR SCHOOLING IS WHAT IS MOST IMPORTANT.

YUCK!

DON'T LISTEN TO HER, VICK. I FAILED SCIENCE. I SAY THERE ARE MORE IMPORTANT THINGS THAN SCHOOLING.

I'VE GOTTA GO TO THAT GAME.

WHAT WAS HER NAME? MS. APPLEBY?

YEA, WHY?

LEAVE IT TO UNCLE ROBBY.

...DRY, PALE SKIN?...

...FINALLY, A TANNER THAT MOISTURIZES AS IT FIRMS...

...CREATING A SLIMMER, SUN-KISSED LOOK...

...SEDUCTIVELY SMOOTH...

...IRRESISTIBLE TO TOUCH...

...CRYSTAL LAKE TANNER AND MOISTURIZER WITH ALOE EXTRACT...

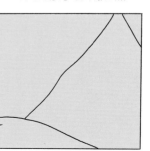

...SMOOTH...
...SOFT...
...SKIN...

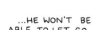

...HE WON'T BE ABLE TO LET GO...

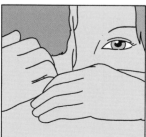

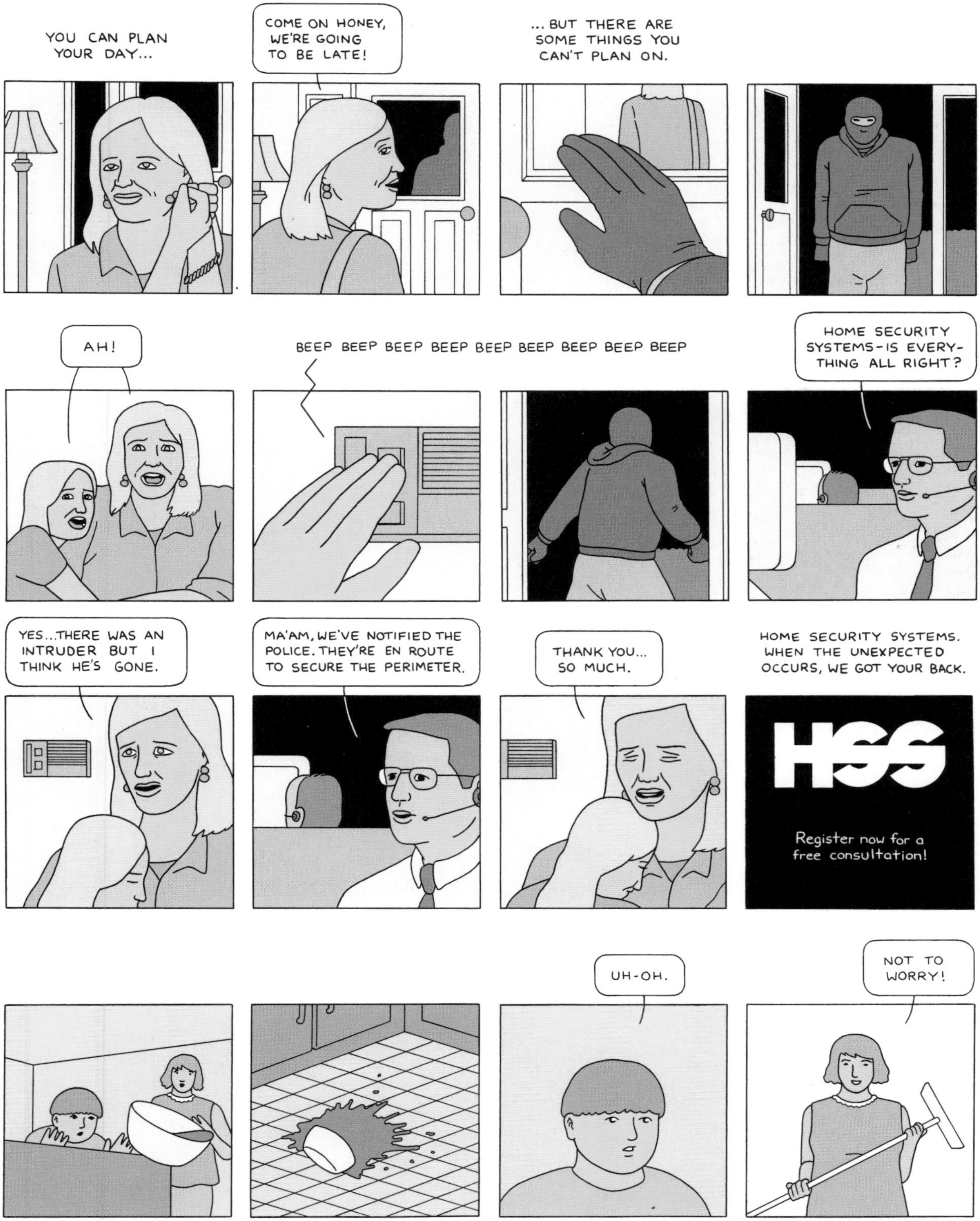

YOU CAN PLAN YOUR DAY...
COME ON HONEY, WE'RE GOING TO BE LATE!
...BUT THERE ARE SOME THINGS YOU CAN'T PLAN ON.
AH!
BEEP BEEP BEEP BEEP BEEP BEEP BEEP BEEP BEEP
HOME SECURITY SYSTEMS-IS EVERYTHING ALL RIGHT?
YES...THERE WAS AN INTRUDER BUT I THINK HE'S GONE.
MA'AM, WE'VE NOTIFIED THE POLICE. THEY'RE EN ROUTE TO SECURE THE PERIMETER.
THANK YOU... SO MUCH.
HOME SECURITY SYSTEMS. WHEN THE UNEXPECTED OCCURS, WE GOT YOUR BACK.
HSS
Register now for a free consultation!
UH-OH.
NOT TO WORRY!

THE RABBIT DUSTER CUTS THROUGH THE TOUGHEST STAINS WITH ADVANCED SHAMMY TECHNOLOGY.

IT MAKES CLEANING...FUN!

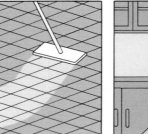

UH...MOM?

THE SLONE RABBIT DUSTER WITH OPTIMAL EXTENSION ARM.

CLEANING HOUSE WAS NEVER THIS MUCH FUN!

SURE YOU AIN'T SEEN THOSE CLUBS, ZACH?

NO.

DADDY, CAN I PLEASE GO TO THE GAME? I PROMISE I'LL STUDY ALL DAY TOMORROW.

ABSOLUTELY NOT.

THIS ISN'T FAIR!

LIFE'S NOT FAIR. SPEAKING OF, KEEP IT DOWN OR YOU'LL WAKE UP GRANDPA.

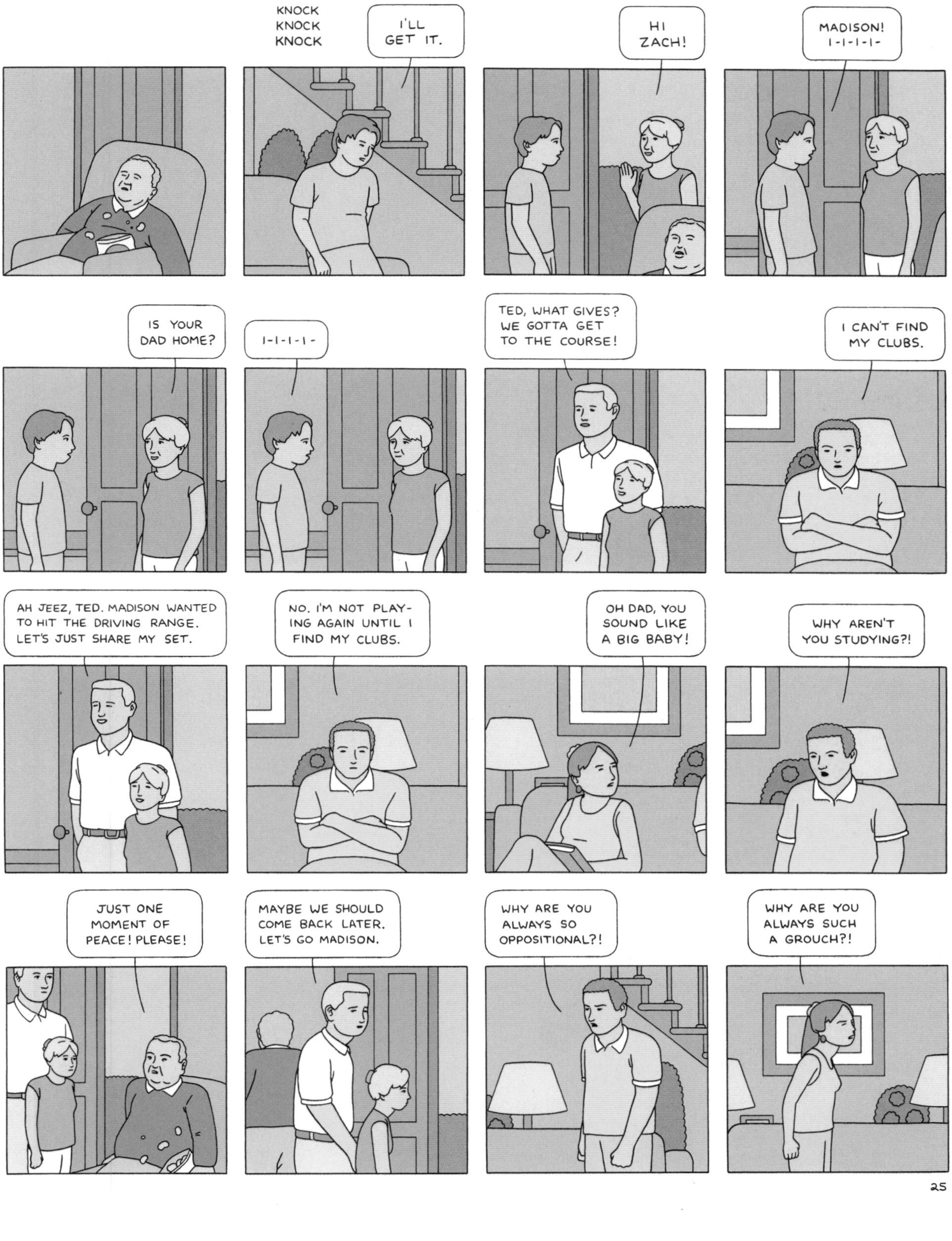
KNOCK KNOCK KNOCK
I'LL GET IT.
HI ZACH!
MADISON! I-I-I-I-
IS YOUR DAD HOME?
I-I-I-I-
TED, WHAT GIVES? WE GOTTA GET TO THE COURSE!
I CAN'T FIND MY CLUBS.
AH JEEZ, TED. MADISON WANTED TO HIT THE DRIVING RANGE. LET'S JUST SHARE MY SET.
NO. I'M NOT PLAY-ING AGAIN UNTIL I FIND MY CLUBS.
OH DAD, YOU SOUND LIKE A BIG BABY!
WHY AREN'T YOU STUDYING?!
JUST ONE MOMENT OF PEACE! PLEASE!
MAYBE WE SHOULD COME BACK LATER. LET'S GO MADISON.
WHY ARE YOU ALWAYS SO OPPOSITIONAL?!
WHY ARE YOU ALWAYS SUCH A GROUCH?!

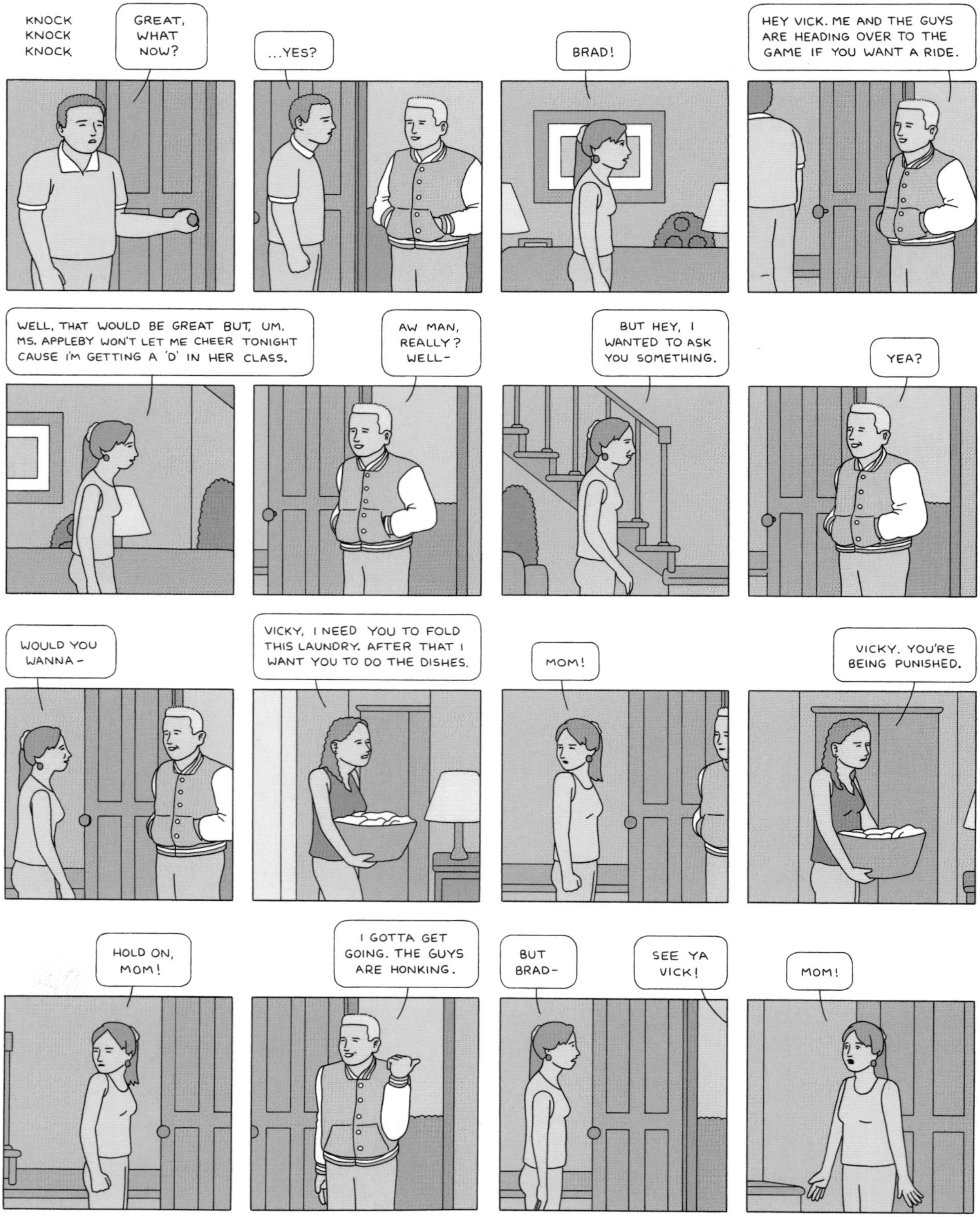
KNOCK KNOCK KNOCK
GREAT, WHAT NOW?
...YES?
BRAD!
HEY VICK. ME AND THE GUYS ARE HEADING OVER TO THE GAME IF YOU WANT A RIDE.
WELL, THAT WOULD BE GREAT BUT, UM. MS. APPLEBY WON'T LET ME CHEER TONIGHT CAUSE I'M GETTING A 'D' IN HER CLASS.
AW MAN, REALLY? WELL-
BUT HEY, I WANTED TO ASK YOU SOMETHING.
YEA?
WOULD YOU WANNA-
VICKY, I NEED YOU TO FOLD THIS LAUNDRY. AFTER THAT I WANT YOU TO DO THE DISHES.
MOM!
VICKY. YOU'RE BEING PUNISHED.
HOLD ON, MOM!
I GOTTA GET GOING. THE GUYS ARE HONKING.
BUT BRAD-
SEE YA VICK!
MOM!

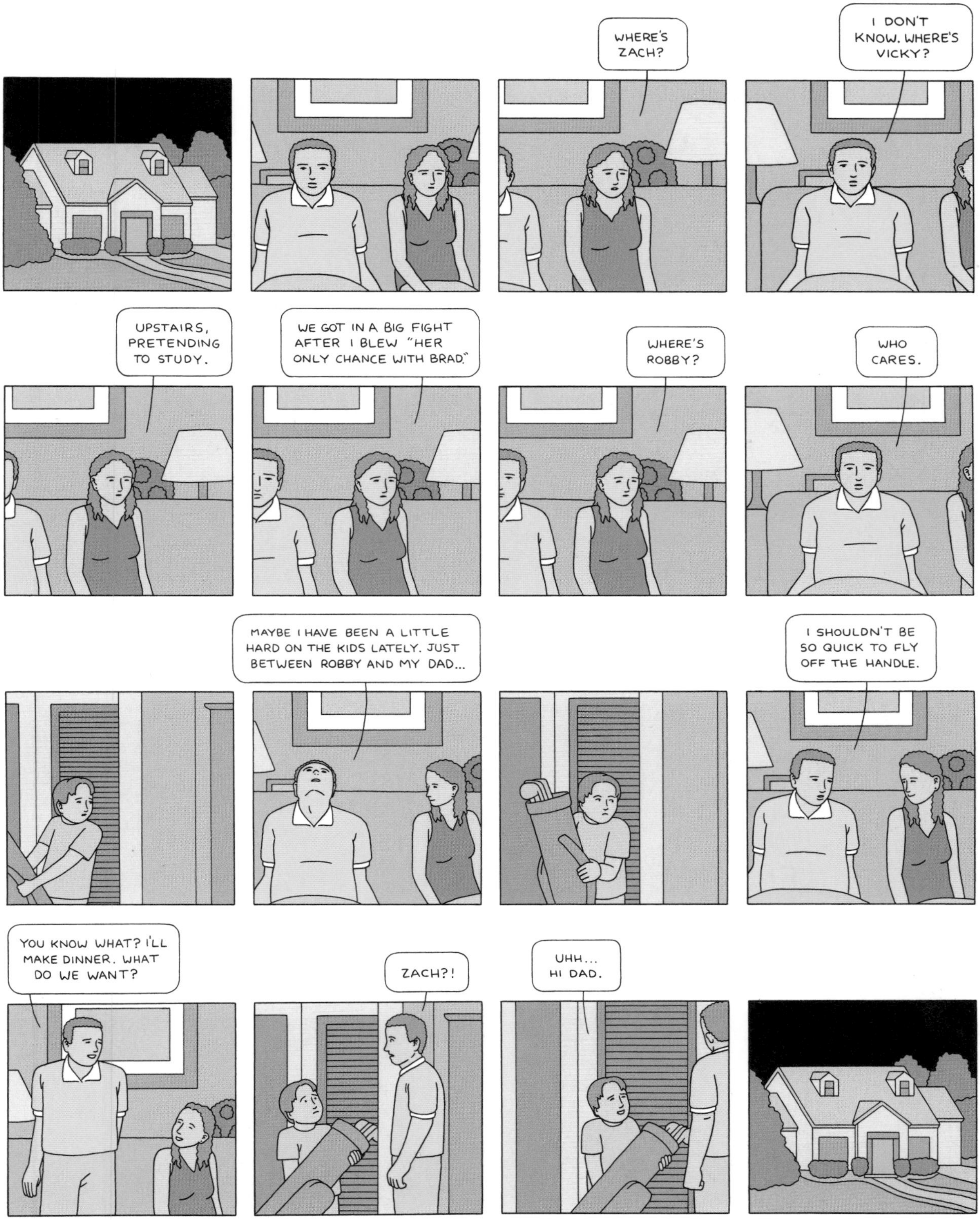
WHERE'S ZACH?
I DON'T KNOW. WHERE'S VICKY?
UPSTAIRS, PRETENDING TO STUDY.
WE GOT IN A BIG FIGHT AFTER I BLEW "HER ONLY CHANCE WITH BRAD."
WHERE'S ROBBY?
WHO CARES.
MAYBE I HAVE BEEN A LITTLE HARD ON THE KIDS LATELY. JUST BETWEEN ROBBY AND MY DAD...
I SHOULDN'T BE SO QUICK TO FLY OFF THE HANDLE.
YOU KNOW WHAT? I'LL MAKE DINNER. WHAT DO WE WANT?
ZACH?!
UHH... HI DAD.

DON'T BORE
YOURSELF...

HMPH.

TRANSFORM
YOURSELF!

TRANSFORM
YOURSELF!

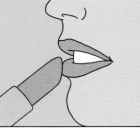

OVER
HERE!

HEY!

TURN
THIS
WAY!

WITH ULTRA BRIGHT
AGE DEFYING
LIP ENHANCER.

ONE COAT. ONE COLOR.
LASTS UP TO TEN HOURS.
SERIOUSLY STRONG.

SERIOUSLY
BOLD.

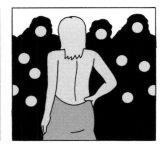

SERIOUSLY
AWESOME.

PICK IT UP,
HONEY. WE GOTTA
GET GOING.

ULTRA BRIGHT.
SERIOUSLY WOW.

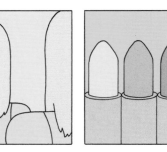

...SOMETIMES, LIFE CAN FEEL
LIKE A MONOTONOUS,
HORRIFYING NIGHTMARE...

...NO OUTLET,
NO END
IN SIGHT...

...MAYBE WE
CAN HELP...

TELL YOUR DOCTOR IF YOUR DE-
PRESSION WORSENS, OR IF YOU
HAVE THOUGHTS OF SUICIDE.

SEVERE LIVER PROBLEMS WERE RE-PORTED. SIGNS INCLUDE ABDOMINAL PAIN AND YELLOWING OF THE SKIN.
FAINTING MAY OCCUR UPON STAND-ING. SIDE EFFECTS INCLUDE DRY MOUTH, NAUSEA, AND CONSTIPATION.
SAUDEROL.
RECLAIM YOUR LIFE.
MY JEANS, ARE MINE!
MY JEANS, ARE MINE!
MY JEANS, ARE MINE!
MY JEANS, ARE MINE!
MY JEANS

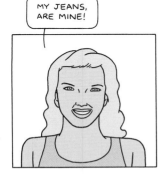

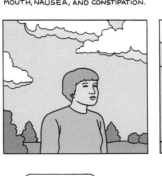

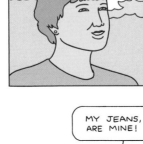

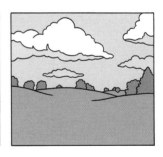

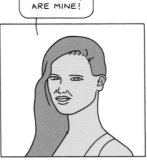

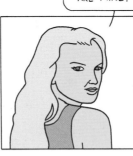

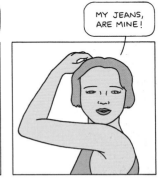

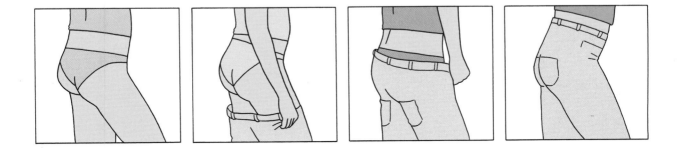

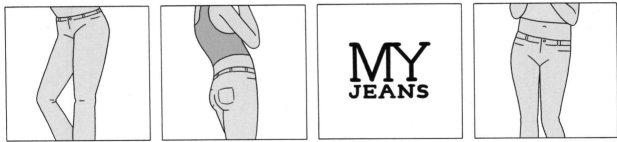

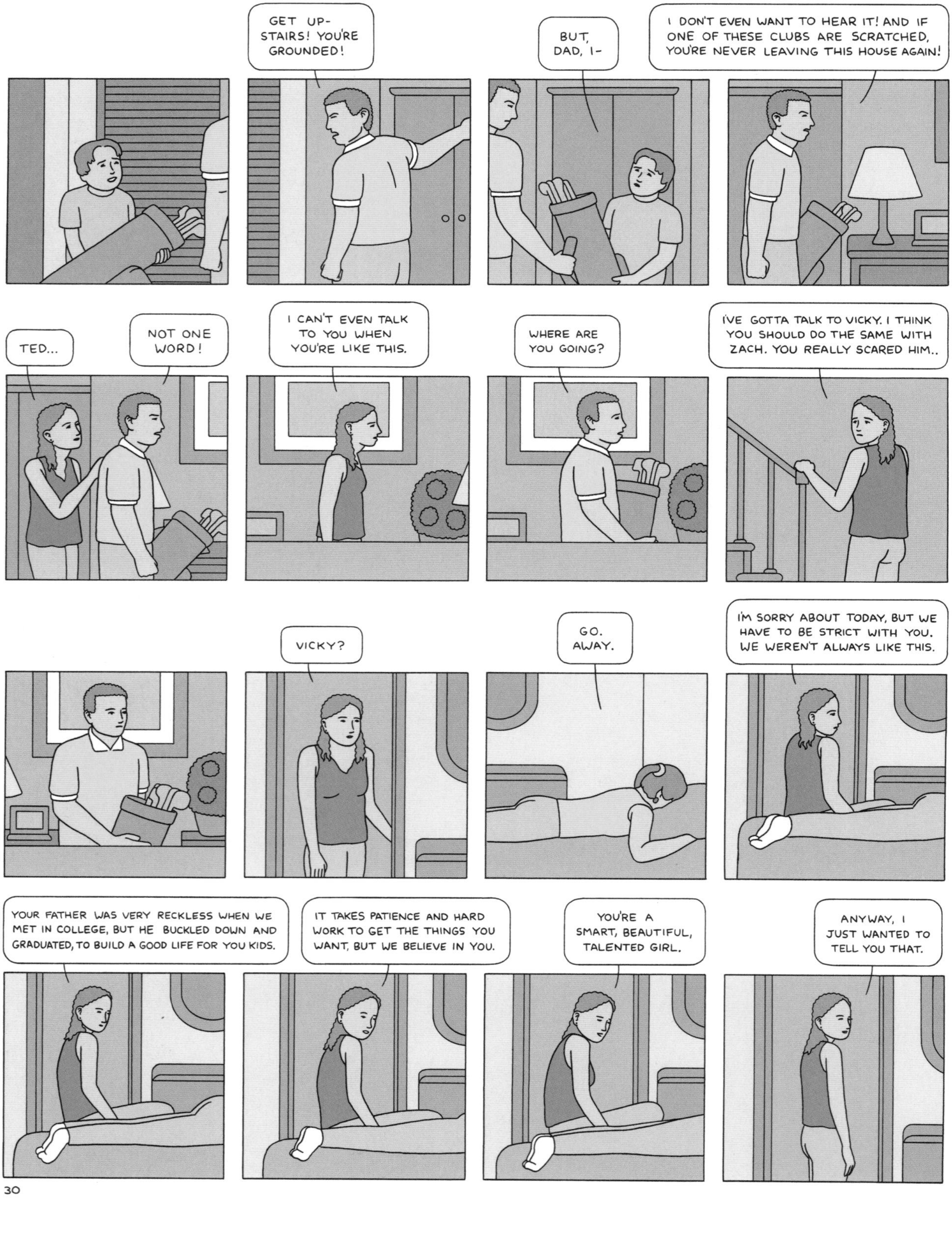
GET UP-STAIRS! YOU'RE GROUNDED!
BUT, DAD, I-
I DON'T EVEN WANT TO HEAR IT! AND IF ONE OF THESE CLUBS ARE SCRATCHED, YOU'RE NEVER LEAVING THIS HOUSE AGAIN!
TED...
NOT ONE WORD!
I CAN'T EVEN TALK TO YOU WHEN YOU'RE LIKE THIS.
WHERE ARE YOU GOING?
I'VE GOTTA TALK TO VICKY. I THINK YOU SHOULD DO THE SAME WITH ZACH. YOU REALLY SCARED HIM..
VICKY?
GO. AWAY.
I'M SORRY ABOUT TODAY, BUT WE HAVE TO BE STRICT WITH YOU. WE WEREN'T ALWAYS LIKE THIS.
YOUR FATHER WAS VERY RECKLESS WHEN WE MET IN COLLEGE, BUT HE BUCKLED DOWN AND GRADUATED, TO BUILD A GOOD LIFE FOR YOU KIDS.
IT TAKES PATIENCE AND HARD WORK TO GET THE THINGS YOU WANT, BUT WE BELIEVE IN YOU.
YOU'RE A SMART, BEAUTIFUL, TALENTED GIRL.
ANYWAY, I JUST WANTED TO TELL YOU THAT.

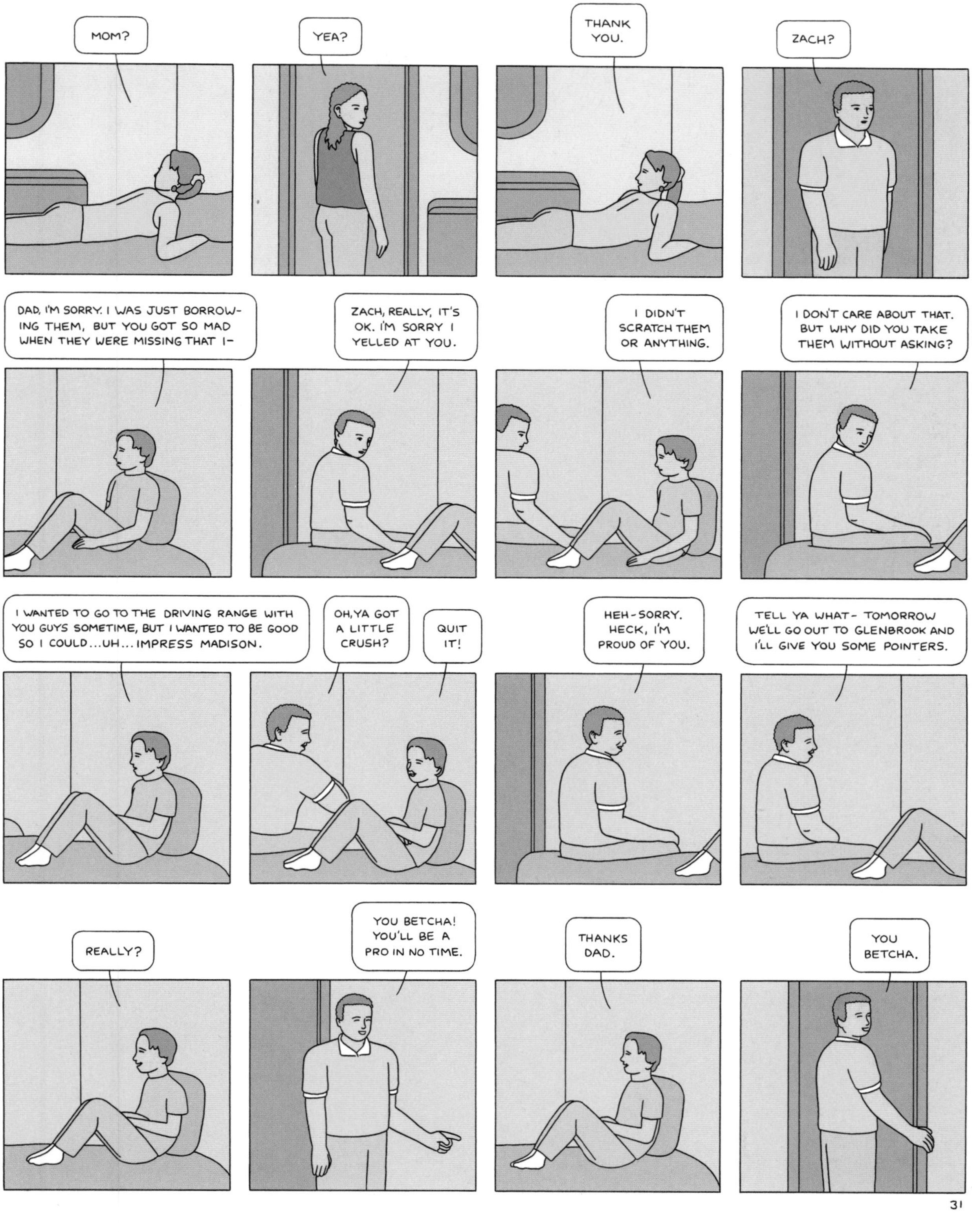
MOM?
YEA?
THANK YOU.
ZACH?
DAD, I'M SORRY. I WAS JUST BORROWING THEM, BUT YOU GOT SO MAD WHEN THEY WERE MISSING THAT I—
ZACH, REALLY, IT'S OK. I'M SORRY I YELLED AT YOU.
I DIDN'T SCRATCH THEM OR ANYTHING.
I DON'T CARE ABOUT THAT. BUT WHY DID YOU TAKE THEM WITHOUT ASKING?
I WANTED TO GO TO THE DRIVING RANGE WITH YOU GUYS SOMETIME, BUT I WANTED TO BE GOOD SO I COULD...UH...IMPRESS MADISON.
OH, YA GOT A LITTLE CRUSH?
QUIT IT!
HEH-SORRY. HECK, I'M PROUD OF YOU.
TELL YA WHAT- TOMORROW WE'LL GO OUT TO GLENBROOK AND I'LL GIVE YOU SOME POINTERS.
REALLY?
YOU BETCHA! YOU'LL BE A PRO IN NO TIME.
THANKS DAD.
YOU BETCHA.

DING DONG!

MS. APPLEBY! WHAT ARE YOU DOING HERE?

YOUR UNCLE ROBBY PERSONALLY ASSURED ME THAT HE'S BEEN TUTORING YOU EVERY NIGHT, AND I THOUGHT THAT WAS SO SWEET.

SO I JUST SPOKE TO COACH YOUNG AND TOLD HER THAT I'M LIFTING YOUR ACADEMIC SUSPENSION.

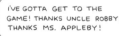

BUT ROBBY, HOW DID YOU—

HE CAN BE VERY CONVINCING.

WHAT CAN I SAY!

I'VE GOTTA GET TO THE GAME! THANKS UNCLE ROBBY! THANKS MS. APPLEBY!

CATCH Y'ALL LATER.

HOW DOES HE DO THAT?

I HAVE NO IDEA.

SEE YA GUYS!

WELL THAT WAS FAST!

BRAD!

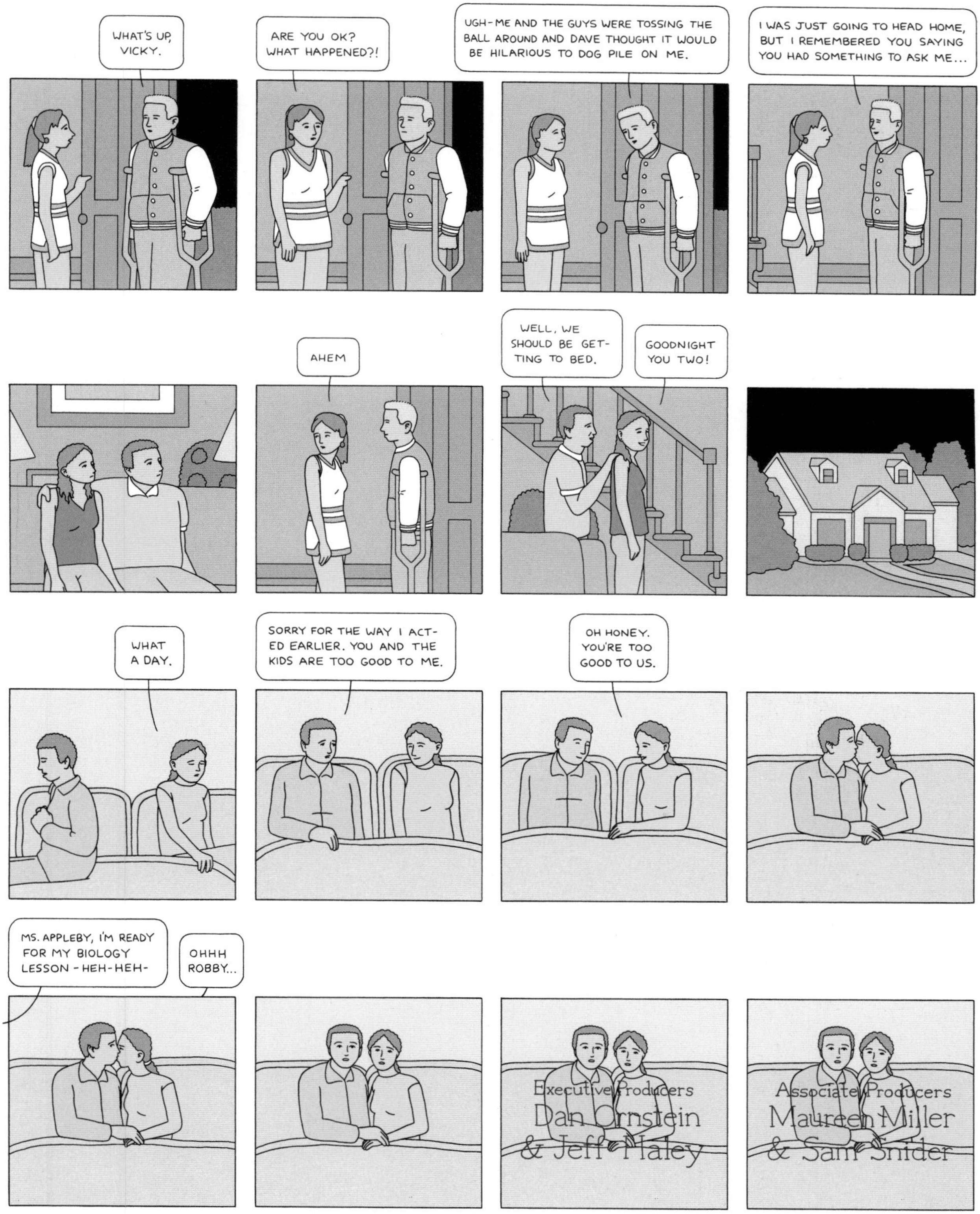
WHAT'S UP, VICKY.
ARE YOU OK? WHAT HAPPENED?!
UGH-ME AND THE GUYS WERE TOSSING THE BALL AROUND AND DAVE THOUGHT IT WOULD BE HILARIOUS TO DOG PILE ON ME.
I WAS JUST GOING TO HEAD HOME, BUT I REMEMBERED YOU SAYING YOU HAD SOMETHING TO ASK ME...
AHEM
WELL, WE SHOULD BE GET-TING TO BED.
GOODNIGHT YOU TWO!
WHAT A DAY.
SORRY FOR THE WAY I ACT-ED EARLIER. YOU AND THE KIDS ARE TOO GOOD TO ME.
OH HONEY. YOU'RE TOO GOOD TO US.
MS. APPLEBY, I'M READY FOR MY BIOLOGY LESSON - HEH-HEH-
OHHH ROBBY...
Executive Producers
Dan Ornstein
& Jeff Haley
Associate Producers
Maureen Miller
& Sam Snider

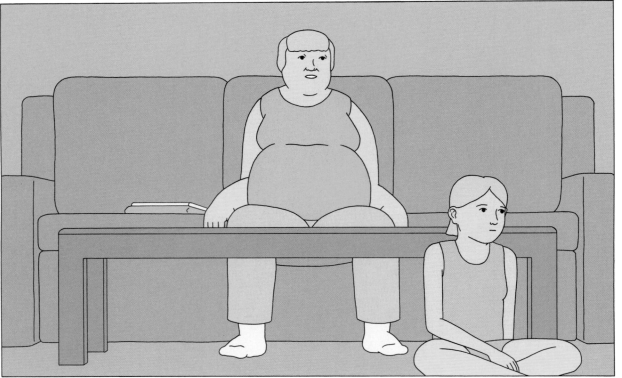

WOW...

THAT WAS REALLY GOOD.

DID YOU LIKE IT, CARA?

LET'S SEE, I JOTTED DOWN SOME NOTES DURING THE COMMERCIALS. WHY DON'T WE REVIEW A BIT BEFORE GETTING INTO THE QUESTIONS.

OK, AT FIRST I THOUGHT THE DAD, TED, WAS NOT LIKABLE ENOUGH AS THE LEAD ACTOR, BUT IT SEEMS LIKE HIS WIFE BALANCES HIM OUT.

I THOUGHT THE KID ACTORS WERE REALLY GOOD. IF THERE'S A QUESTION ABOUT THEM, I'M GOING TO SUGGEST THAT WE SEE MORE DEVELOPMENT IN THEIR PERSONAL LIVES.

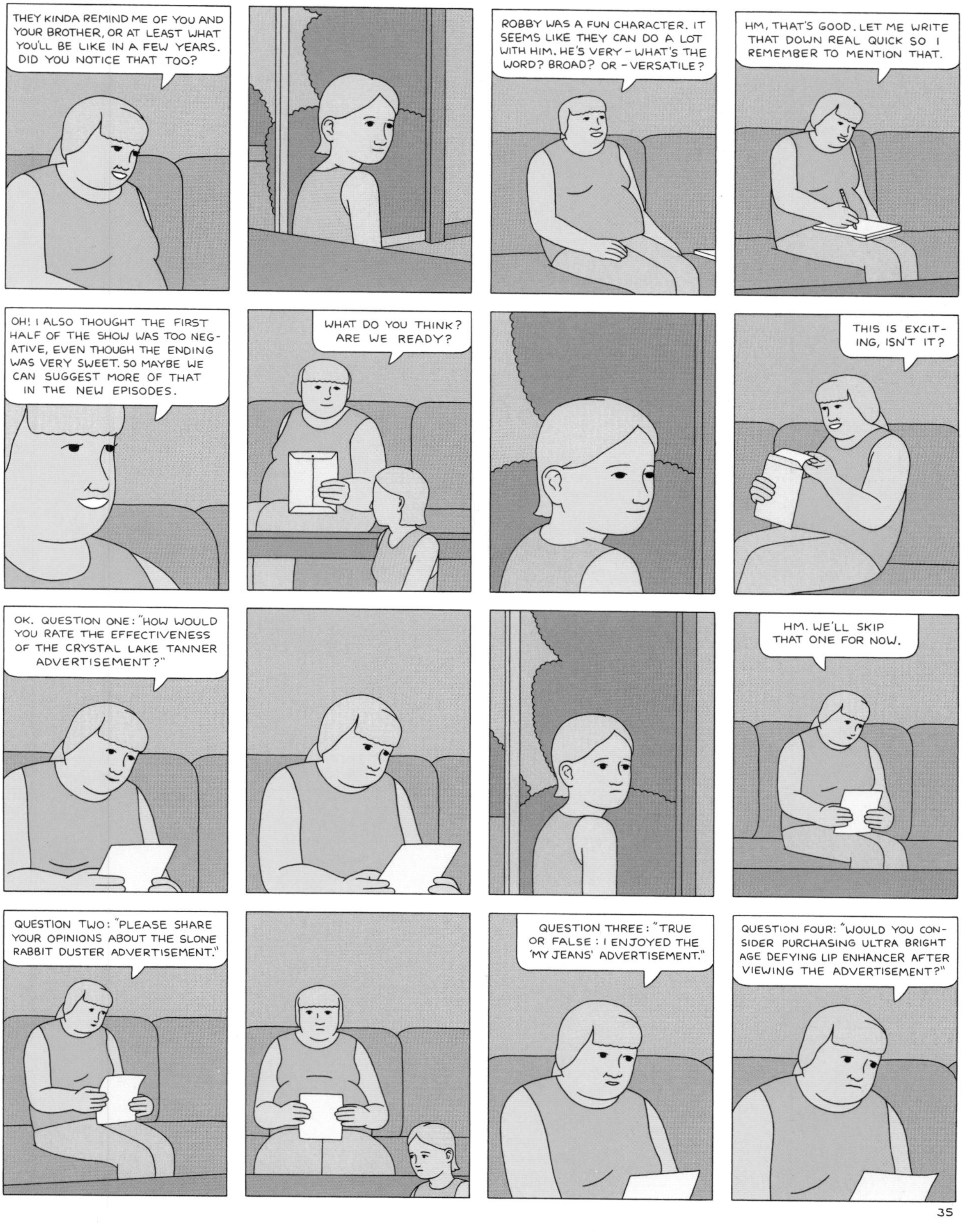
THEY KINDA REMIND ME OF YOU AND YOUR BROTHER, OR AT LEAST WHAT YOU'LL BE LIKE IN A FEW YEARS. DID YOU NOTICE THAT TOO?
ROBBY WAS A FUN CHARACTER. IT SEEMS LIKE THEY CAN DO A LOT WITH HIM. HE'S VERY - WHAT'S THE WORD? BROAD? OR - VERSATILE?
HM, THAT'S GOOD. LET ME WRITE THAT DOWN REAL QUICK SO I REMEMBER TO MENTION THAT.
OH! I ALSO THOUGHT THE FIRST HALF OF THE SHOW WAS TOO NEGATIVE, EVEN THOUGH THE ENDING WAS VERY SWEET. SO MAYBE WE CAN SUGGEST MORE OF THAT IN THE NEW EPISODES.
WHAT DO YOU THINK? ARE WE READY?
THIS IS EXCITING, ISN'T IT?
OK. QUESTION ONE: "HOW WOULD YOU RATE THE EFFECTIVENESS OF THE CRYSTAL LAKE TANNER ADVERTISEMENT?"
HM. WE'LL SKIP THAT ONE FOR NOW.
QUESTION TWO: "PLEASE SHARE YOUR OPINIONS ABOUT THE SLONE RABBIT DUSTER ADVERTISEMENT."
QUESTION THREE: "TRUE OR FALSE: I ENJOYED THE 'MY JEANS' ADVERTISEMENT."
QUESTION FOUR: "WOULD YOU CONSIDER PURCHASING ULTRA BRIGHT AGE DEFYING LIP ENHANCER AFTER VIEWING THE ADVERTISEMENT?"

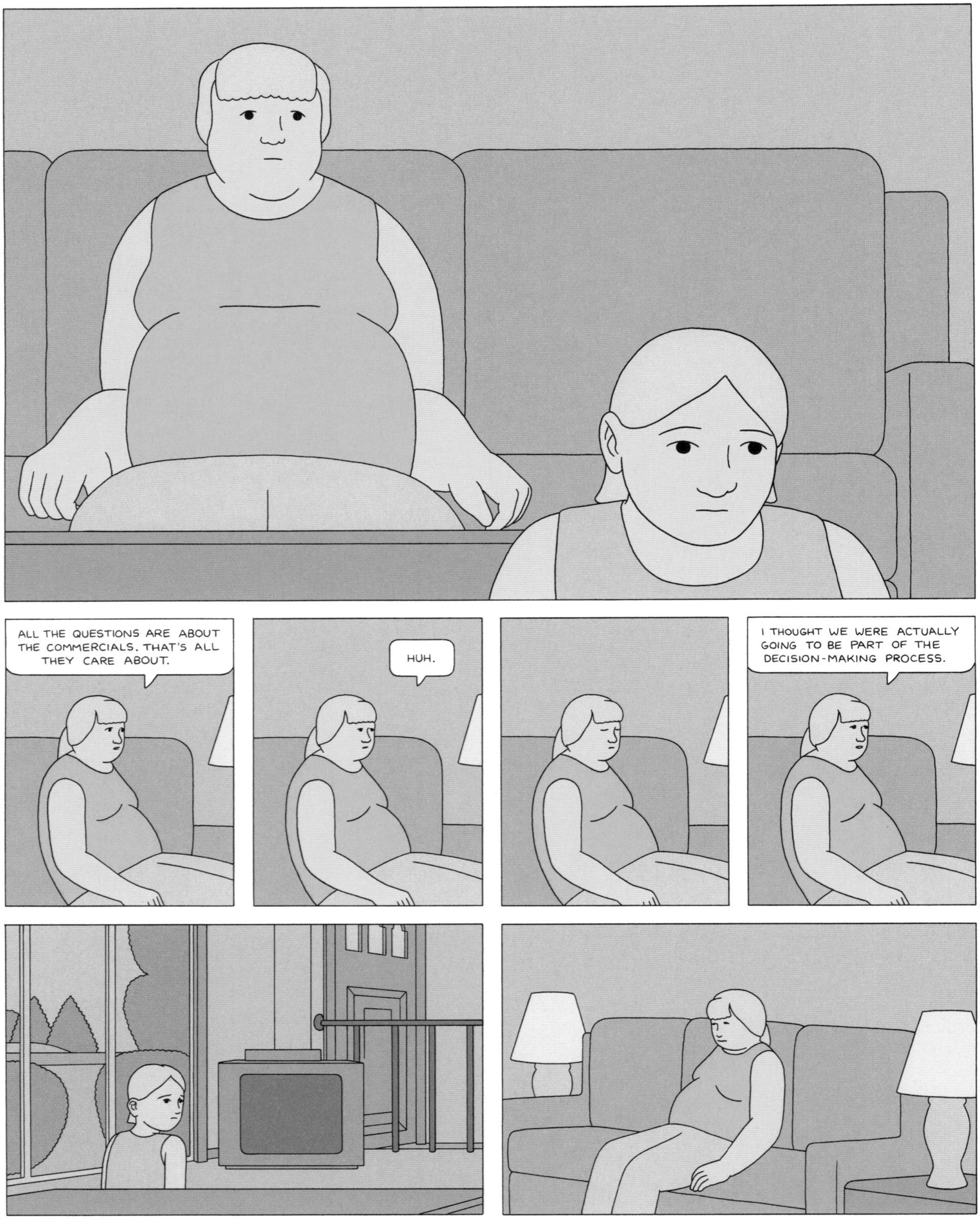
ALL THE QUESTIONS ARE ABOUT THE COMMERCIALS. THAT'S ALL THEY CARE ABOUT.
HUH.
I THOUGHT WE WERE ACTUALLY GOING TO BE PART OF THE DECISION-MAKING PROCESS.

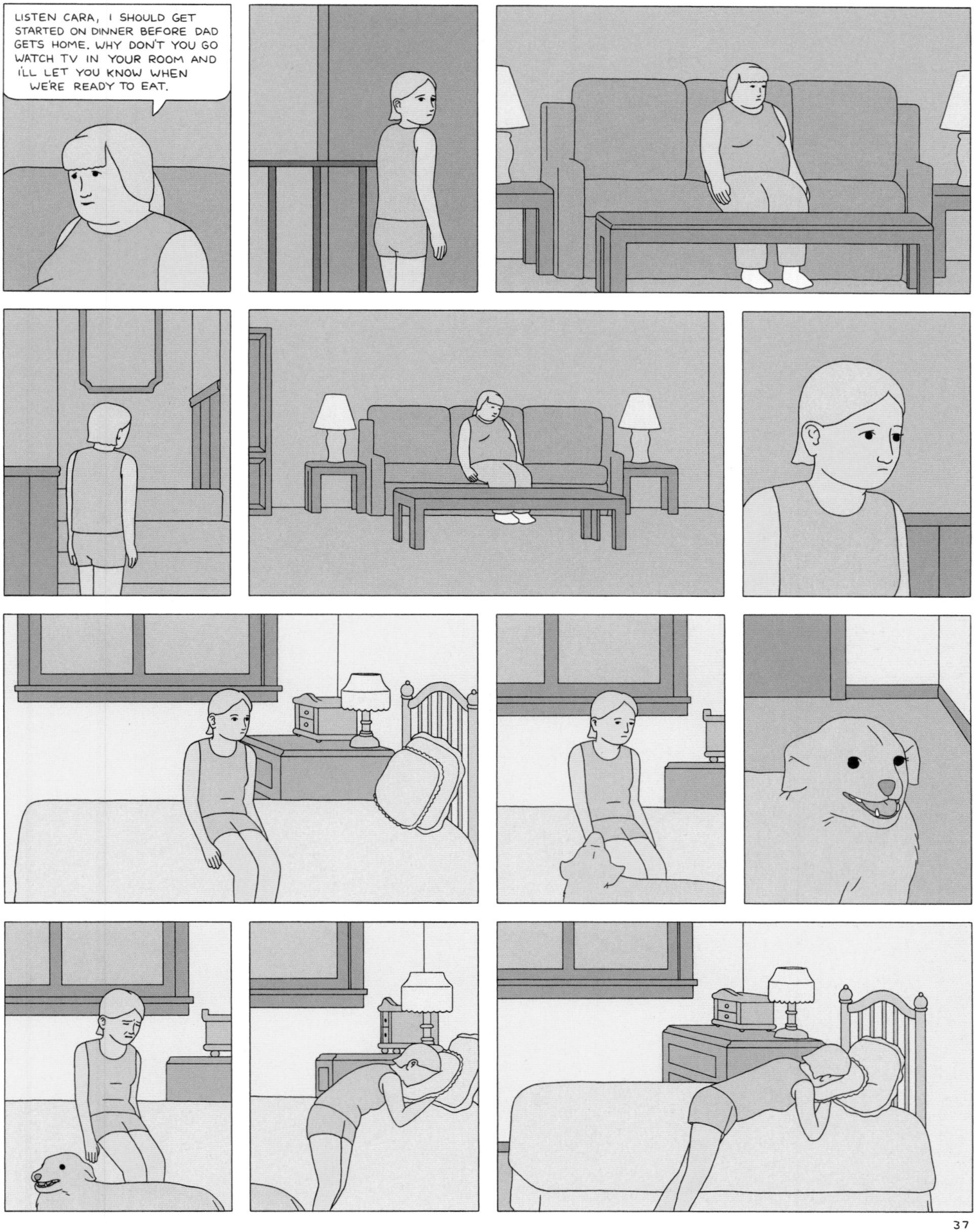
LISTEN CARA, I SHOULD GET STARTED ON DINNER BEFORE DAD GETS HOME. WHY DON'T YOU GO WATCH TV IN YOUR ROOM AND I'LL LET YOU KNOW WHEN WE'RE READY TO EAT.

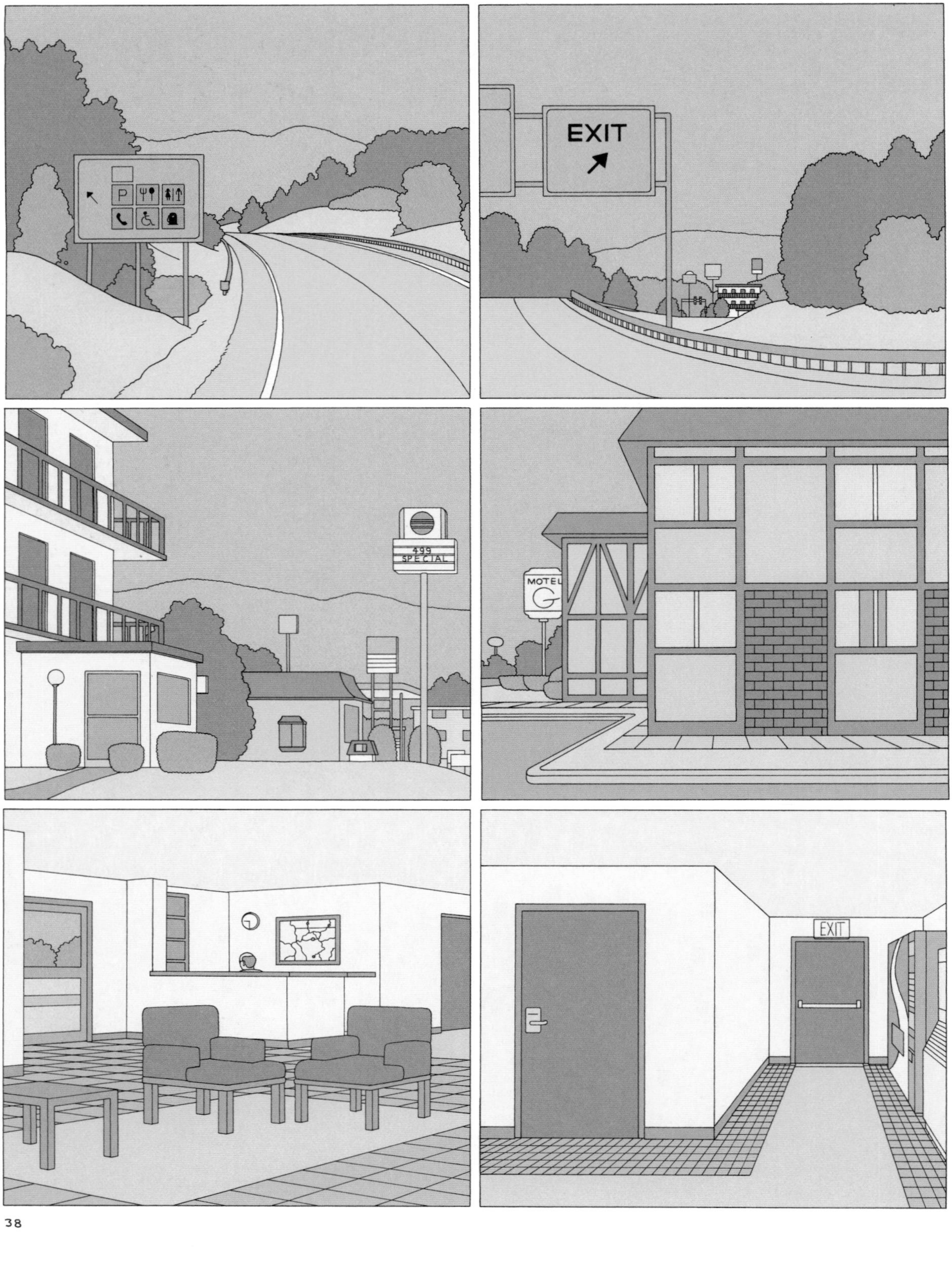
P
EXIT
499
SPECIAL
MOTEL
EXIT

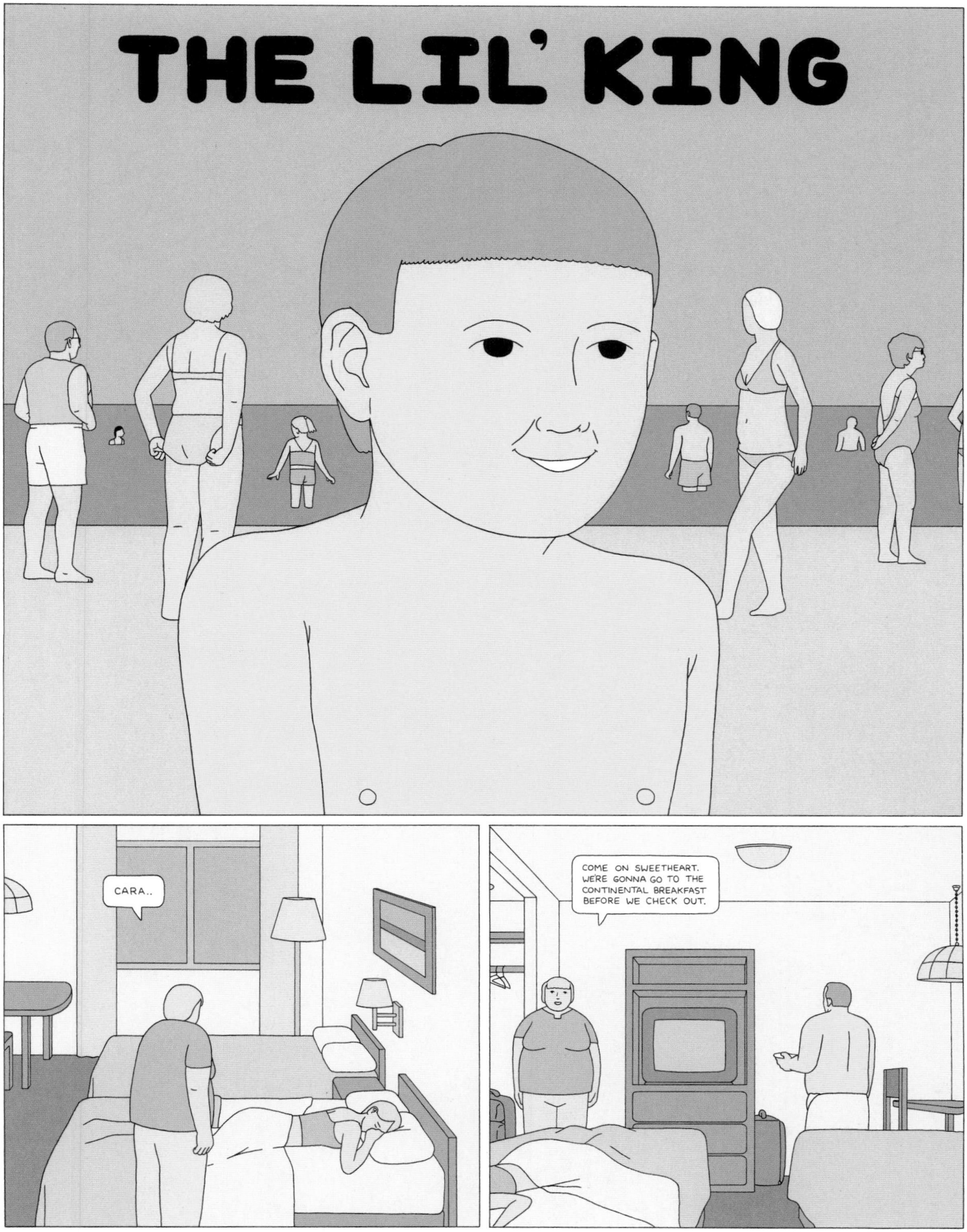
THE LIL' KING
CARA..
COME ON SWEETHEART. WE'RE GONNA GO TO THE CONTINENTAL BREAKFAST BEFORE WE CHECK OUT.

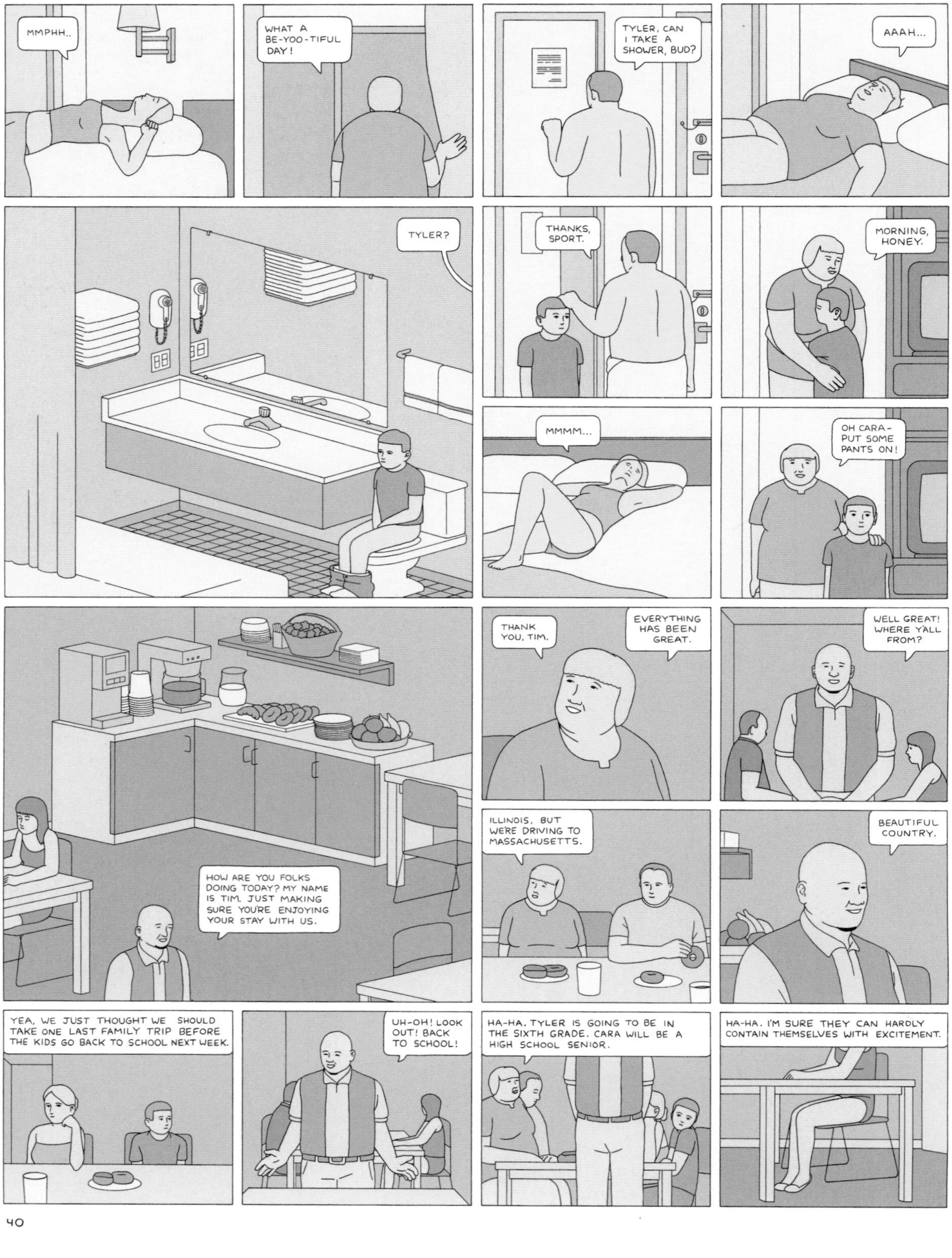
MMPHH..
WHAT A BE-YOO-TIFUL DAY!
TYLER, CAN I TAKE A SHOWER, BUD?
AAAH...
TYLER?
THANKS, SPORT.
MORNING, HONEY.
MMMM...
OH CARA - PUT SOME PANTS ON!
HOW ARE YOU FOLKS DOING TODAY? MY NAME IS TIM. JUST MAKING SURE YOU'RE ENJOYING YOUR STAY WITH US.
THANK YOU, TIM.
EVERYTHING HAS BEEN GREAT.
WELL GREAT! WHERE Y'ALL FROM?
ILLINOIS, BUT WE'RE DRIVING TO MASSACHUSETTS.
BEAUTIFUL COUNTRY.
YEA, WE JUST THOUGHT WE SHOULD TAKE ONE LAST FAMILY TRIP BEFORE THE KIDS GO BACK TO SCHOOL NEXT WEEK.
UH-OH! LOOK OUT! BACK TO SCHOOL!
HA-HA. TYLER IS GOING TO BE IN THE SIXTH GRADE. CARA WILL BE A HIGH SCHOOL SENIOR.
HA-HA. I'M SURE THEY CAN HARDLY CONTAIN THEMSELVES WITH EXCITEMENT.

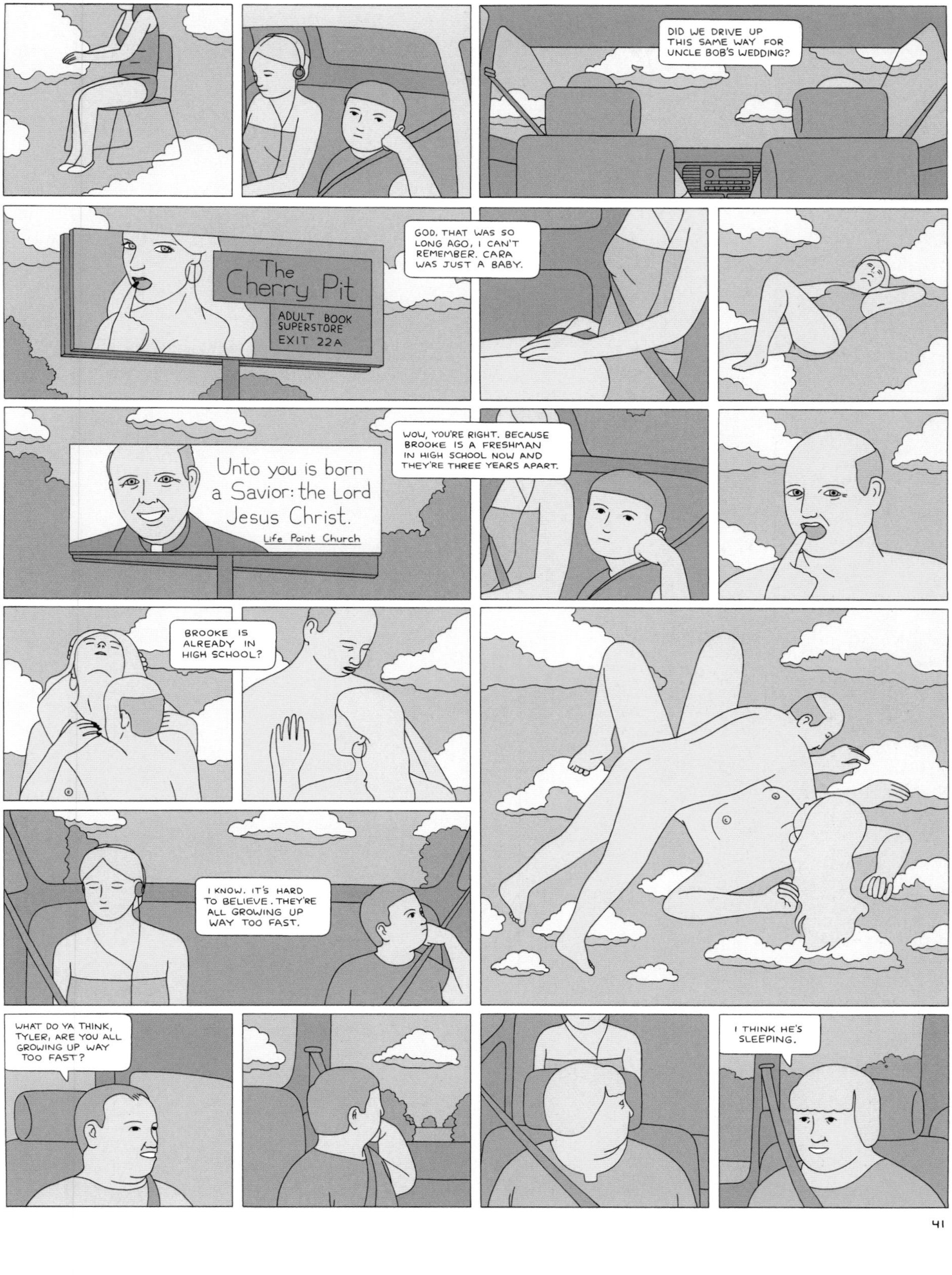
DID WE DRIVE UP THIS SAME WAY FOR UNCLE BOB'S WEDDING?
The Cherry Pit
ADULT BOOK SUPERSTORE
EXIT 22A
GOD, THAT WAS SO LONG AGO, I CAN'T REMEMBER. CARA WAS JUST A BABY.
Unto you is born a Savior: the Lord Jesus Christ.
Life Point Church
WOW, YOU'RE RIGHT. BECAUSE BROOKE IS A FRESHMAN IN HIGH SCHOOL NOW AND THEY'RE THREE YEARS APART.
BROOKE IS ALREADY IN HIGH SCHOOL?
I KNOW. IT'S HARD TO BELIEVE. THEY'RE ALL GROWING UP WAY TOO FAST.
WHAT DO YA THINK, TYLER, ARE YOU ALL GROWING UP WAY TOO FAST?
I THINK HE'S SLEEPING.

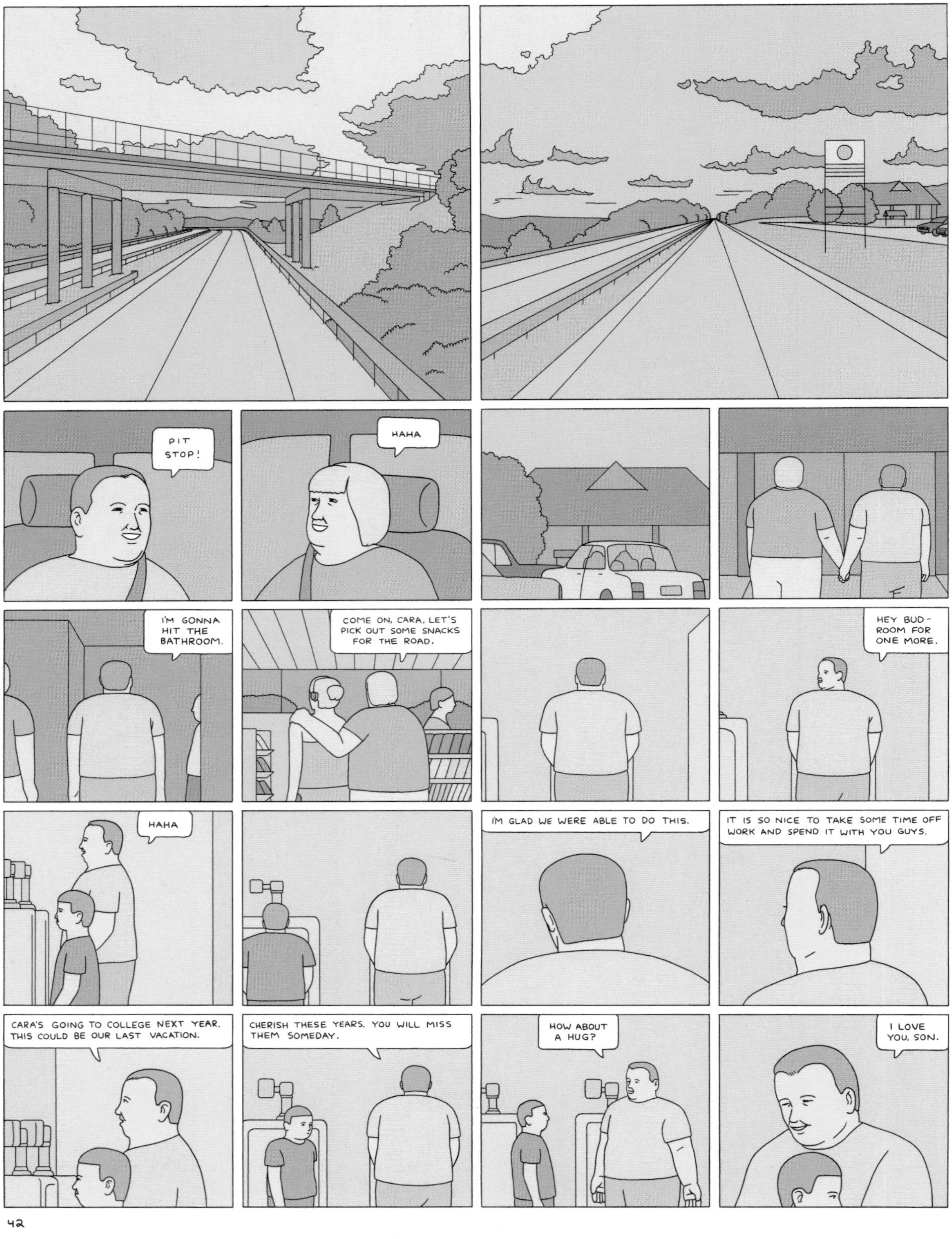
PIT STOP!
HAHA
I'M GONNA HIT THE BATHROOM.
COME ON, CARA, LET'S PICK OUT SOME SNACKS FOR THE ROAD.
HEY BUD - ROOM FOR ONE MORE.
HAHA
I'M GLAD WE WERE ABLE TO DO THIS.
IT IS SO NICE TO TAKE SOME TIME OFF WORK AND SPEND IT WITH YOU GUYS.
CARA'S GOING TO COLLEGE NEXT YEAR. THIS COULD BE OUR LAST VACATION.
CHERISH THESE YEARS. YOU WILL MISS THEM SOMEDAY.
HOW ABOUT A HUG?
I LOVE YOU, SON.

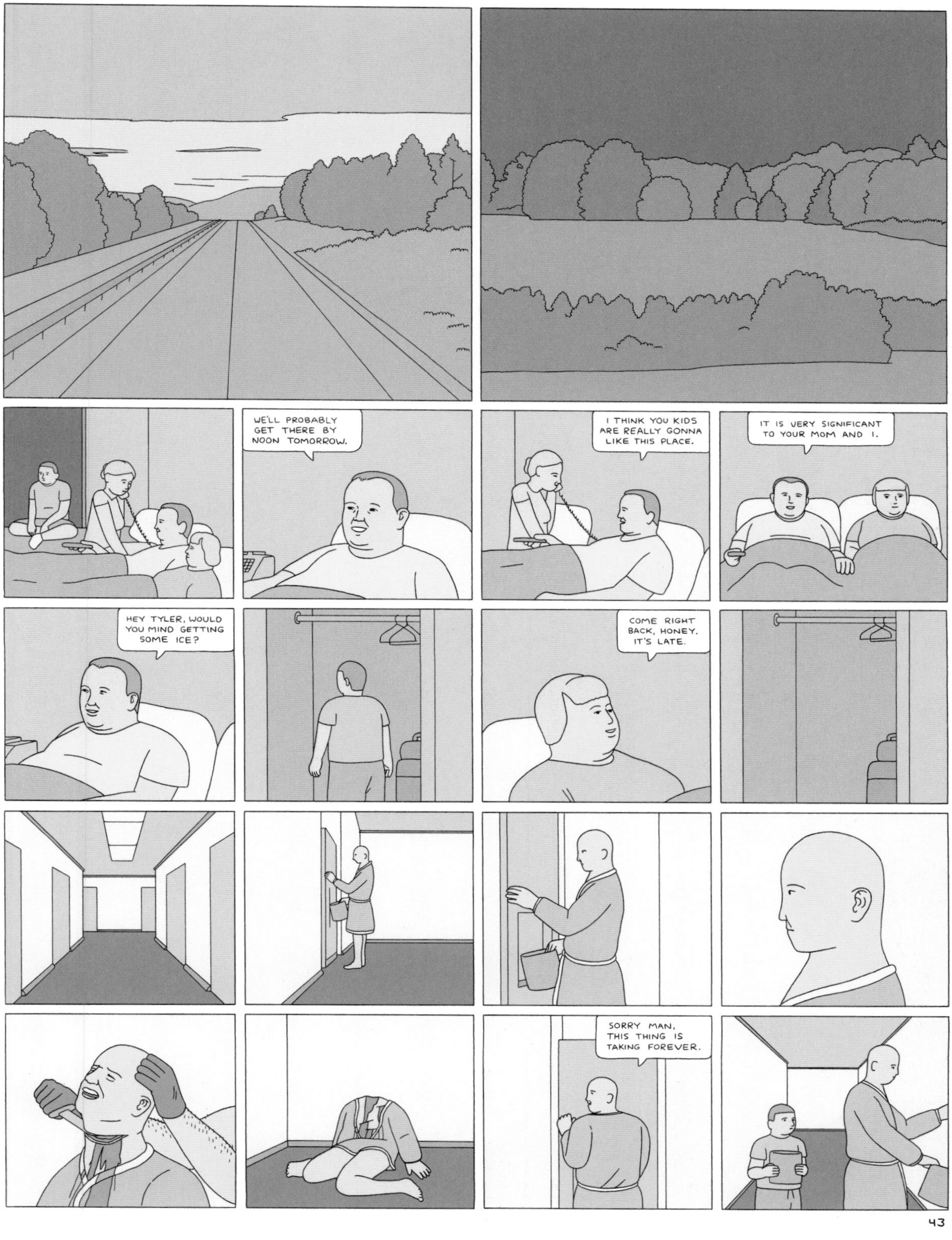
WE'LL PROBABLY GET THERE BY NOON TOMORROW.
I THINK YOU KIDS ARE REALLY GONNA LIKE THIS PLACE.
IT IS VERY SIGNIFICANT TO YOUR MOM AND I.
HEY TYLER, WOULD YOU MIND GETTING SOME ICE?
COME RIGHT BACK, HONEY. IT'S LATE.
SORRY MAN, THIS THING IS TAKING FOREVER.

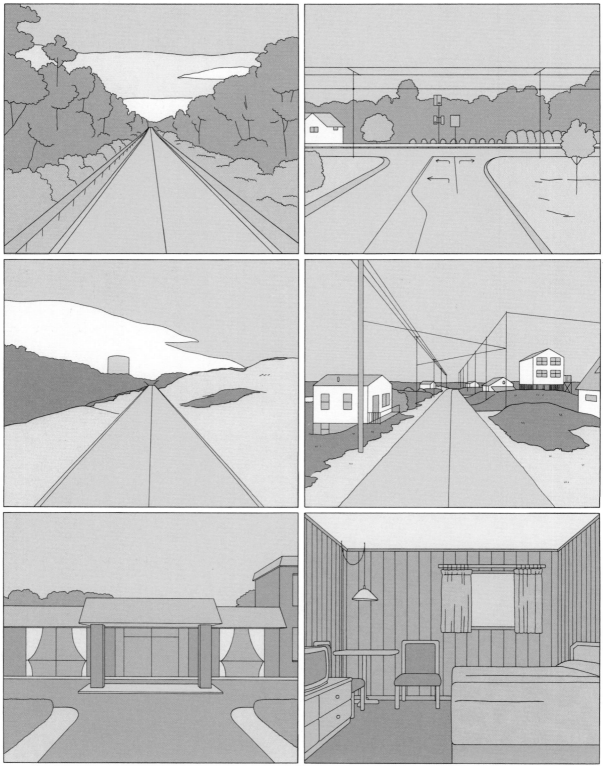

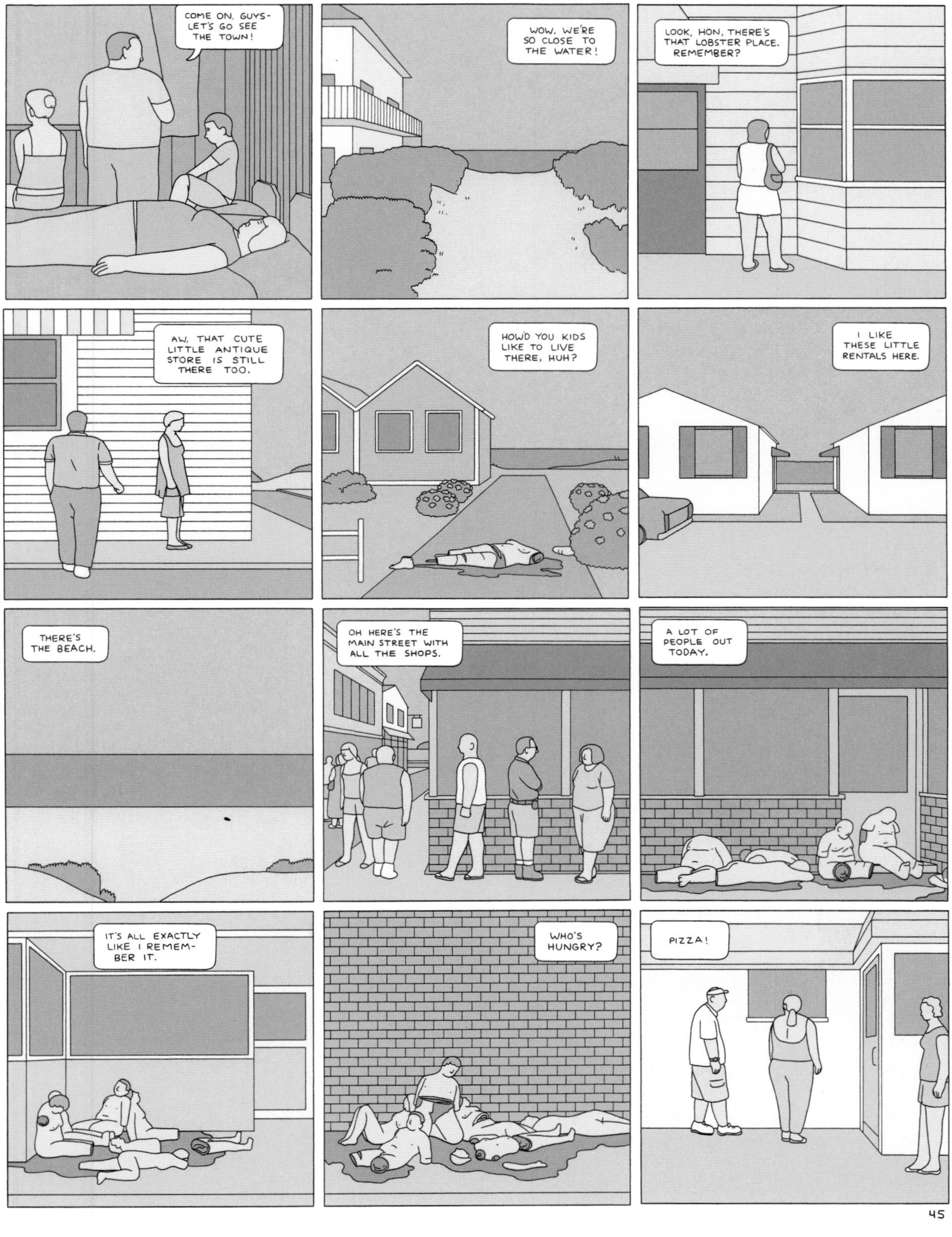
COME ON, GUYS- LET'S GO SEE THE TOWN!
WOW, WE'RE SO CLOSE TO THE WATER!
LOOK, HON, THERE'S THAT LOBSTER PLACE. REMEMBER?
AW, THAT CUTE LITTLE ANTIQUE STORE IS STILL THERE TOO.
HOW'D YOU KIDS LIKE TO LIVE THERE, HUH?
I LIKE THESE LITTLE RENTALS HERE.
THERE'S THE BEACH.
OH HERE'S THE MAIN STREET WITH ALL THE SHOPS.
A LOT OF PEOPLE OUT TODAY.
IT'S ALL EXACTLY LIKE I REMEMBER IT.
WHO'S HUNGRY?
PIZZA!

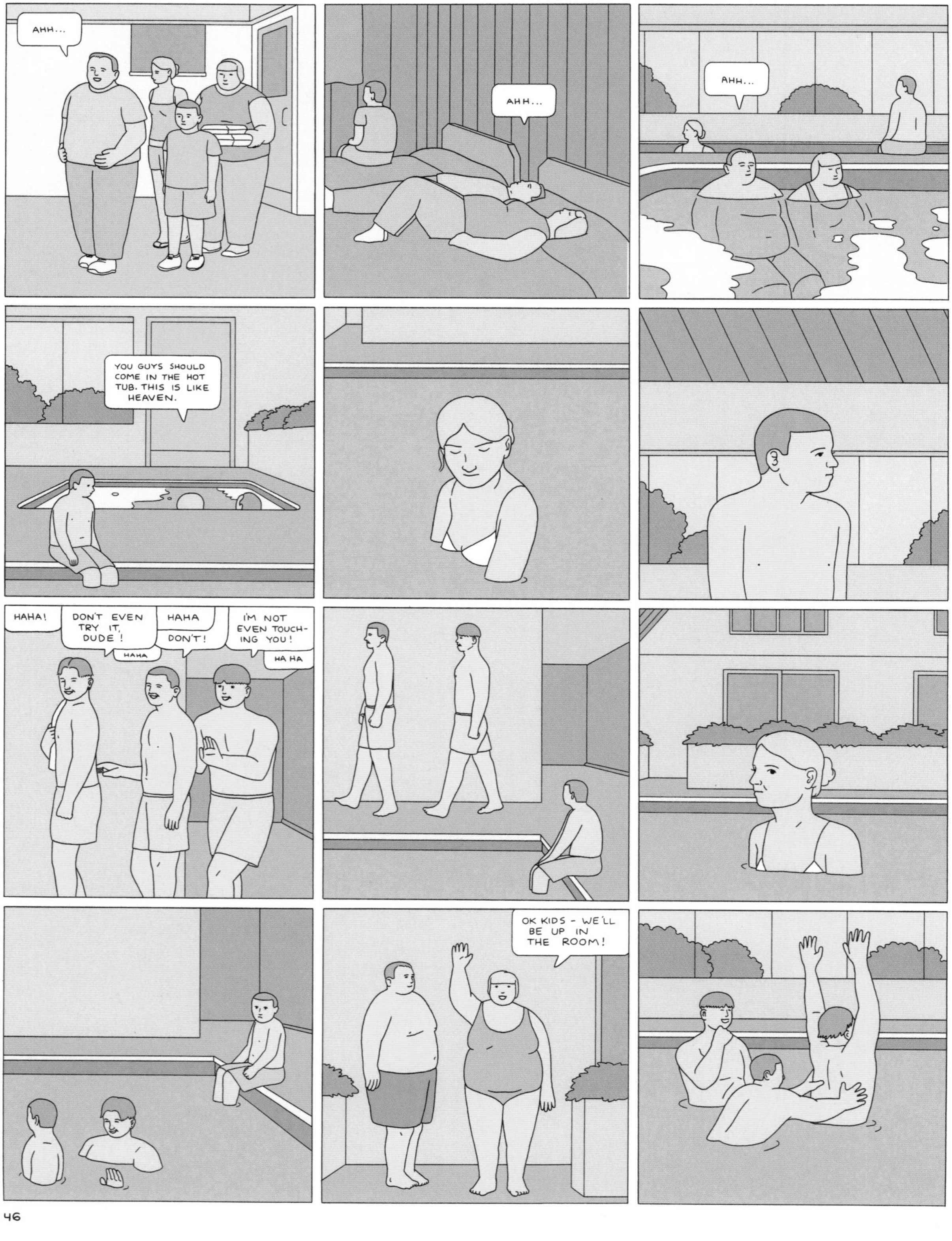
AHH...
AHH...
AHH...
YOU GUYS SHOULD COME IN THE HOT TUB. THIS IS LIKE HEAVEN.
HAHA!
DON'T EVEN TRY IT, DUDE!
HAHA
HAHA DON'T!
I'M NOT EVEN TOUCHING YOU!
HA HA
OK KIDS - WE'LL BE UP IN THE ROOM!

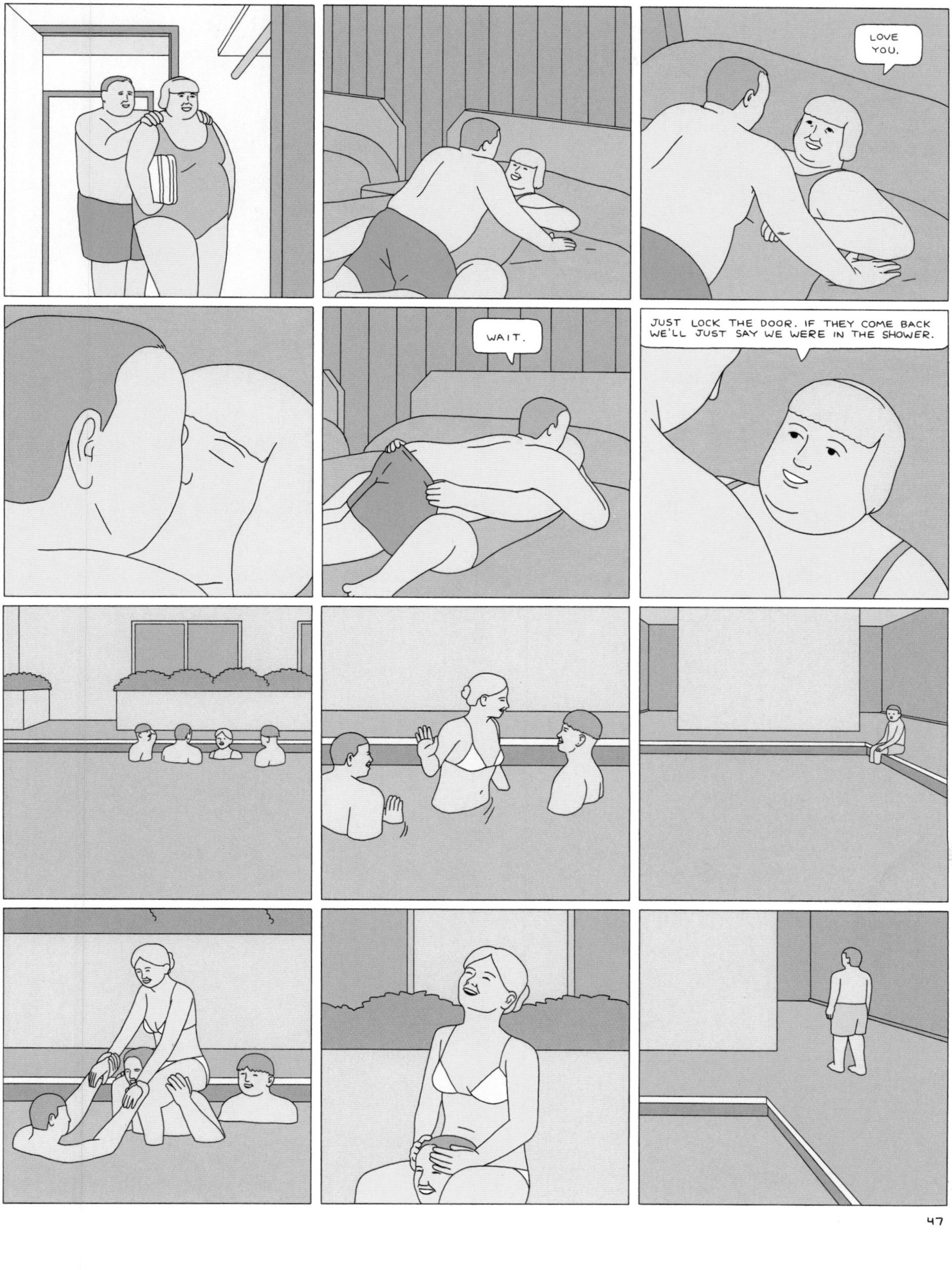
LOVE YOU.
WAIT.
JUST LOCK THE DOOR. IF THEY COME BACK WE'LL JUST SAY WE WERE IN THE SHOWER.

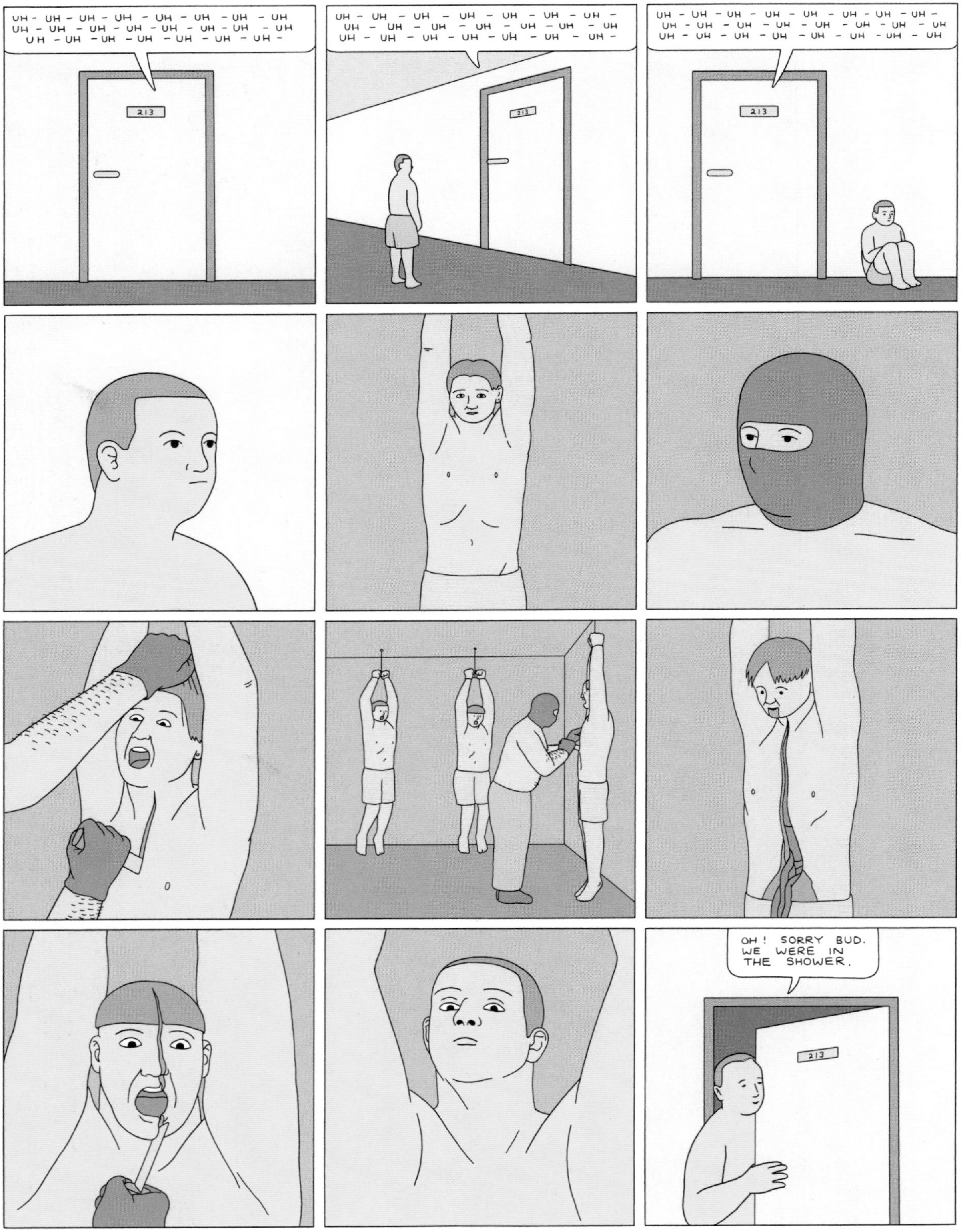
UH - UH - UH - UH - UH - UH - UH - UH
UH - UH - UH - UH - UH - UH - UH - UH
UH - UH - UH - UH - UH - UH - UH -
UH - UH - UH - UH - UH - UH - UH -
UH - UH - UH - UH - UH - UH - UH
UH - UH - UH - UH - UH - UH - UH -
UH - UH - UH - UH - UH - UH - UH - UH -
UH - UH - UH - UH - UH - UH - UH - UH
UH - UH - UH - UH - UH - UH - UH - UH
213
OH! SORRY BUD.
WE WERE IN
THE SHOWER.

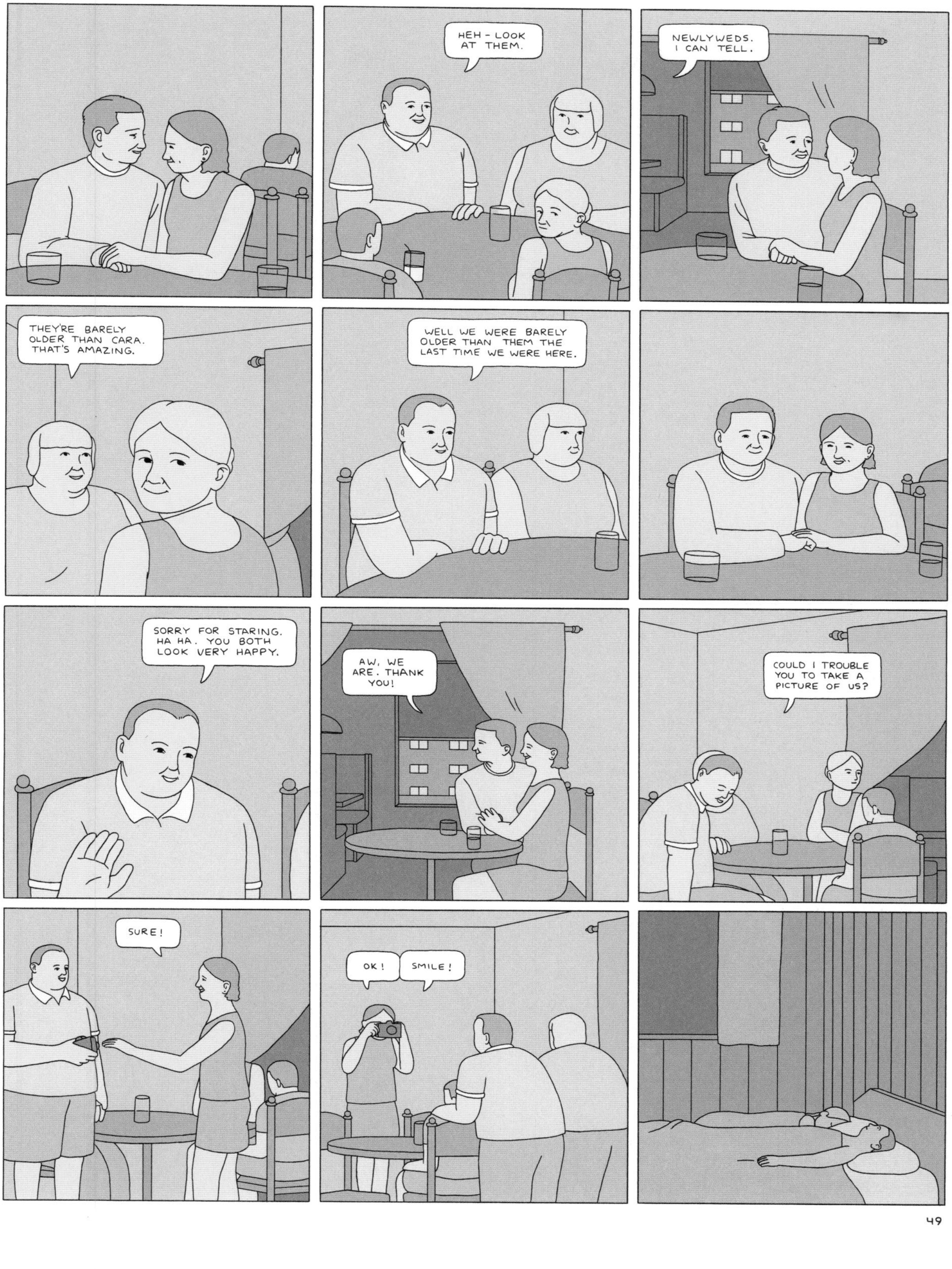
HEH - LOOK AT THEM.
NEWLYWEDS. I CAN TELL.
THEY'RE BARELY OLDER THAN CARA. THAT'S AMAZING.
WELL WE WERE BARELY OLDER THAN THEM THE LAST TIME WE WERE HERE.
SORRY FOR STARING. HA HA. YOU BOTH LOOK VERY HAPPY.
AW, WE ARE. THANK YOU!
COULD I TROUBLE YOU TO TAKE A PICTURE OF US?
SURE!
OK!
SMILE!

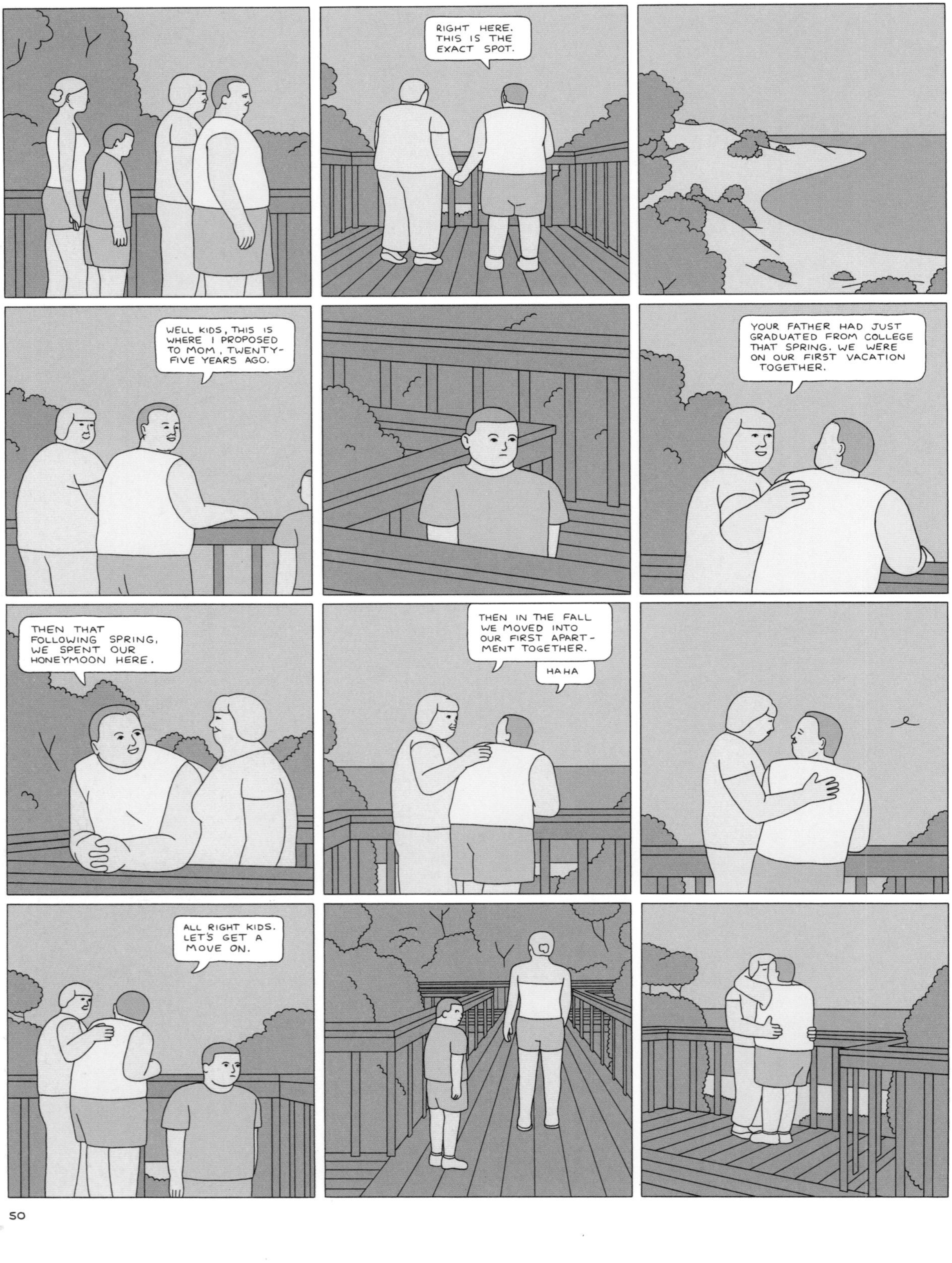
RIGHT HERE. THIS IS THE EXACT SPOT.
WELL KIDS, THIS IS WHERE I PROPOSED TO MOM, TWENTY-FIVE YEARS AGO.
YOUR FATHER HAD JUST GRADUATED FROM COLLEGE THAT SPRING. WE WERE ON OUR FIRST VACATION TOGETHER.
THEN THAT FOLLOWING SPRING, WE SPENT OUR HONEYMOON HERE.
THEN IN THE FALL WE MOVED INTO OUR FIRST APART-MENT TOGETHER.
HAHA
ALL RIGHT KIDS. LET'S GET A MOVE ON.

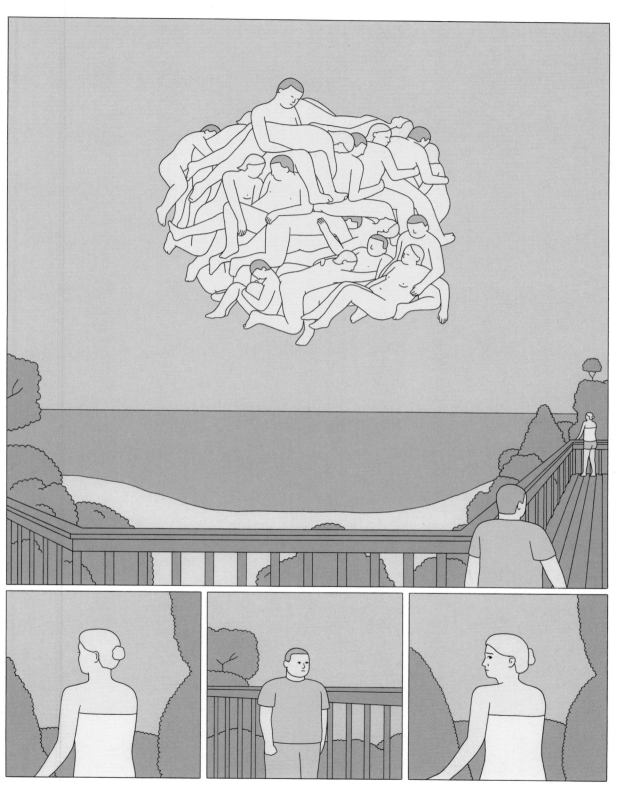

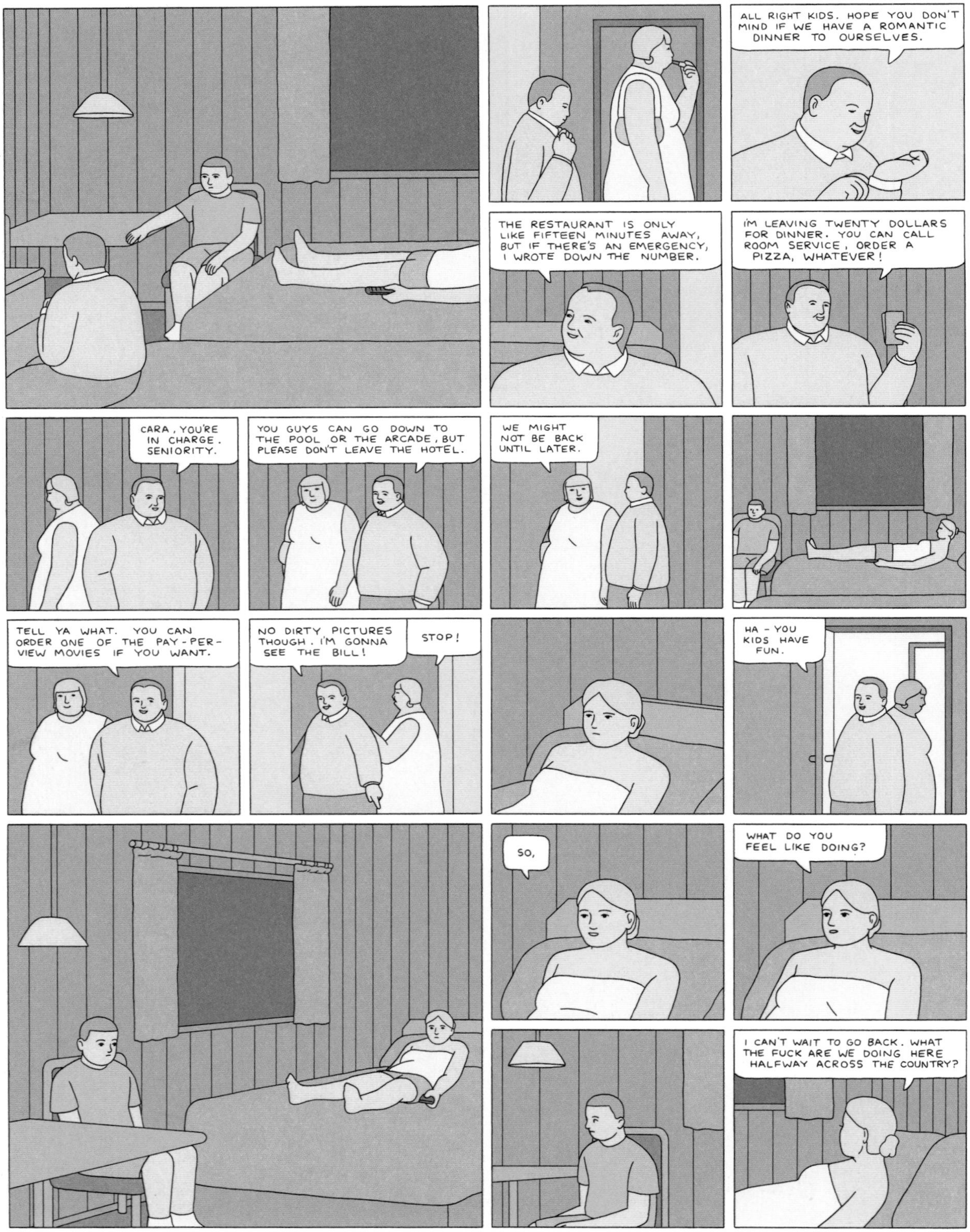
ALL RIGHT KIDS. HOPE YOU DON'T MIND IF WE HAVE A ROMANTIC DINNER TO OURSELVES.
THE RESTAURANT IS ONLY LIKE FIFTEEN MINUTES AWAY, BUT IF THERE'S AN EMERGENCY, I WROTE DOWN THE NUMBER.
I'M LEAVING TWENTY DOLLARS FOR DINNER. YOU CAN CALL ROOM SERVICE, ORDER A PIZZA, WHATEVER!
CARA, YOU'RE IN CHARGE. SENIORITY.
YOU GUYS CAN GO DOWN TO THE POOL OR THE ARCADE, BUT PLEASE DON'T LEAVE THE HOTEL.
WE MIGHT NOT BE BACK UNTIL LATER.
TELL YA WHAT. YOU CAN ORDER ONE OF THE PAY-PER-VIEW MOVIES IF YOU WANT.
NO DIRTY PICTURES THOUGH. I'M GONNA SEE THE BILL!
STOP!
HA - YOU KIDS HAVE FUN.
SO,
WHAT DO YOU FEEL LIKE DOING?
I CAN'T WAIT TO GO BACK. WHAT THE FUCK ARE WE DOING HERE HALFWAY ACROSS THE COUNTRY?

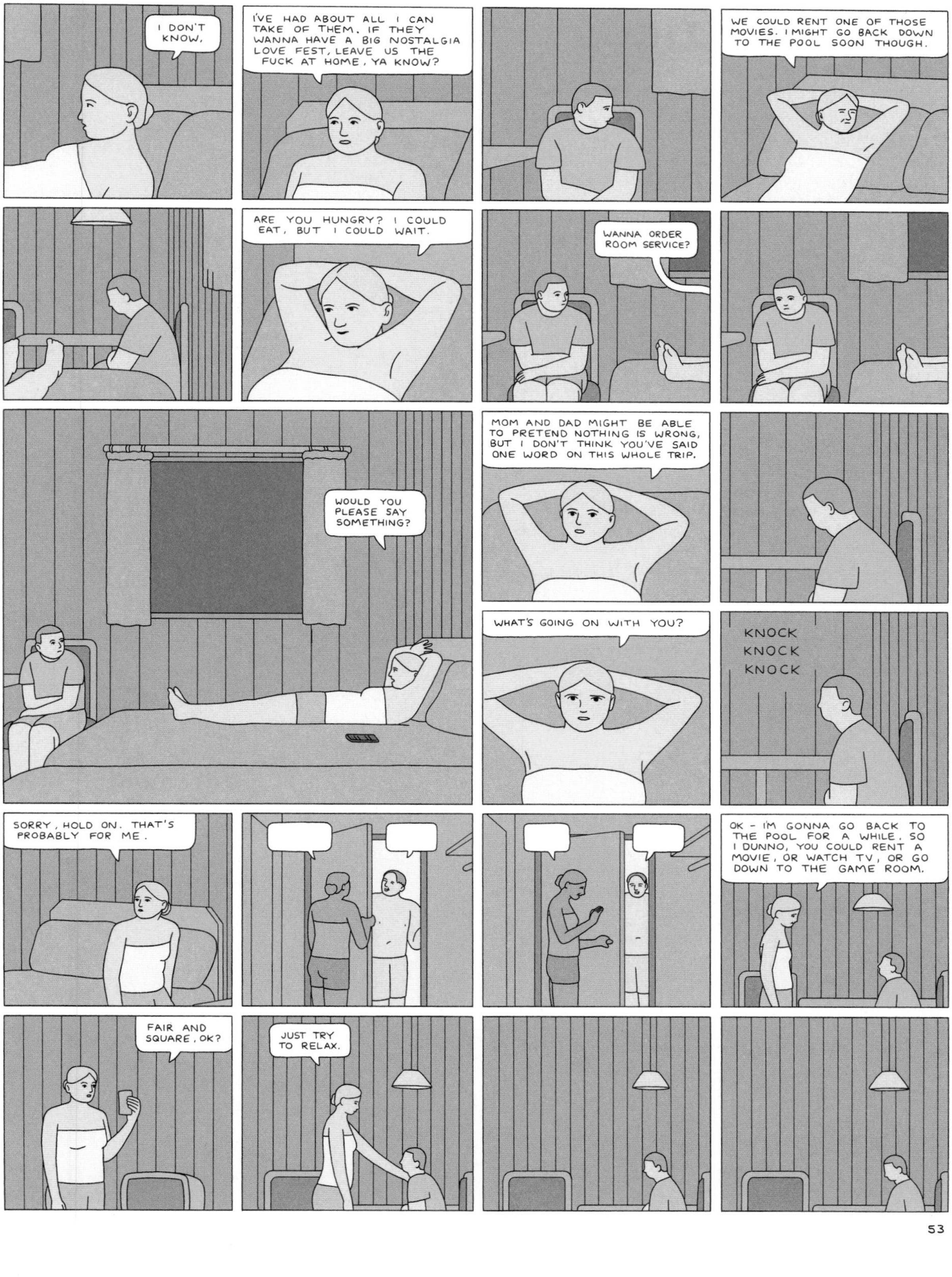
I DON'T KNOW,
I'VE HAD ABOUT ALL I CAN TAKE OF THEM. IF THEY WANNA HAVE A BIG NOSTALGIA LOVE FEST, LEAVE US THE FUCK AT HOME, YA KNOW?
WE COULD RENT ONE OF THOSE MOVIES. I MIGHT GO BACK DOWN TO THE POOL SOON THOUGH.
ARE YOU HUNGRY? I COULD EAT, BUT I COULD WAIT.
WANNA ORDER ROOM SERVICE?
WOULD YOU PLEASE SAY SOMETHING?
MOM AND DAD MIGHT BE ABLE TO PRETEND NOTHING IS WRONG, BUT I DON'T THINK YOU'VE SAID ONE WORD ON THIS WHOLE TRIP.
WHAT'S GOING ON WITH YOU?
KNOCK
KNOCK
KNOCK
SORRY, HOLD ON. THAT'S PROBABLY FOR ME.
OK - I'M GONNA GO BACK TO THE POOL FOR A WHILE. SO I DUNNO, YOU COULD RENT A MOVIE, OR WATCH TV, OR GO DOWN TO THE GAME ROOM.
FAIR AND SQUARE, OK?
JUST TRY TO RELAX.

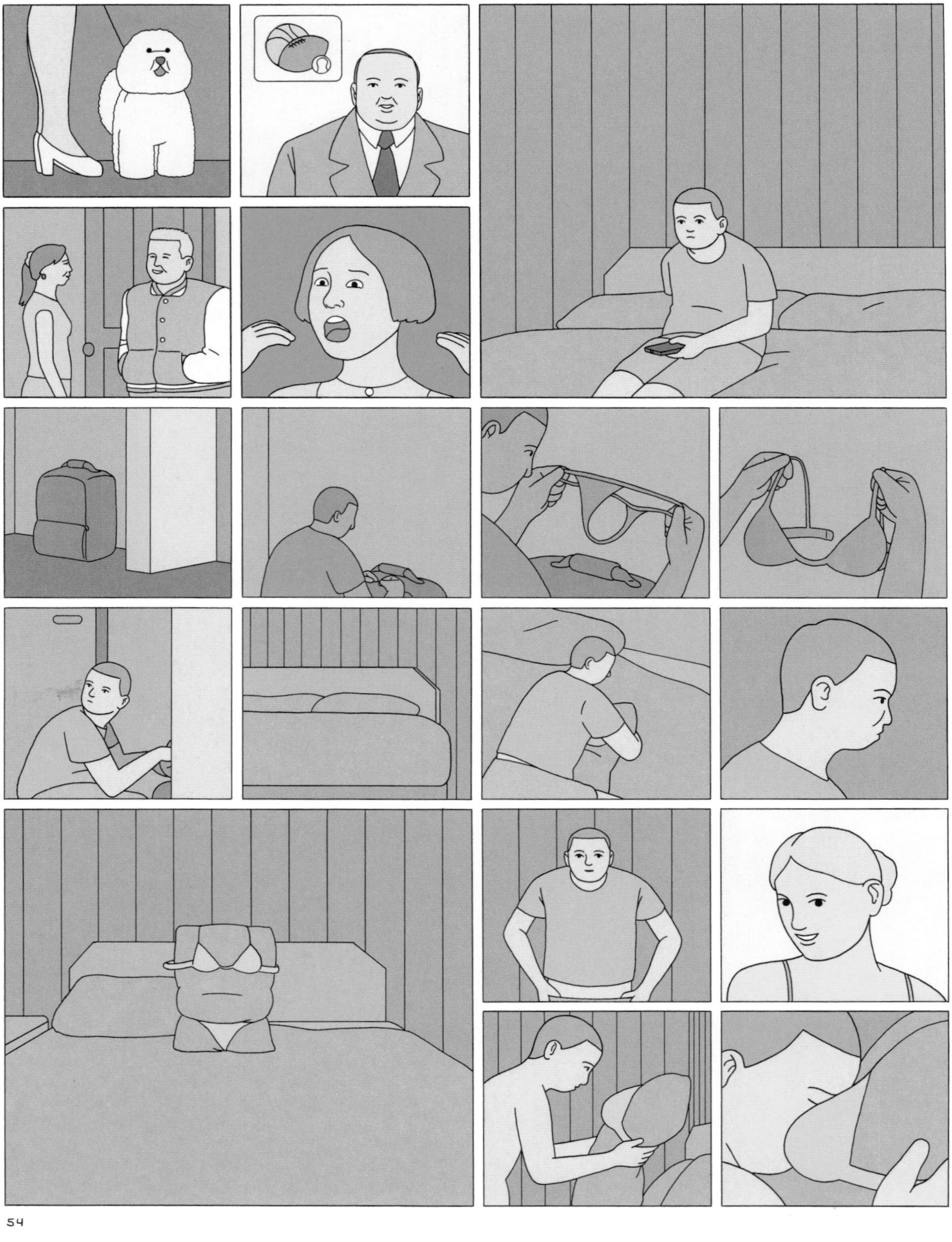

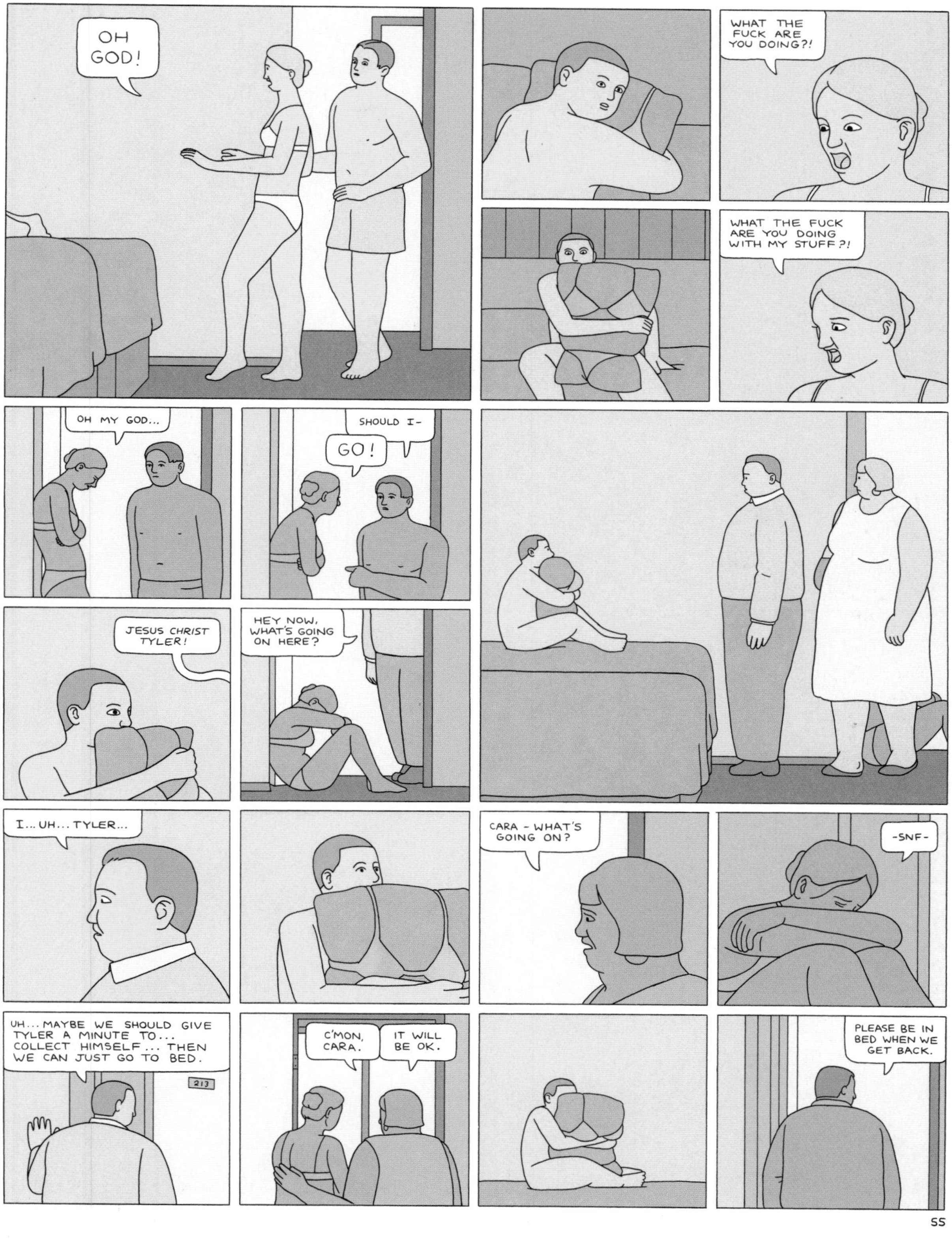
OH GOD!
WHAT THE FUCK ARE YOU DOING?!
WHAT THE FUCK ARE YOU DOING WITH MY STUFF?!
OH MY GOD...
SHOULD I-
GO!
JESUS CHRIST TYLER!
HEY NOW, WHAT'S GOING ON HERE?
I... UH... TYLER...
CARA - WHAT'S GOING ON?
-SNF-
UH... MAYBE WE SHOULD GIVE TYLER A MINUTE TO... COLLECT HIMSELF... THEN WE CAN JUST GO TO BED.
213
C'MON, CARA.
IT WILL BE OK.
PLEASE BE IN BED WHEN WE GET BACK.

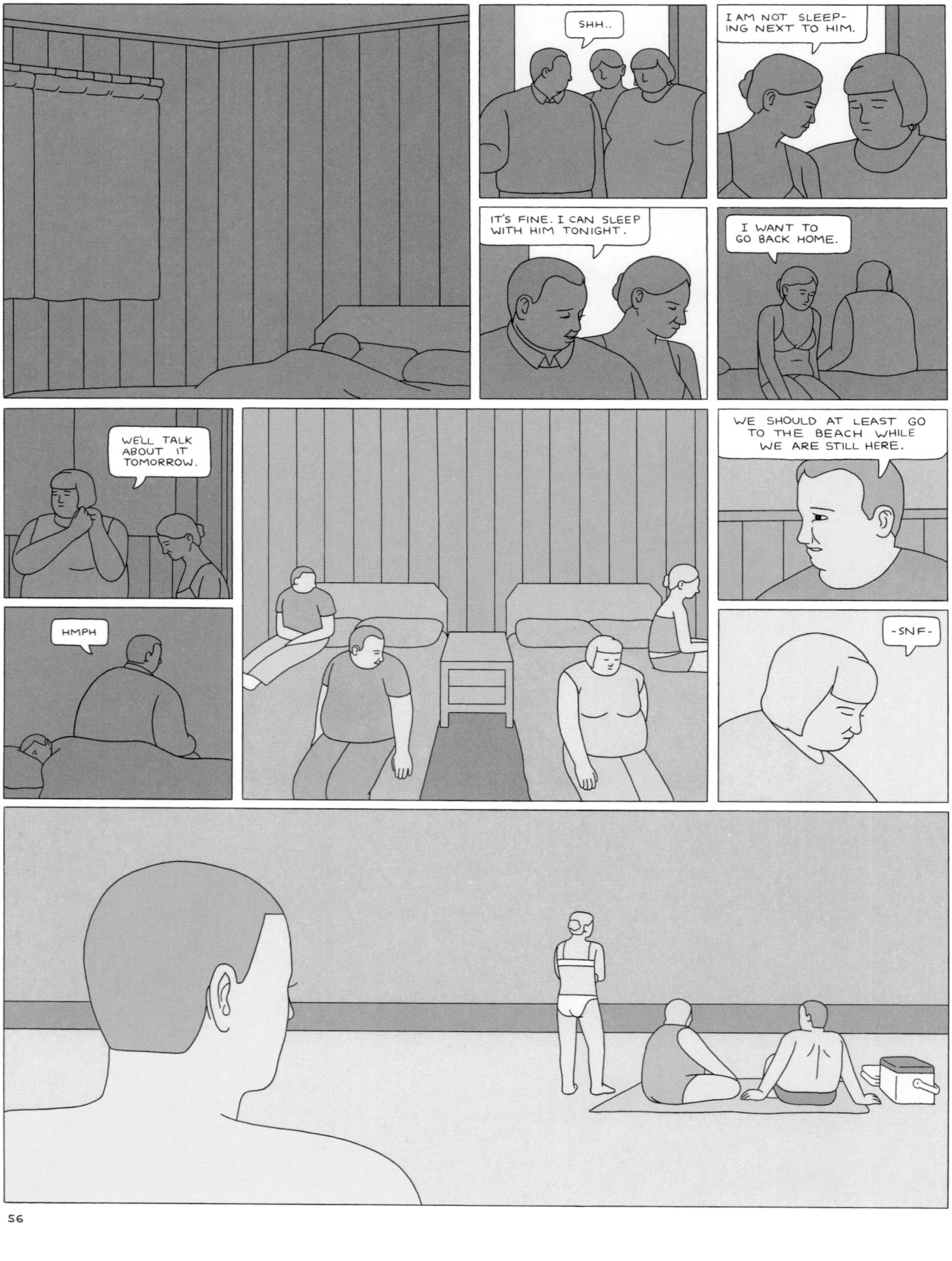
SHH..
I AM NOT SLEEP-ING NEXT TO HIM.
IT'S FINE. I CAN SLEEP WITH HIM TONIGHT.
I WANT TO GO BACK HOME.
WE'LL TALK ABOUT IT TOMORROW.
HMPH
WE SHOULD AT LEAST GO TO THE BEACH WHILE WE ARE STILL HERE.
-SNF-

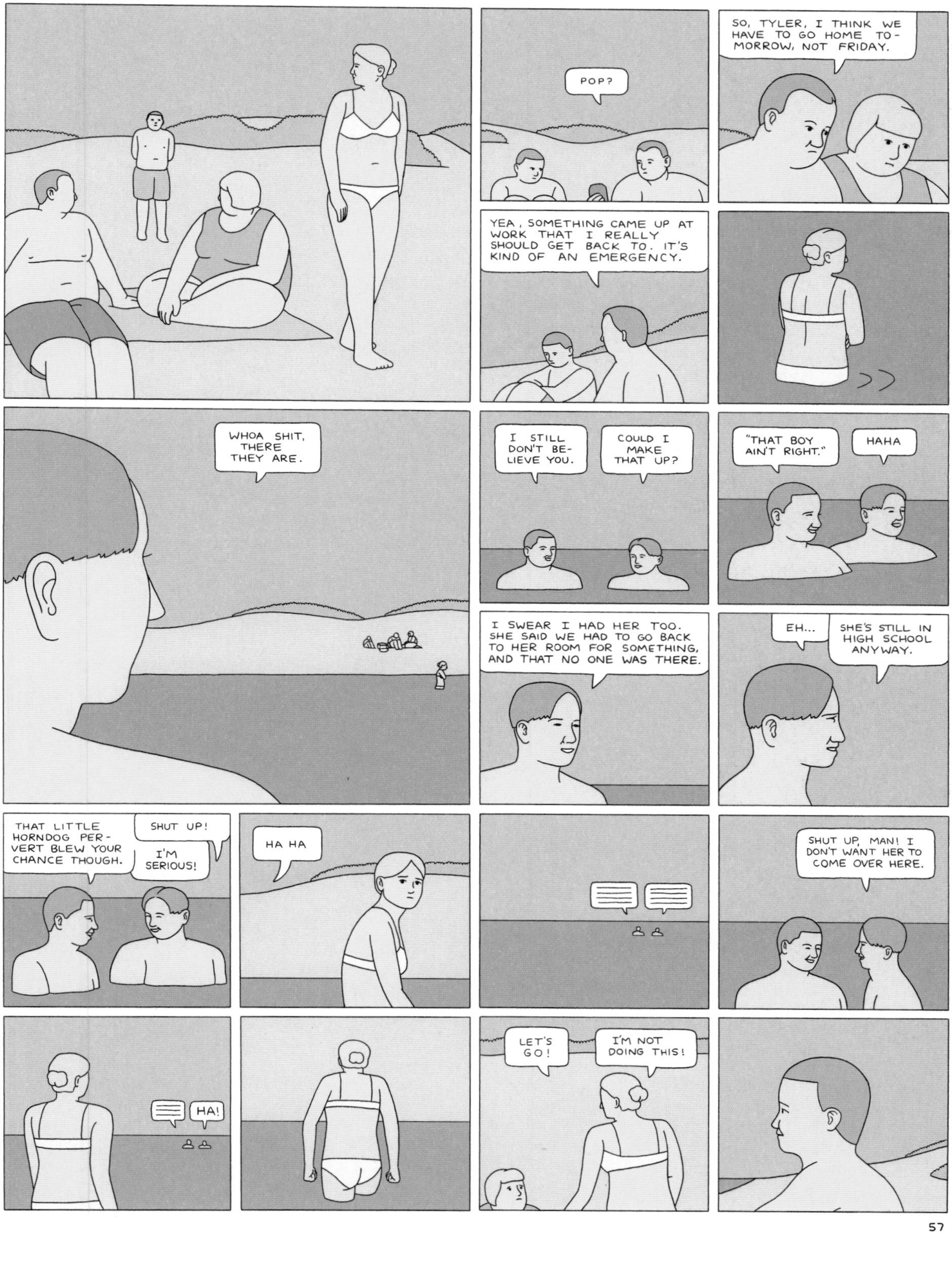
POP?
SO, TYLER, I THINK WE HAVE TO GO HOME TO-MORROW, NOT FRIDAY.
YEA, SOMETHING CAME UP AT WORK THAT I REALLY SHOULD GET BACK TO. IT'S KIND OF AN EMERGENCY.
WHOA SHIT, THERE THEY ARE.
I STILL DON'T BE-LIEVE YOU.
COULD I MAKE THAT UP?
"THAT BOY AIN'T RIGHT."
HAHA
I SWEAR I HAD HER TOO. SHE SAID WE HAD TO GO BACK TO HER ROOM FOR SOMETHING, AND THAT NO ONE WAS THERE.
EH...
SHE'S STILL IN HIGH SCHOOL ANYWAY.
THAT LITTLE HORNDOG PER-VERT BLEW YOUR CHANCE THOUGH.
SHUT UP!
I'M SERIOUS!
HA HA
SHUT UP, MAN! I DON'T WANT HER TO COME OVER HERE.
HA!
LET'S GO!
I'M NOT DOING THIS!

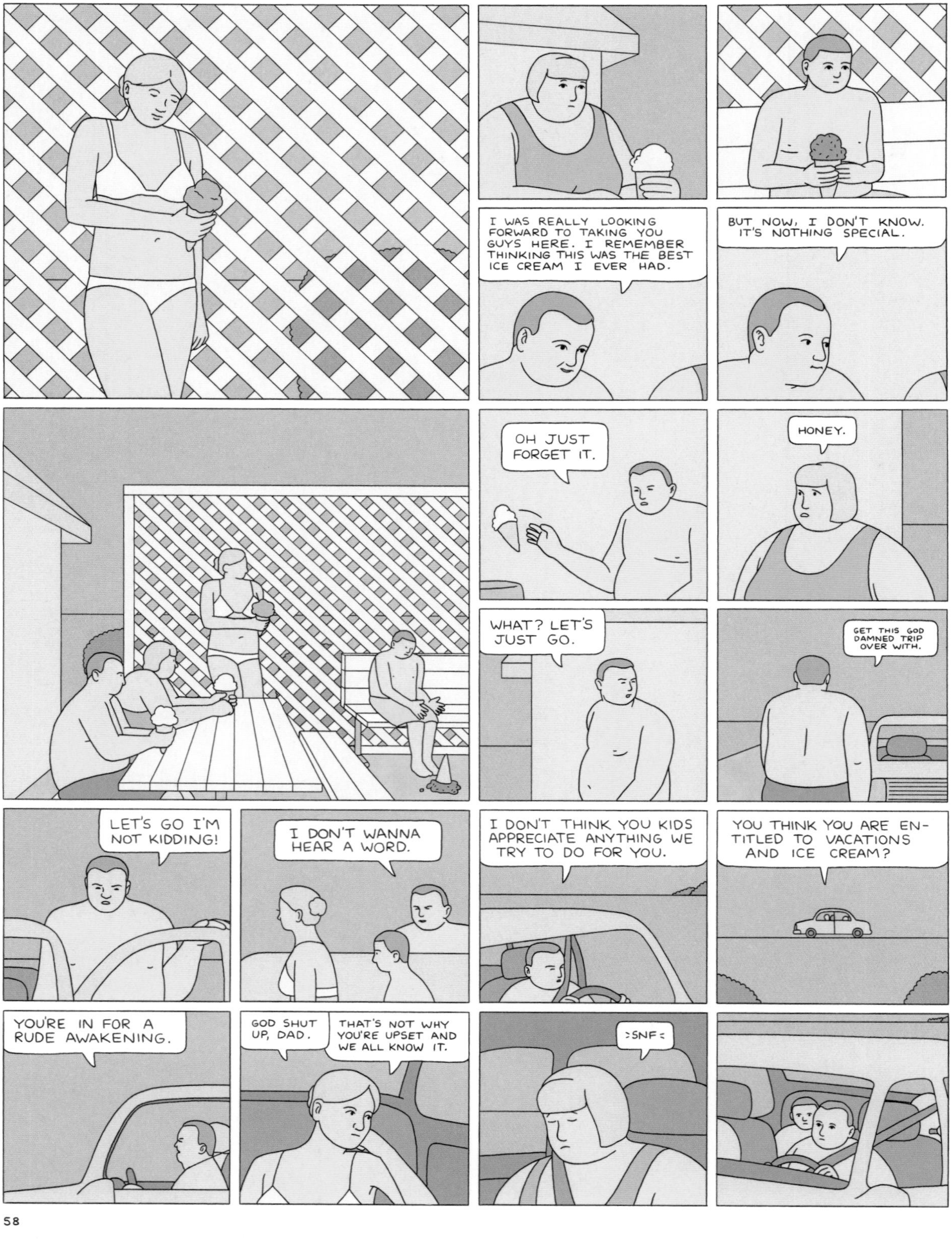
I WAS REALLY LOOKING FORWARD TO TAKING YOU GUYS HERE. I REMEMBER THINKING THIS WAS THE BEST ICE CREAM I EVER HAD.
BUT NOW, I DON'T KNOW. IT'S NOTHING SPECIAL.
OH JUST FORGET IT.
HONEY.
WHAT? LET'S JUST GO.
GET THIS GOD DAMNED TRIP OVER WITH.
LET'S GO I'M NOT KIDDING!
I DON'T WANNA HEAR A WORD.
I DON'T THINK YOU KIDS APPRECIATE ANYTHING WE TRY TO DO FOR YOU.
YOU THINK YOU ARE EN-TITLED TO VACATIONS AND ICE CREAM?
YOU'RE IN FOR A RUDE AWAKENING.
GOD SHUT UP, DAD.
THAT'S NOT WHY YOU'RE UPSET AND WE ALL KNOW IT.
>SNF<

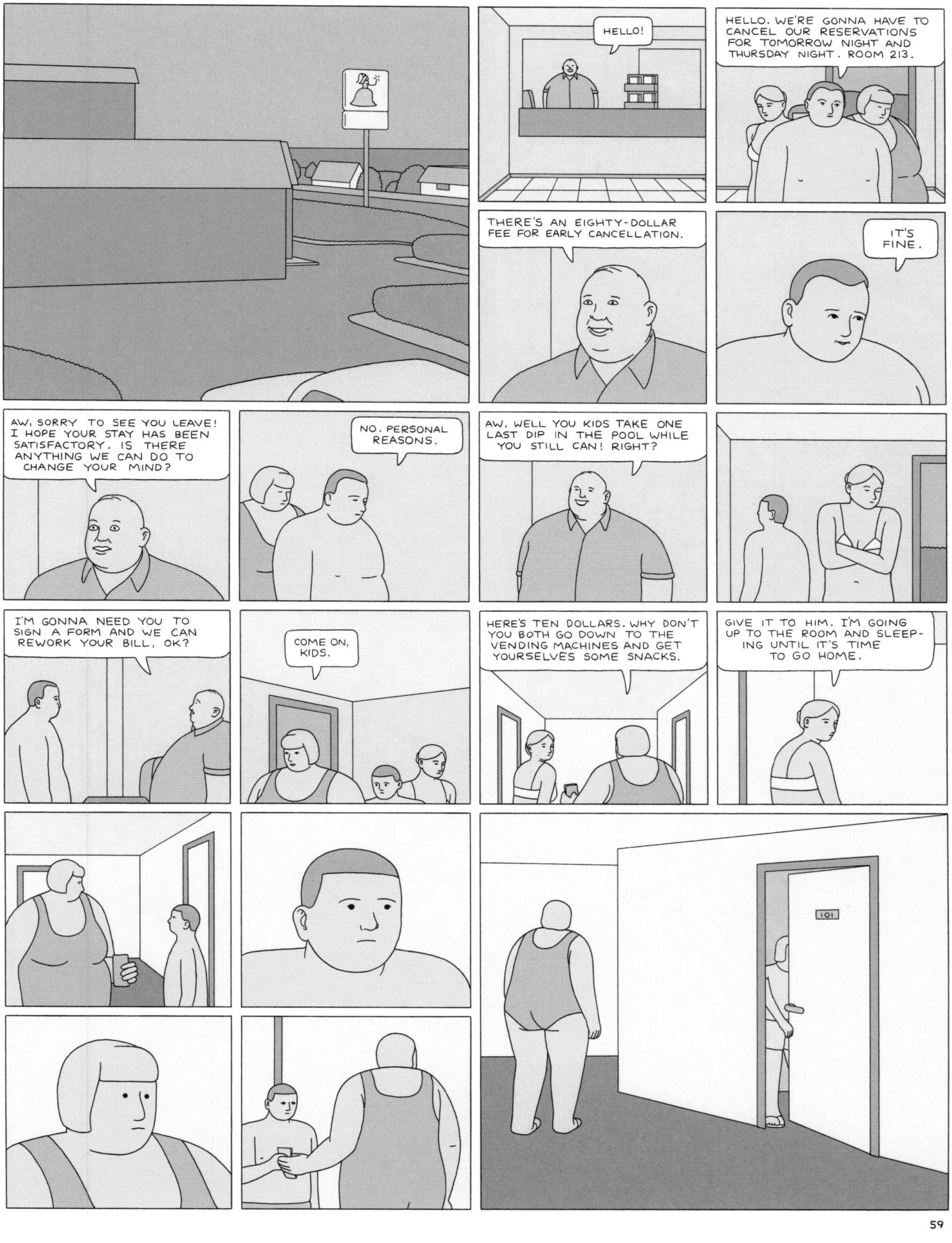
HELLO!
HELLO. WE'RE GONNA HAVE TO CANCEL OUR RESERVATIONS FOR TOMORROW NIGHT AND THURSDAY NIGHT. ROOM 213.
THERE'S AN EIGHTY-DOLLAR FEE FOR EARLY CANCELLATION.
IT'S FINE.
AW, SORRY TO SEE YOU LEAVE! I HOPE YOUR STAY HAS BEEN SATISFACTORY. IS THERE ANYTHING WE CAN DO TO CHANGE YOUR MIND?
NO. PERSONAL REASONS.
AW, WELL YOU KIDS TAKE ONE LAST DIP IN THE POOL WHILE YOU STILL CAN! RIGHT?
I'M GONNA NEED YOU TO SIGN A FORM AND WE CAN REWORK YOUR BILL, OK?
COME ON, KIDS.
HERE'S TEN DOLLARS. WHY DON'T YOU BOTH GO DOWN TO THE VENDING MACHINES AND GET YOURSELVES SOME SNACKS.
GIVE IT TO HIM. I'M GOING UP TO THE ROOM AND SLEEPING UNTIL IT'S TIME TO GO HOME.
101

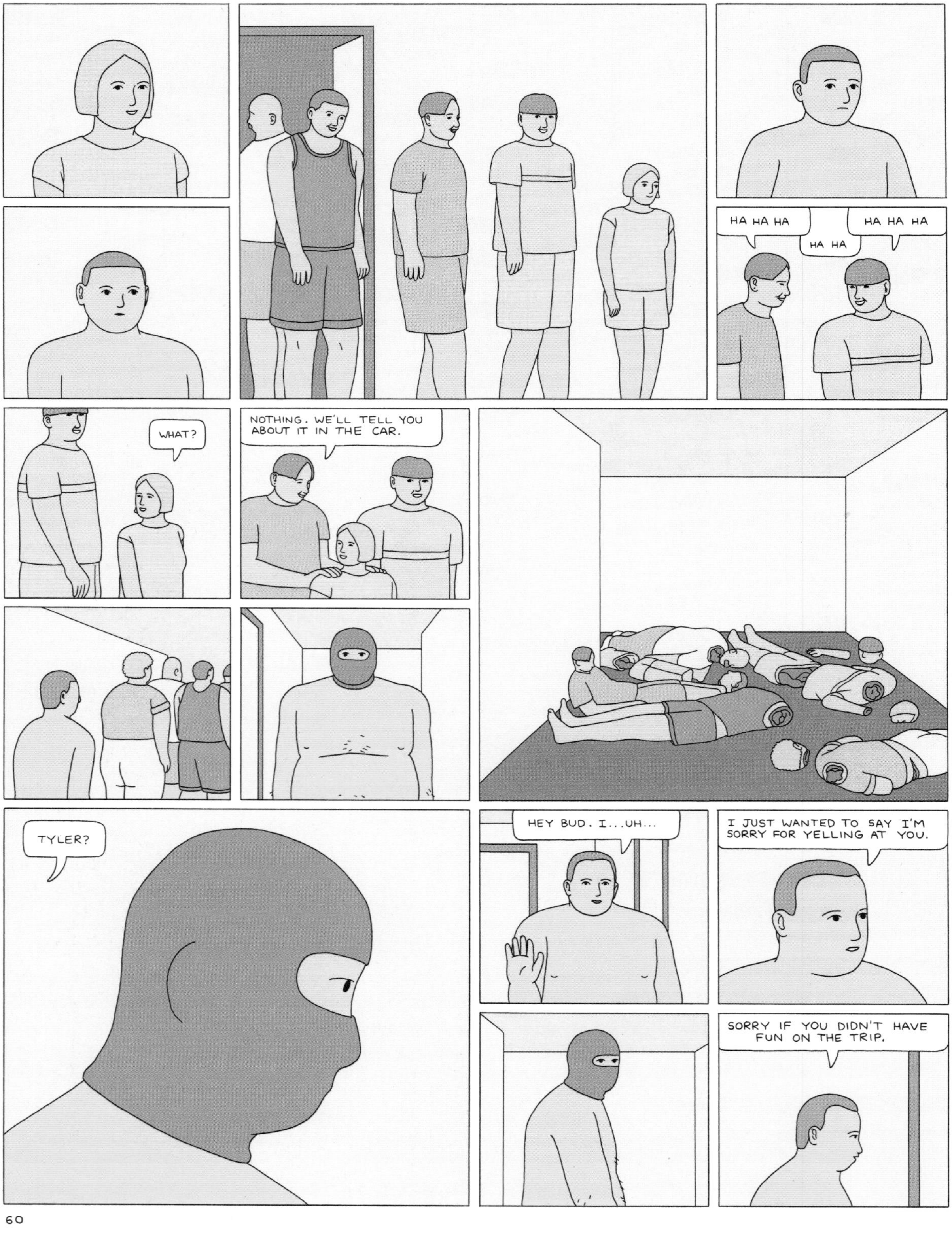
HA HA HA
HA HA
HA HA HA
WHAT?
NOTHING. WE'LL TELL YOU ABOUT IT IN THE CAR.
TYLER?
HEY BUD. I...UH...
I JUST WANTED TO SAY I'M SORRY FOR YELLING AT YOU.
SORRY IF YOU DIDN'T HAVE FUN ON THE TRIP.

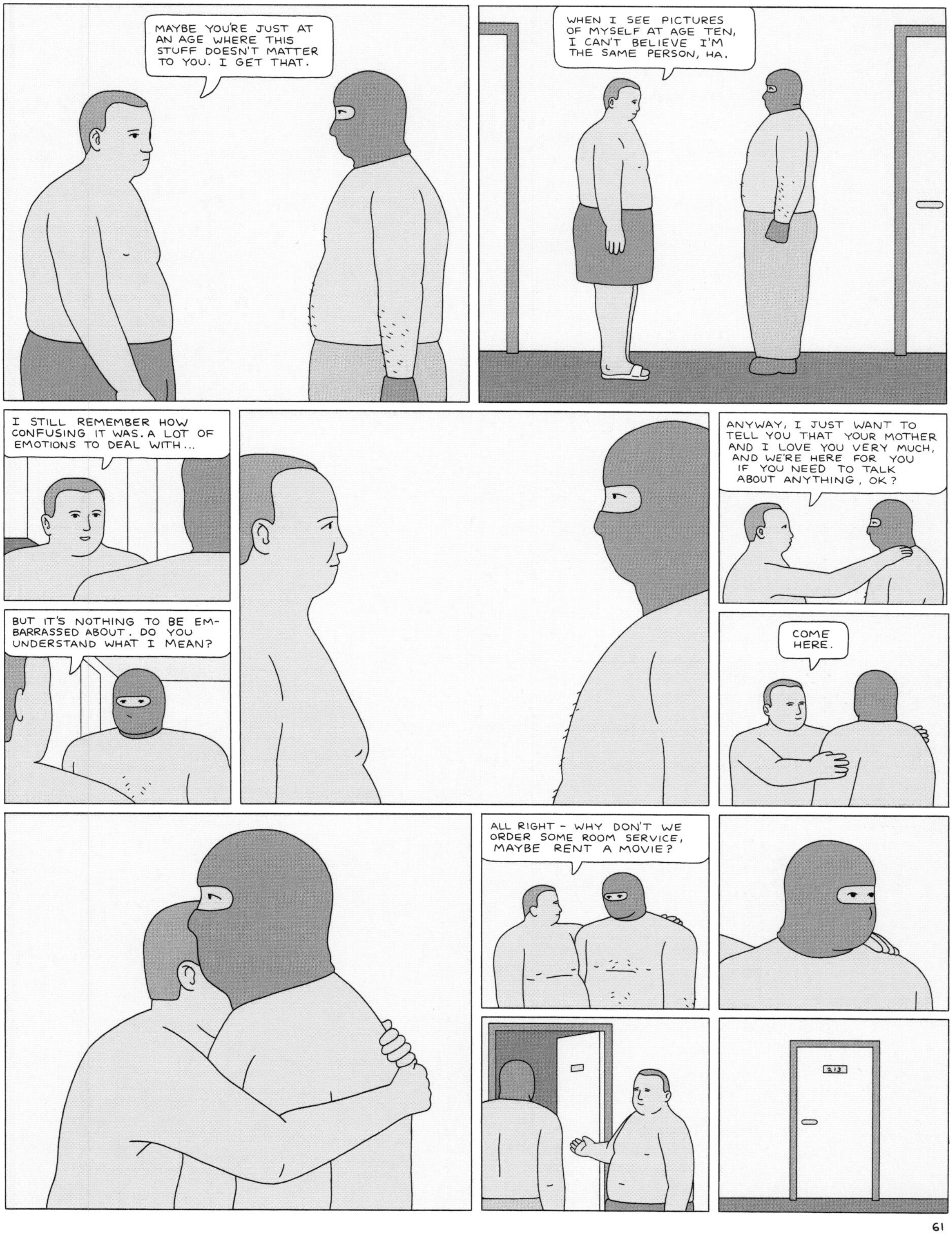

MAYBE YOU'RE JUST AT AN AGE WHERE THIS STUFF DOESN'T MATTER TO YOU. I GET THAT.
WHEN I SEE PICTURES OF MYSELF AT AGE TEN, I CAN'T BELIEVE I'M THE SAME PERSON, HA.
I STILL REMEMBER HOW CONFUSING IT WAS. A LOT OF EMOTIONS TO DEAL WITH...
BUT IT'S NOTHING TO BE EM-BARRASSED ABOUT. DO YOU UNDERSTAND WHAT I MEAN?
ANYWAY, I JUST WANT TO TELL YOU THAT YOUR MOTHER AND I LOVE YOU VERY MUCH, AND WE'RE HERE FOR YOU IF YOU NEED TO TALK ABOUT ANYTHING, OK?
COME HERE.
ALL RIGHT - WHY DON'T WE ORDER SOME ROOM SERVICE, MAYBE RENT A MOVIE?
213

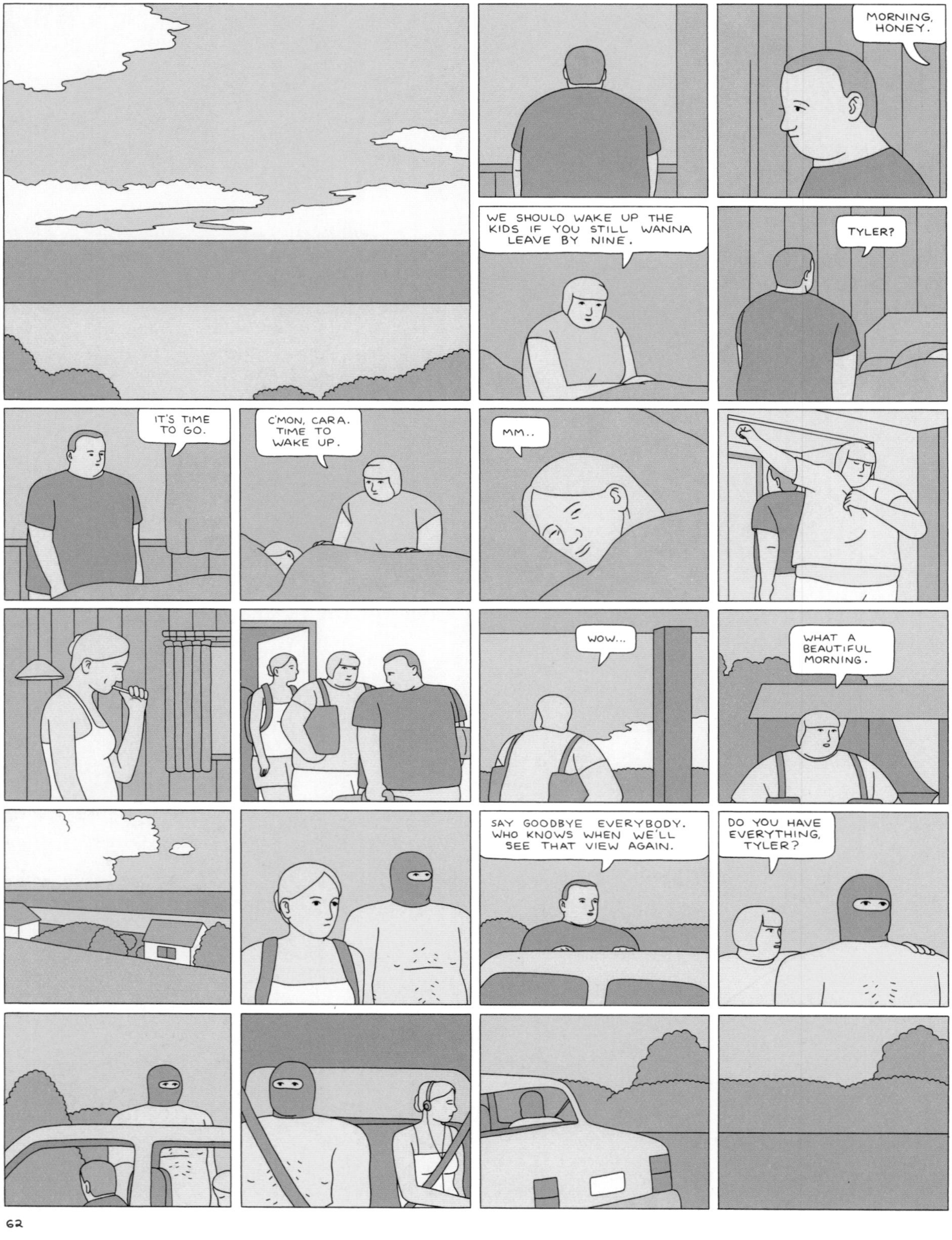
MORNING, HONEY.
WE SHOULD WAKE UP THE KIDS IF YOU STILL WANNA LEAVE BY NINE.
TYLER?
IT'S TIME TO GO.
C'MON, CARA. TIME TO WAKE UP.
MM..
WOW...
WHAT A BEAUTIFUL MORNING.
SAY GOODBYE EVERYBODY. WHO KNOWS WHEN WE'LL SEE THAT VIEW AGAIN.
DO YOU HAVE EVERYTHING, TYLER?

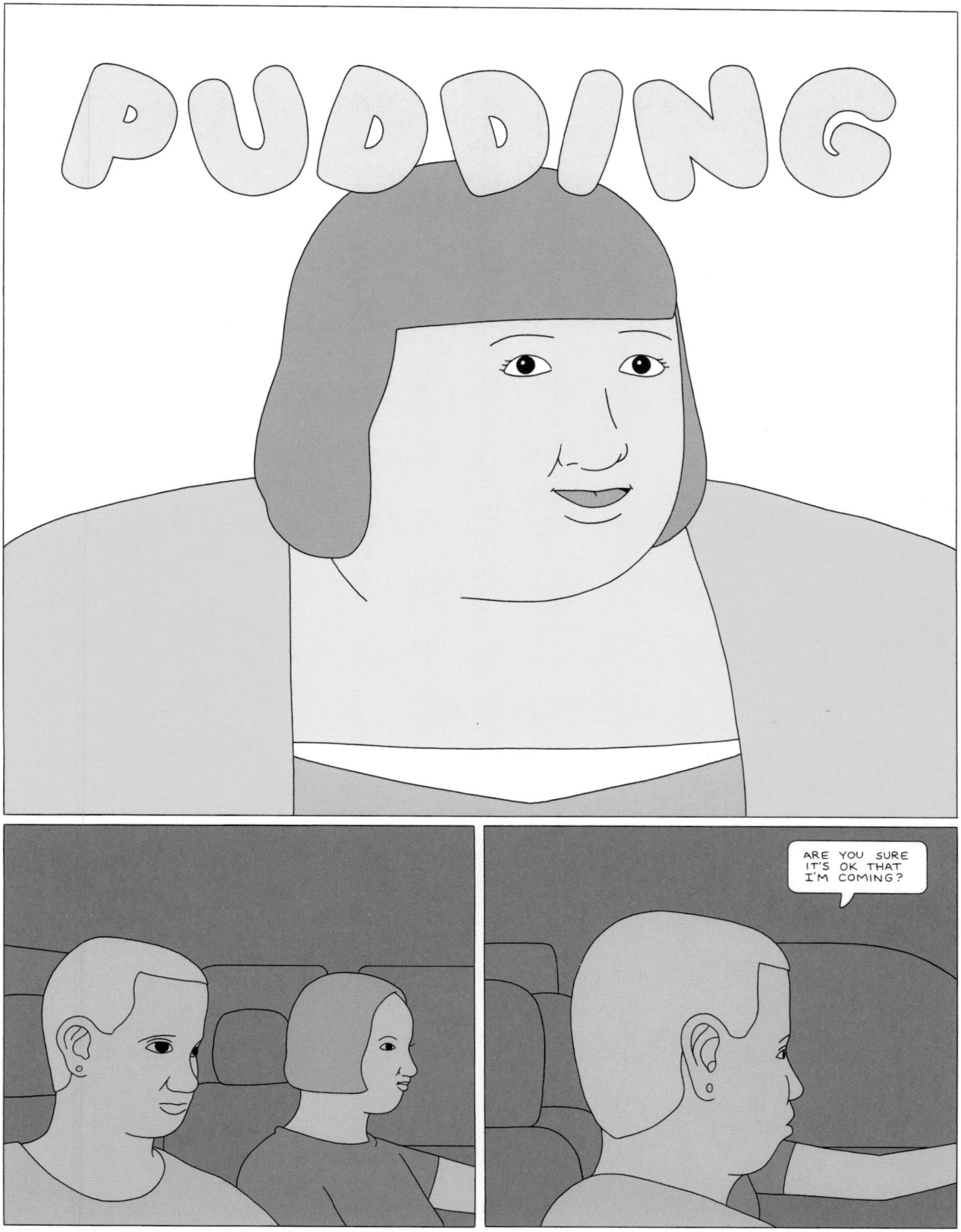
PUDDING
ARE YOU SURE IT'S OK THAT I'M COMING?

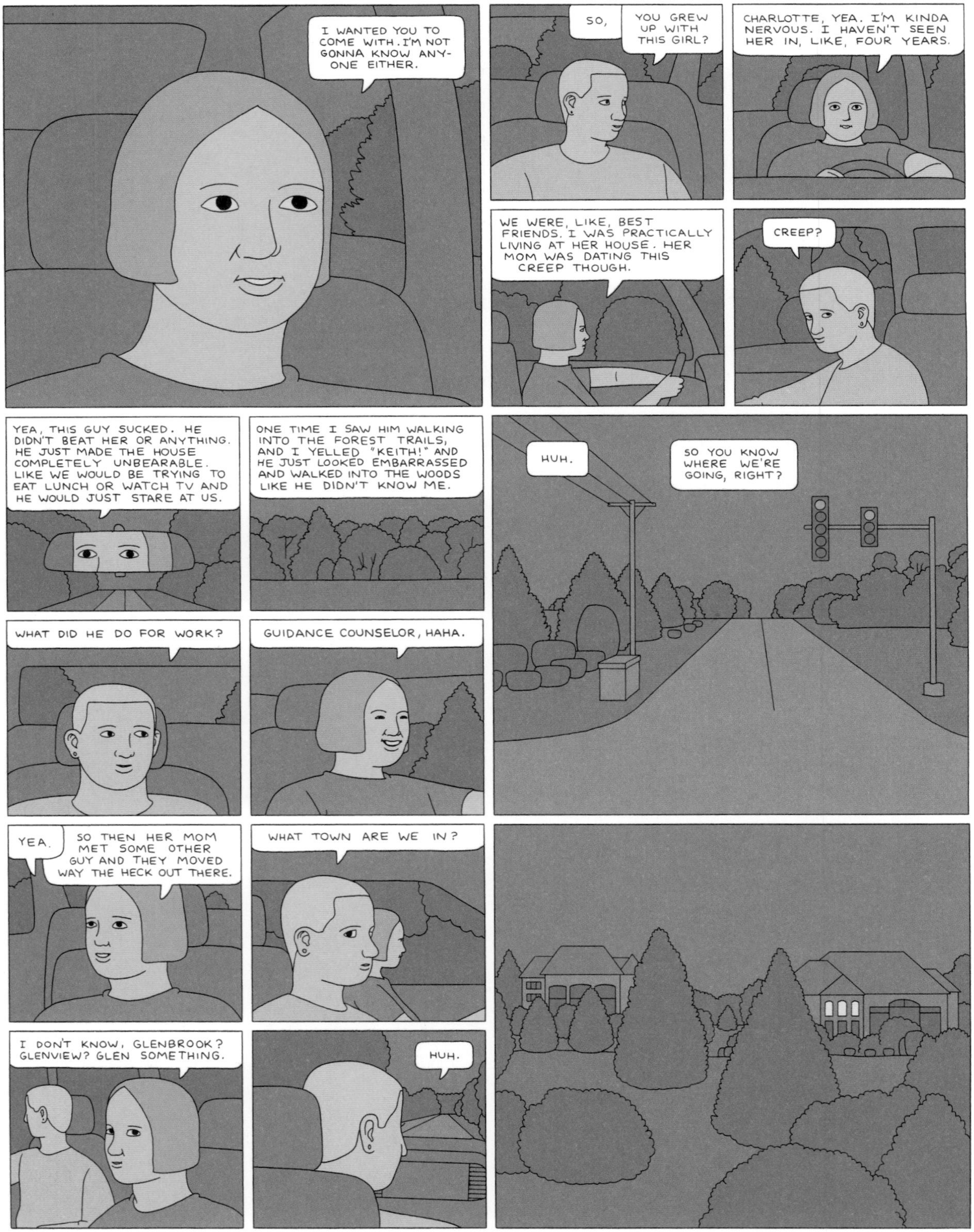
I WANTED YOU TO COME WITH. I'M NOT GONNA KNOW ANY-ONE EITHER.
SO,
YOU GREW UP WITH THIS GIRL?
CHARLOTTE, YEA. I'M KINDA NERVOUS. I HAVEN'T SEEN HER IN, LIKE, FOUR YEARS.
WE WERE, LIKE, BEST FRIENDS. I WAS PRACTICALLY LIVING AT HER HOUSE. HER MOM WAS DATING THIS CREEP THOUGH.
CREEP?
YEA, THIS GUY SUCKED. HE DIDN'T BEAT HER OR ANYTHING. HE JUST MADE THE HOUSE COMPLETELY UNBEARABLE. LIKE WE WOULD BE TRYING TO EAT LUNCH OR WATCH TV AND HE WOULD JUST STARE AT US.
ONE TIME I SAW HIM WALKING INTO THE FOREST TRAILS, AND I YELLED "KEITH!" AND HE JUST LOOKED EMBARRASSED AND WALKED INTO THE WOODS LIKE HE DIDN'T KNOW ME.
WHAT DID HE DO FOR WORK?
GUIDANCE COUNSELOR, HAHA.
HUH.
SO YOU KNOW WHERE WE'RE GOING, RIGHT?
YEA.
SO THEN HER MOM MET SOME OTHER GUY AND THEY MOVED WAY THE HECK OUT THERE.
WHAT TOWN ARE WE IN?
I DON'T KNOW, GLENBROOK? GLENVIEW? GLEN SOMETHING.
HUH.

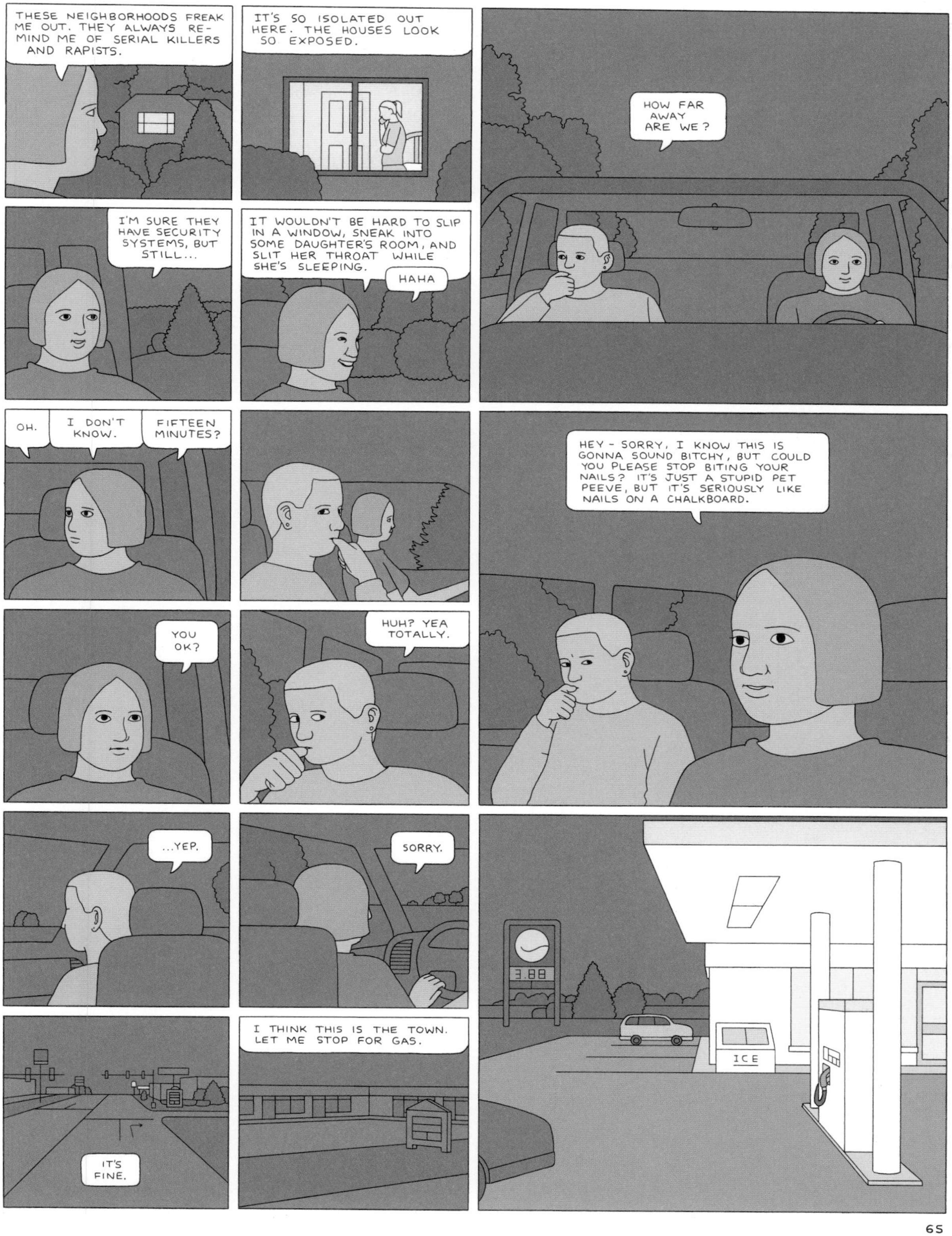
THESE NEIGHBORHOODS FREAK ME OUT. THEY ALWAYS RE-MIND ME OF SERIAL KILLERS AND RAPISTS.
IT'S SO ISOLATED OUT HERE. THE HOUSES LOOK SO EXPOSED.
HOW FAR AWAY ARE WE?
I'M SURE THEY HAVE SECURITY SYSTEMS, BUT STILL...
IT WOULDN'T BE HARD TO SLIP IN A WINDOW, SNEAK INTO SOME DAUGHTER'S ROOM, AND SLIT HER THROAT WHILE SHE'S SLEEPING.
HAHA
OH.
I DON'T KNOW.
FIFTEEN MINUTES?
HEY - SORRY, I KNOW THIS IS GONNA SOUND BITCHY, BUT COULD YOU PLEASE STOP BITING YOUR NAILS? IT'S JUST A STUPID PET PEEVE, BUT IT'S SERIOUSLY LIKE NAILS ON A CHALKBOARD.
YOU OK?
HUH? YEA TOTALLY.
...YEP.
SORRY.
IT'S FINE.
I THINK THIS IS THE TOWN. LET ME STOP FOR GAS.
3.88
ICE

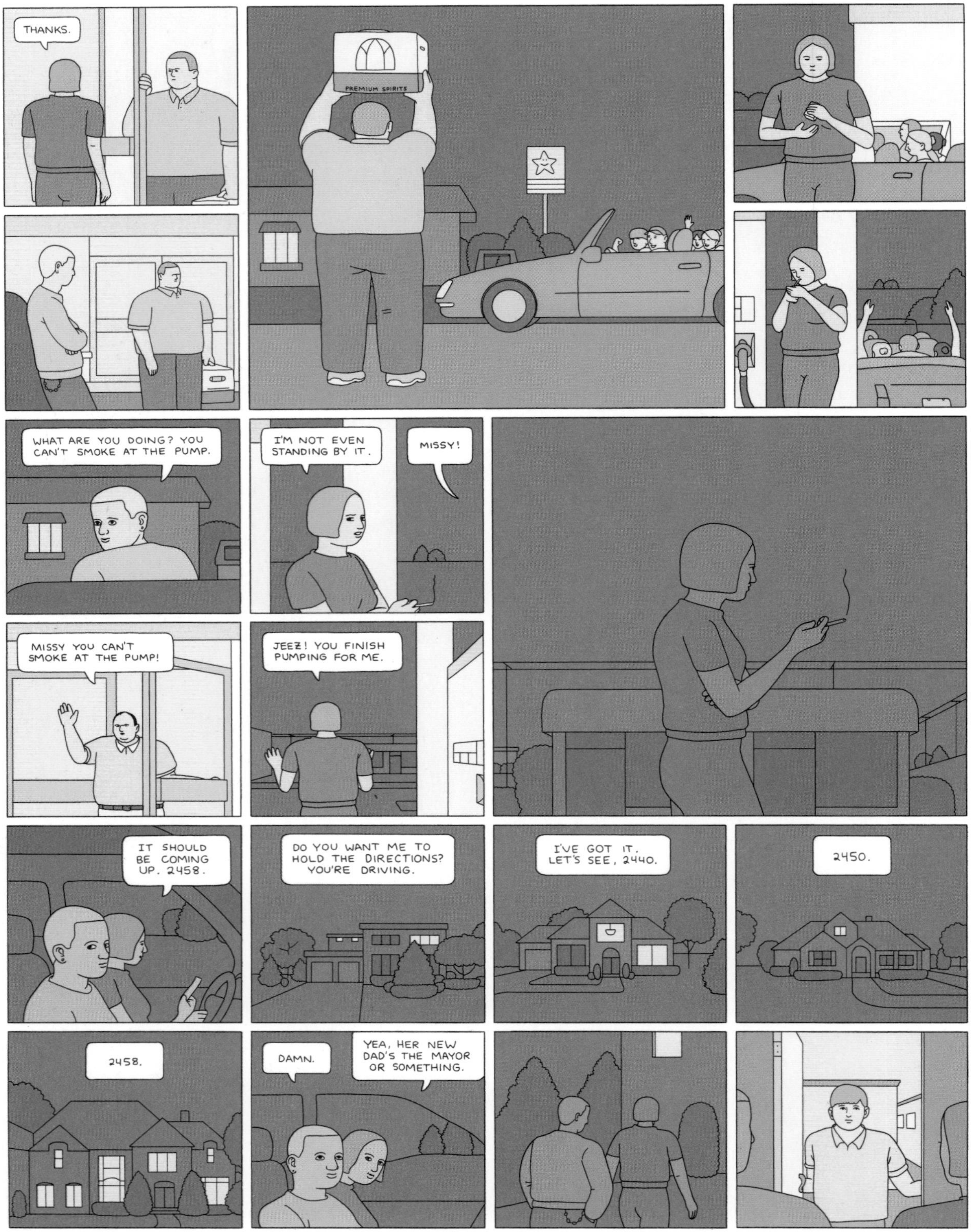
THANKS.
PREMIUM SPIRITS
WHAT ARE YOU DOING? YOU CAN'T SMOKE AT THE PUMP.
I'M NOT EVEN STANDING BY IT.
MISSY!
MISSY YOU CAN'T SMOKE AT THE PUMP!
JEEZ! YOU FINISH PUMPING FOR ME.
IT SHOULD BE COMING UP. 2458.
DO YOU WANT ME TO HOLD THE DIRECTIONS? YOU'RE DRIVING.
I'VE GOT IT. LET'S SEE, 2440.
2450.
2458.
DAMN.
YEA, HER NEW DAD'S THE MAYOR OR SOMETHING.

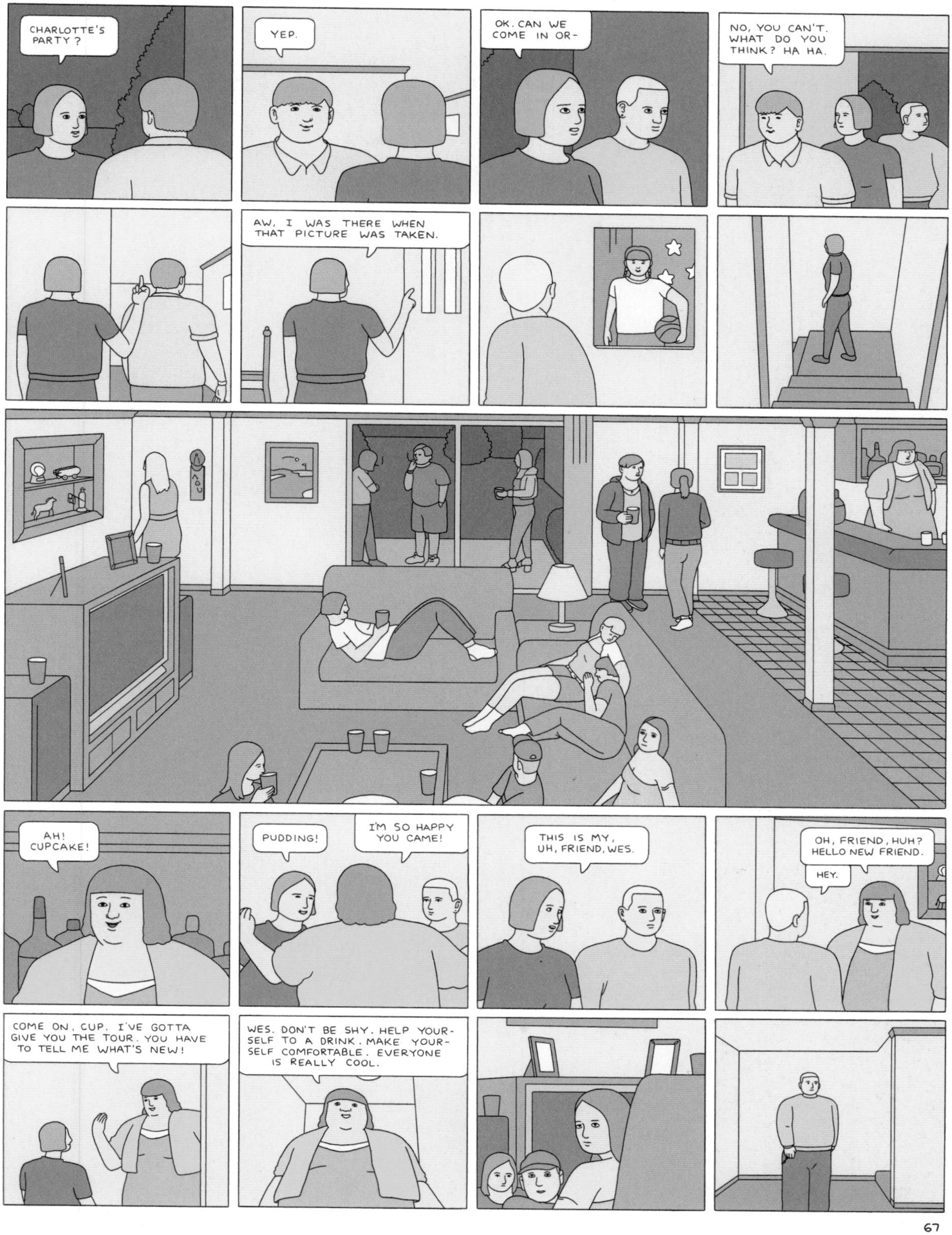

CHARLOTTE'S PARTY?
YEP.
OK. CAN WE COME IN OR-
NO, YOU CAN'T. WHAT DO YOU THINK? HA HA.
AW, I WAS THERE WHEN THAT PICTURE WAS TAKEN.
AH! CUPCAKE!
PUDDING!
I'M SO HAPPY YOU CAME!
THIS IS MY, UH, FRIEND, WES.
OH, FRIEND, HUH? HELLO NEW FRIEND.
HEY.
COME ON, CUP. I'VE GOTTA GIVE YOU THE TOUR. YOU HAVE TO TELL ME WHAT'S NEW!
WES. DON'T BE SHY. HELP YOURSELF TO A DRINK. MAKE YOURSELF COMFORTABLE. EVERYONE IS REALLY COOL.

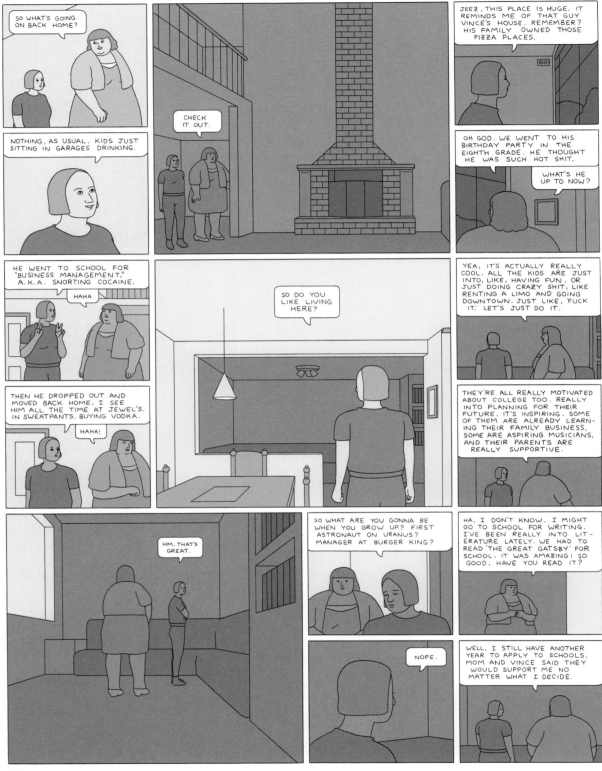

SO WHAT'S GOING ON BACK HOME?

NOTHING, AS USUAL. KIDS JUST SITTING IN GARAGES DRINKING.

CHECK IT OUT.

JEEZ, THIS PLACE IS HUGE. IT REMINDS ME OF THAT GUY VINCE'S HOUSE. REMEMBER? HIS FAMILY OWNED THOSE PIZZA PLACES.

OH GOD. WE WENT TO HIS BIRTHDAY PARTY IN THE EIGHTH GRADE. HE THOUGHT HE WAS SUCH HOT SHIT.

WHAT'S HE UP TO NOW?

HE WENT TO SCHOOL FOR "BUSINESS MANAGEMENT," A.K.A. SNORTING COCAINE.

HAHA

THEN HE DROPPED OUT AND MOVED BACK HOME. I SEE HIM ALL THE TIME AT JEWEL'S. IN SWEATPANTS. BUYING VODKA.

HAHA!

SO DO YOU LIKE LIVING HERE?

YEA, IT'S ACTUALLY REALLY COOL. ALL THE KIDS ARE JUST INTO, LIKE, HAVING FUN. OR JUST DOING CRAZY SHIT, LIKE RENTING A LIMO AND GOING DOWNTOWN. JUST LIKE, 'FUCK IT,' LET'S JUST DO IT.

THEY'RE ALL REALLY MOTIVATED ABOUT COLLEGE TOO. REALLY INTO PLANNING FOR THEIR FUTURE. IT'S INSPIRING. SOME OF THEM ARE ALREADY LEARN-ING THEIR FAMILY BUSINESS, SOME ARE ASPIRING MUSICIANS, AND THEIR PARENTS ARE REALLY SUPPORTIVE.

HM. THAT'S GREAT.

SO WHAT ARE YOU GONNA BE WHEN YOU GROW UP? FIRST ASTRONAUT ON URANUS? MANAGER AT BURGER KING?

HA, I DON'T KNOW. I MIGHT GO TO SCHOOL FOR WRITING. I'VE BEEN REALLY INTO LIT-ERATURE LATELY. WE HAD TO READ 'THE GREAT GATSBY' FOR SCHOOL. IT WAS AMAZING! SO GOOD. HAVE YOU READ IT?

NOPE.

WELL, I STILL HAVE ANOTHER YEAR TO APPLY TO SCHOOLS. MOM AND VINCE SAID THEY WOULD SUPPORT ME NO MATTER WHAT I DECIDE.

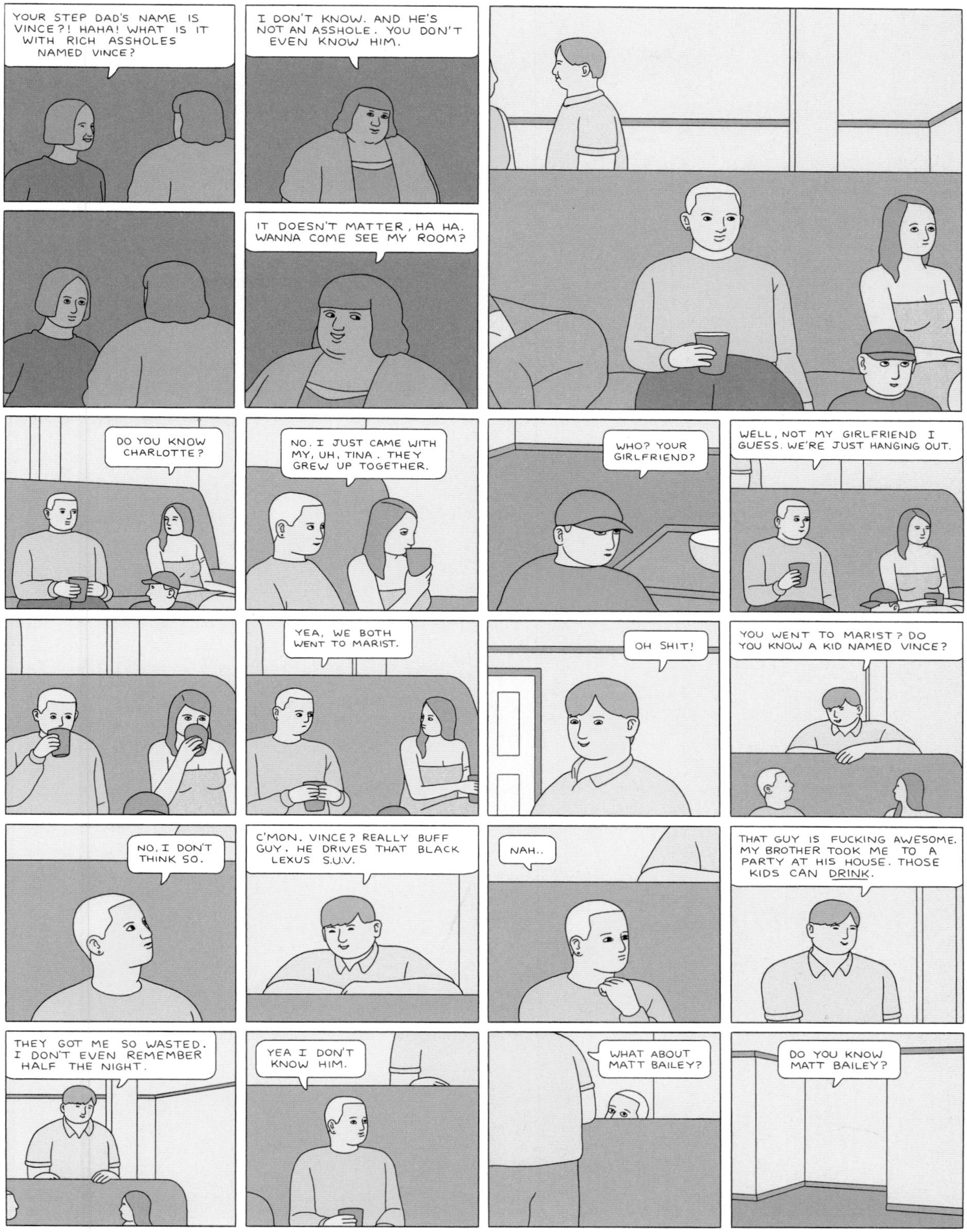
YOUR STEP DAD'S NAME IS VINCE?! HAHA! WHAT IS IT WITH RICH ASSHOLES NAMED VINCE?
I DON'T KNOW. AND HE'S NOT AN ASSHOLE. YOU DON'T EVEN KNOW HIM.
IT DOESN'T MATTER, HA HA. WANNA COME SEE MY ROOM?
DO YOU KNOW CHARLOTTE?
NO. I JUST CAME WITH MY, UH, TINA. THEY GREW UP TOGETHER.
WHO? YOUR GIRLFRIEND?
WELL, NOT MY GIRLFRIEND I GUESS. WE'RE JUST HANGING OUT.
YEA, WE BOTH WENT TO MARIST.
OH SHIT!
YOU WENT TO MARIST? DO YOU KNOW A KID NAMED VINCE?
NO, I DON'T THINK SO.
C'MON. VINCE? REALLY BUFF GUY. HE DRIVES THAT BLACK LEXUS S.U.V.
NAH..
THAT GUY IS FUCKING AWESOME. MY BROTHER TOOK ME TO A PARTY AT HIS HOUSE. THOSE KIDS CAN DRINK.
THEY GOT ME SO WASTED. I DON'T EVEN REMEMBER HALF THE NIGHT.
YEA I DON'T KNOW HIM.
WHAT ABOUT MATT BAILEY?
DO YOU KNOW MATT BAILEY?

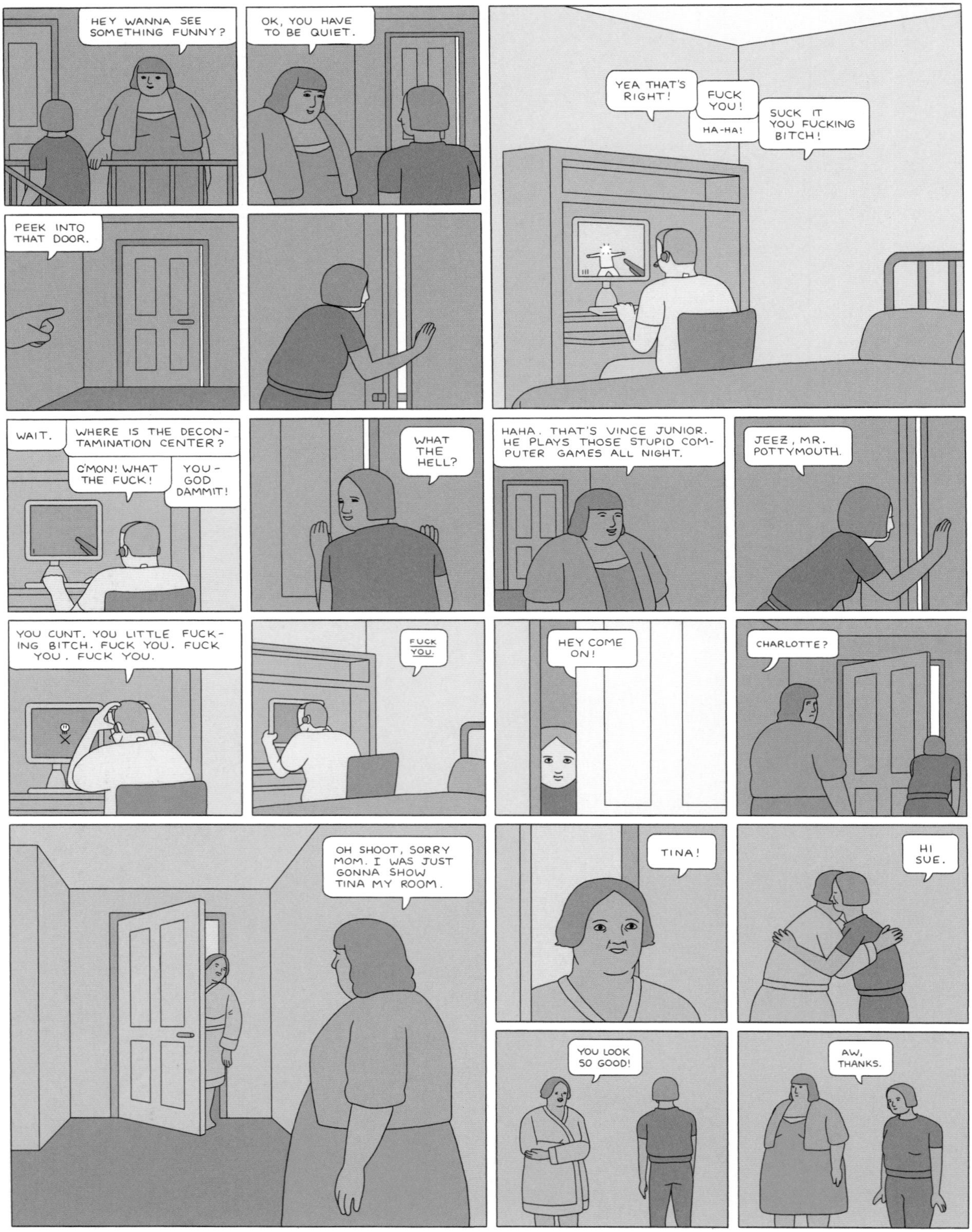
HEY WANNA SEE SOMETHING FUNNY?
OK, YOU HAVE TO BE QUIET.
PEEK INTO THAT DOOR.
YEA THAT'S RIGHT!
FUCK YOU!
HA-HA!
SUCK IT YOU FUCKING BITCH!
WAIT.
WHERE IS THE DECON-TAMINATION CENTER?
C'MON! WHAT THE FUCK!
YOU-GOD DAMMIT!
WHAT THE HELL?
HAHA. THAT'S VINCE JUNIOR. HE PLAYS THOSE STUPID COM-PUTER GAMES ALL NIGHT.
JEEZ, MR. POTTYMOUTH.
YOU CUNT. YOU LITTLE FUCK-ING BITCH. FUCK YOU. FUCK YOU. FUCK YOU.
FUCK YOU.
HEY COME ON!
CHARLOTTE?
OH SHOOT, SORRY MOM. I WAS JUST GONNA SHOW TINA MY ROOM.
TINA!
HI SUE.
YOU LOOK SO GOOD!
AW, THANKS.

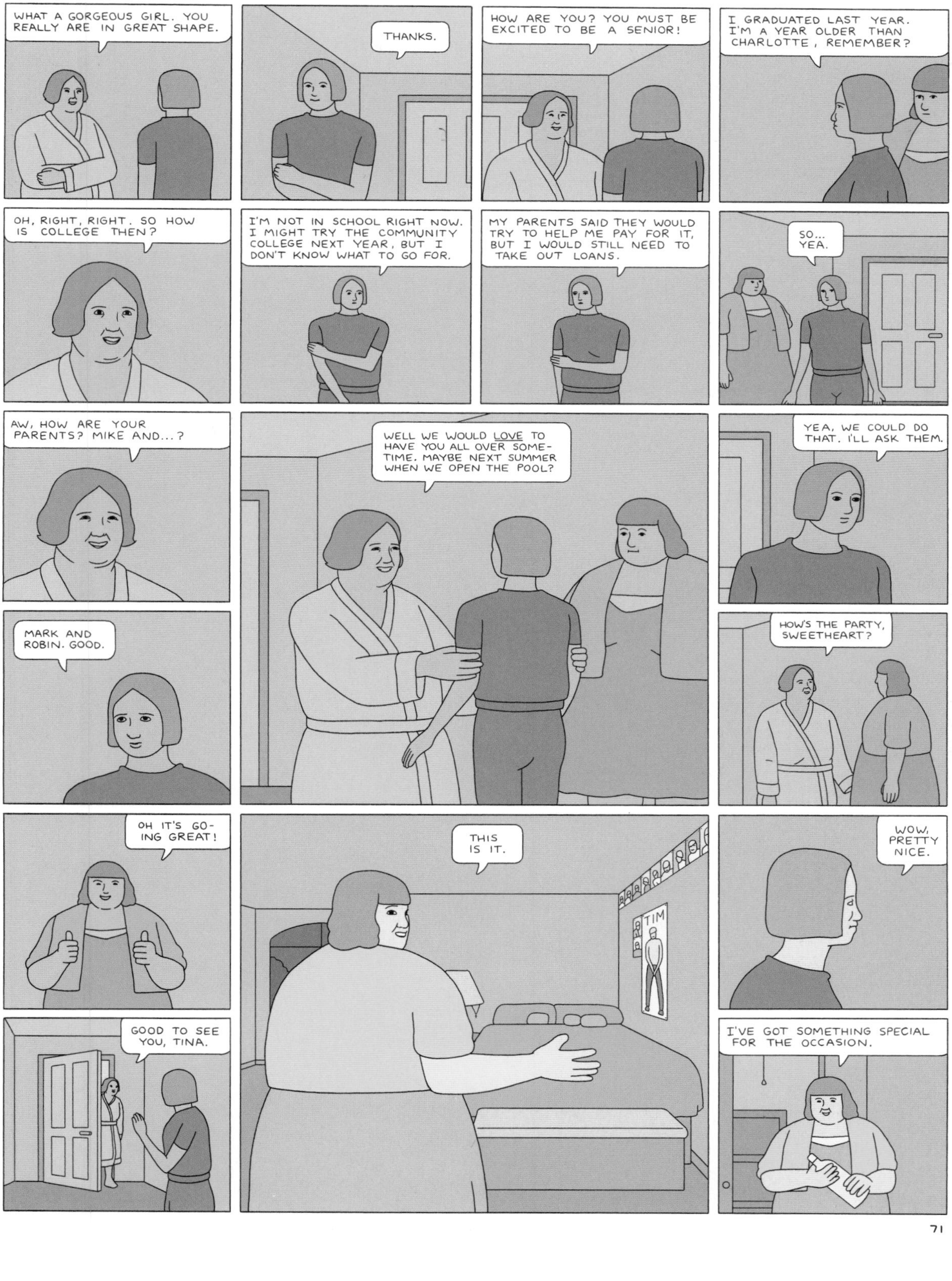
WHAT A GORGEOUS GIRL. YOU REALLY ARE IN GREAT SHAPE.
THANKS.
HOW ARE YOU? YOU MUST BE EXCITED TO BE A SENIOR!
I GRADUATED LAST YEAR. I'M A YEAR OLDER THAN CHARLOTTE, REMEMBER?
OH, RIGHT, RIGHT. SO HOW IS COLLEGE THEN?
I'M NOT IN SCHOOL RIGHT NOW. I MIGHT TRY THE COMMUNITY COLLEGE NEXT YEAR, BUT I DON'T KNOW WHAT TO GO FOR.
MY PARENTS SAID THEY WOULD TRY TO HELP ME PAY FOR IT, BUT I WOULD STILL NEED TO TAKE OUT LOANS.
SO... YEA.
AW, HOW ARE YOUR PARENTS? MIKE AND...?
MARK AND ROBIN. GOOD.
WELL WE WOULD LOVE TO HAVE YOU ALL OVER SOME-TIME. MAYBE NEXT SUMMER WHEN WE OPEN THE POOL?
YEA, WE COULD DO THAT. I'LL ASK THEM.
HOW'S THE PARTY, SWEETHEART?
OH IT'S GO-ING GREAT!
GOOD TO SEE YOU, TINA.
THIS IS IT.
TIM
WOW, PRETTY NICE.
I'VE GOT SOMETHING SPECIAL FOR THE OCCASION.

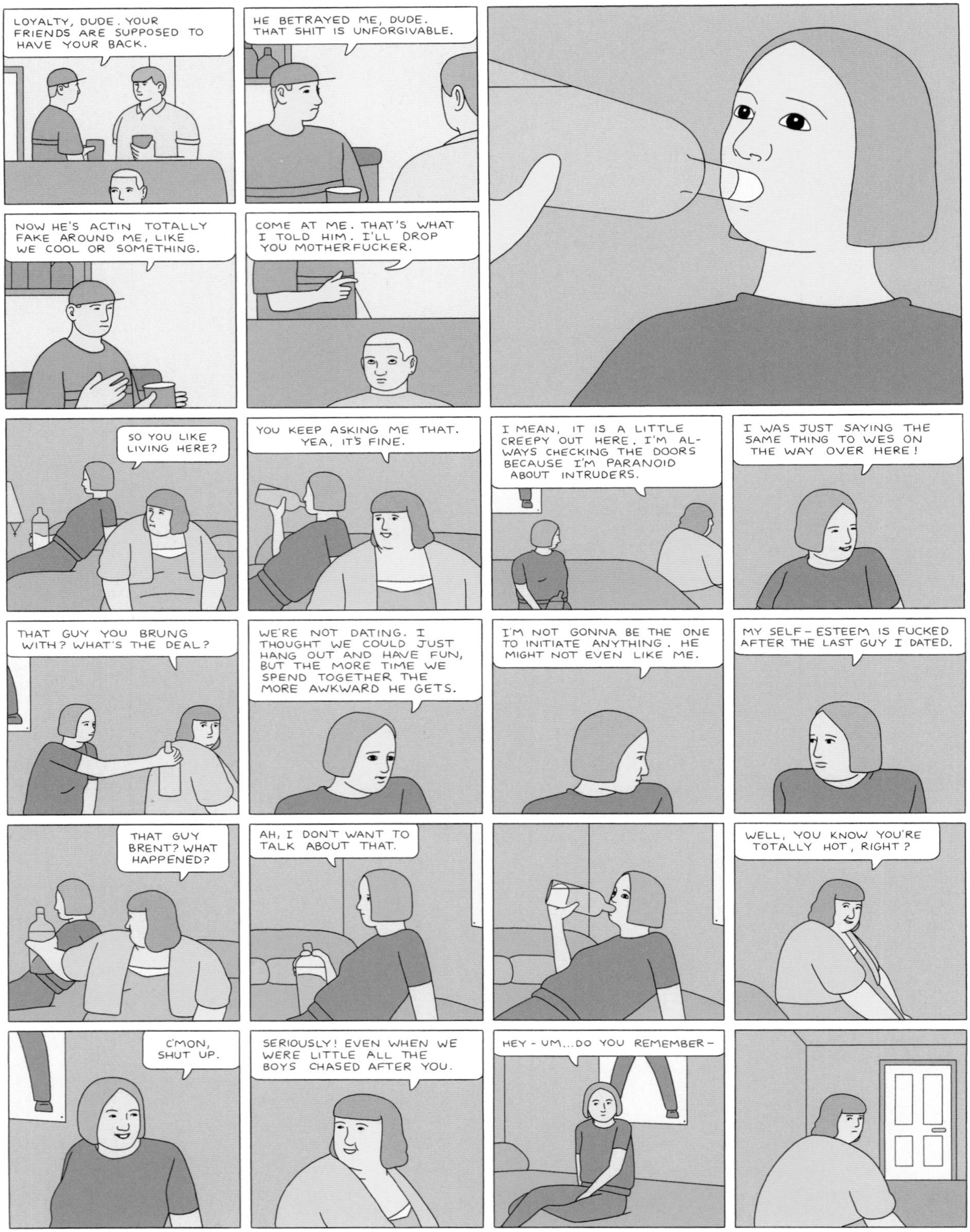
LOYALTY, DUDE. YOUR FRIENDS ARE SUPPOSED TO HAVE YOUR BACK.
HE BETRAYED ME, DUDE. THAT SHIT IS UNFORGIVABLE.
NOW HE'S ACTIN TOTALLY FAKE AROUND ME, LIKE WE COOL OR SOMETHING.
COME AT ME. THAT'S WHAT I TOLD HIM. I'LL DROP YOU MOTHERFUCKER.
SO YOU LIKE LIVING HERE?
YOU KEEP ASKING ME THAT. YEA, IT'S FINE.
I MEAN, IT IS A LITTLE CREEPY OUT HERE. I'M AL- WAYS CHECKING THE DOORS BECAUSE I'M PARANOID ABOUT INTRUDERS.
I WAS JUST SAYING THE SAME THING TO WES ON THE WAY OVER HERE!
THAT GUY YOU BRUNG WITH? WHAT'S THE DEAL?
WE'RE NOT DATING. I THOUGHT WE COULD JUST HANG OUT AND HAVE FUN, BUT THE MORE TIME WE SPEND TOGETHER THE MORE AWKWARD HE GETS.
I'M NOT GONNA BE THE ONE TO INITIATE ANYTHING. HE MIGHT NOT EVEN LIKE ME.
MY SELF-ESTEEM IS FUCKED AFTER THE LAST GUY I DATED.
THAT GUY BRENT? WHAT HAPPENED?
AH, I DON'T WANT TO TALK ABOUT THAT.
WELL, YOU KNOW YOU'RE TOTALLY HOT, RIGHT?
C'MON, SHUT UP.
SERIOUSLY! EVEN WHEN WE WERE LITTLE ALL THE BOYS CHASED AFTER YOU.
HEY-UM...DO YOU REMEMBER-

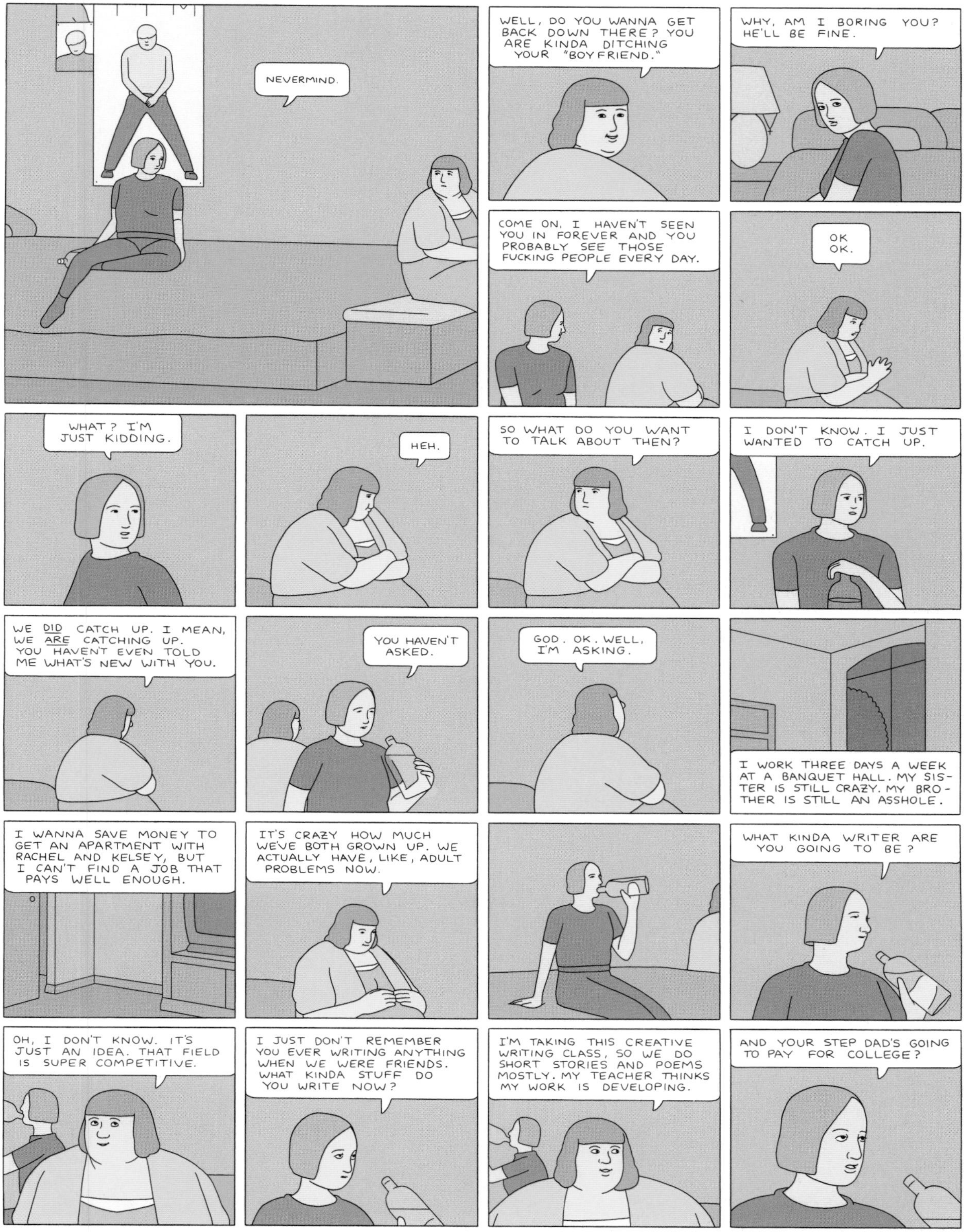
NEVERMIND.
WELL, DO YOU WANNA GET BACK DOWN THERE? YOU ARE KINDA DITCHING YOUR "BOYFRIEND."
WHY, AM I BORING YOU? HE'LL BE FINE.
COME ON, I HAVEN'T SEEN YOU IN FOREVER AND YOU PROBABLY SEE THOSE FUCKING PEOPLE EVERY DAY.
OK OK.
WHAT? I'M JUST KIDDING.
HEH.
SO WHAT DO YOU WANT TO TALK ABOUT THEN?
I DON'T KNOW. I JUST WANTED TO CATCH UP.
WE DID CATCH UP. I MEAN, WE ARE CATCHING UP. YOU HAVEN'T EVEN TOLD ME WHAT'S NEW WITH YOU.
YOU HAVEN'T ASKED.
GOD. OK. WELL, I'M ASKING.
I WORK THREE DAYS A WEEK AT A BANQUET HALL. MY SISTER IS STILL CRAZY. MY BROTHER IS STILL AN ASSHOLE.
I WANNA SAVE MONEY TO GET AN APARTMENT WITH RACHEL AND KELSEY, BUT I CAN'T FIND A JOB THAT PAYS WELL ENOUGH.
IT'S CRAZY HOW MUCH WE'VE BOTH GROWN UP. WE ACTUALLY HAVE, LIKE, ADULT PROBLEMS NOW.
WHAT KINDA WRITER ARE YOU GOING TO BE?
OH, I DON'T KNOW. IT'S JUST AN IDEA. THAT FIELD IS SUPER COMPETITIVE.
I JUST DON'T REMEMBER YOU EVER WRITING ANYTHING WHEN WE WERE FRIENDS. WHAT KINDA STUFF DO YOU WRITE NOW?
I'M TAKING THIS CREATIVE WRITING CLASS, SO WE DO SHORT STORIES AND POEMS MOSTLY. MY TEACHER THINKS MY WORK IS DEVELOPING.
AND YOUR STEP DAD'S GOING TO PAY FOR COLLEGE?

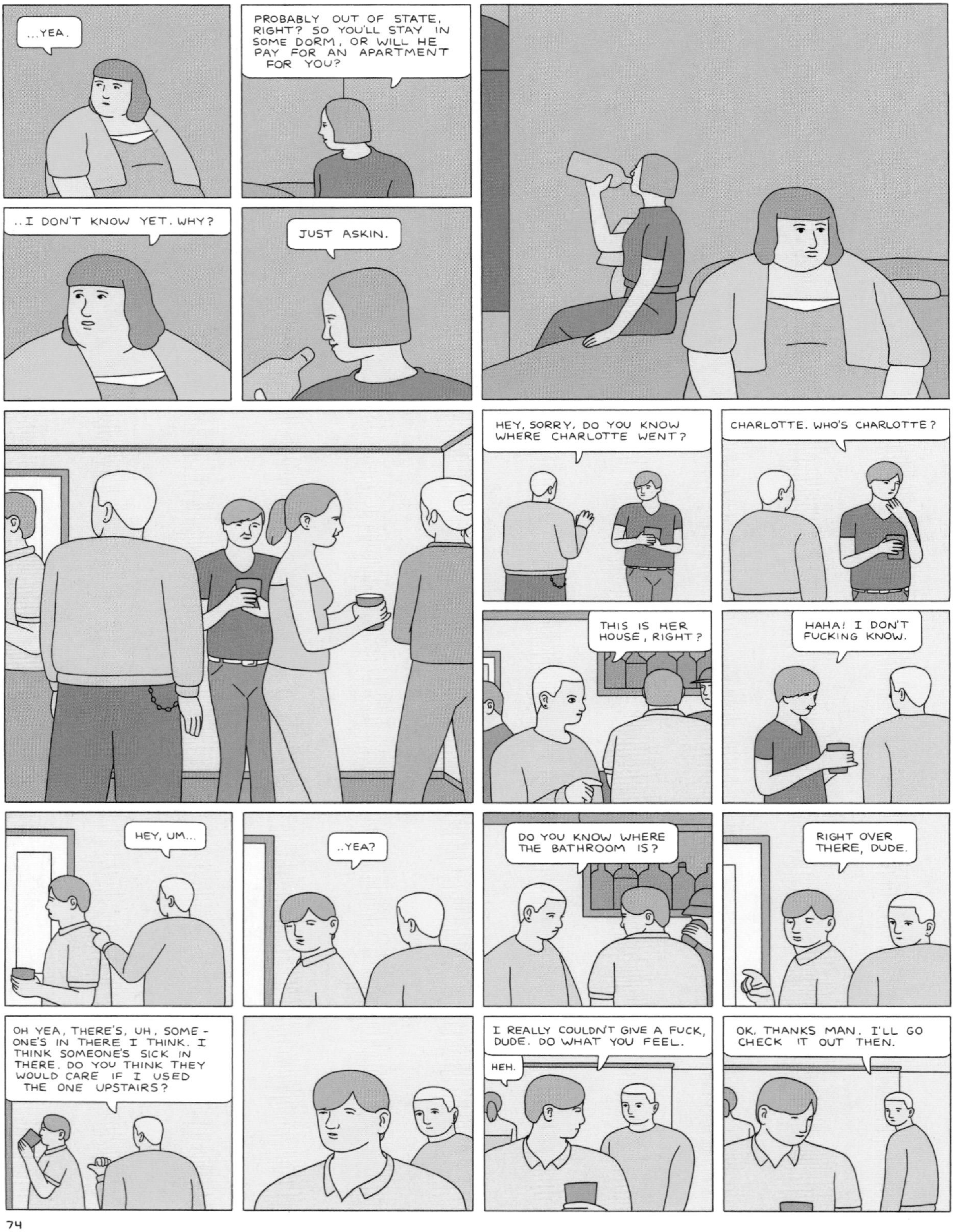

...YEA.
PROBABLY OUT OF STATE, RIGHT? SO YOU'LL STAY IN SOME DORM, OR WILL HE PAY FOR AN APARTMENT FOR YOU?
..I DON'T KNOW YET. WHY?
JUST ASKIN.
HEY, SORRY, DO YOU KNOW WHERE CHARLOTTE WENT?
CHARLOTTE. WHO'S CHARLOTTE?
THIS IS HER HOUSE, RIGHT?
HAHA! I DON'T FUCKING KNOW.
HEY, UM...
..YEA?
DO YOU KNOW WHERE THE BATHROOM IS?
RIGHT OVER THERE, DUDE.
OH YEA, THERE'S, UH, SOME-ONE'S IN THERE I THINK. I THINK SOMEONE'S SICK IN THERE. DO YOU THINK THEY WOULD CARE IF I USED THE ONE UPSTAIRS?
I REALLY COULDN'T GIVE A FUCK, DUDE. DO WHAT YOU FEEL.
HEH.
OK, THANKS MAN. I'LL GO CHECK IT OUT THEN.

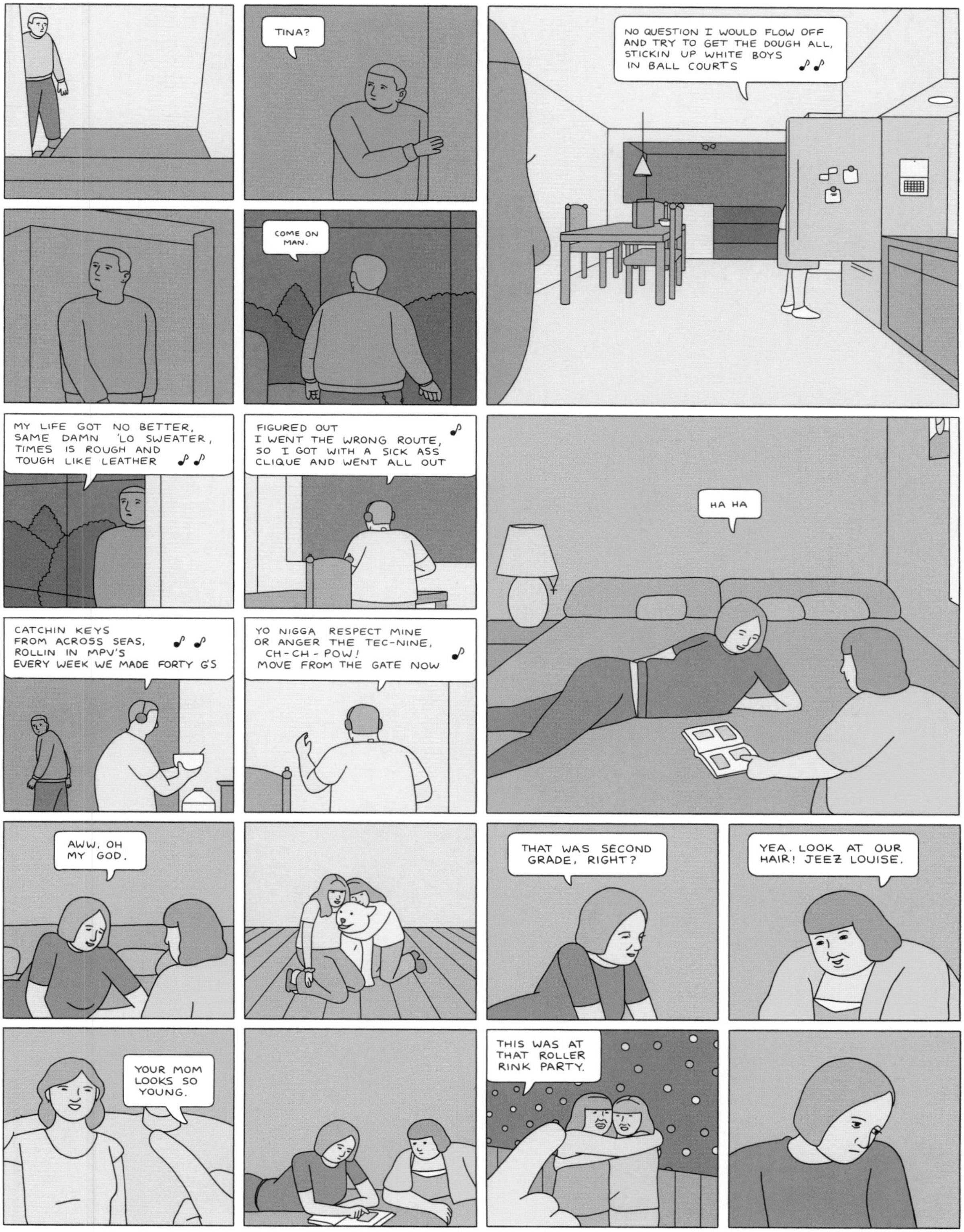

TINA?
NO QUESTION I WOULD FLOW OFF AND TRY TO GET THE DOUGH ALL, STICKIN UP WHITE BOYS IN BALL COURTS
COME ON MAN.
MY LIFE GOT NO BETTER, SAME DAMN 'LO SWEATER, TIMES IS ROUGH AND TOUGH LIKE LEATHER
FIGURED OUT I WENT THE WRONG ROUTE, SO I GOT WITH A SICK ASS CLIQUE AND WENT ALL OUT
HA HA
CATCHIN KEYS FROM ACROSS SEAS, ROLLIN IN MPV'S EVERY WEEK WE MADE FORTY G'S
YO NIGGA RESPECT MINE OR ANGER THE TEC-NINE, CH-CH-POW! MOVE FROM THE GATE NOW
AWW, OH MY GOD.
THAT WAS SECOND GRADE, RIGHT?
YEA. LOOK AT OUR HAIR! JEEZ LOUISE.
YOUR MOM LOOKS SO YOUNG.
THIS WAS AT THAT ROLLER RINK PARTY.

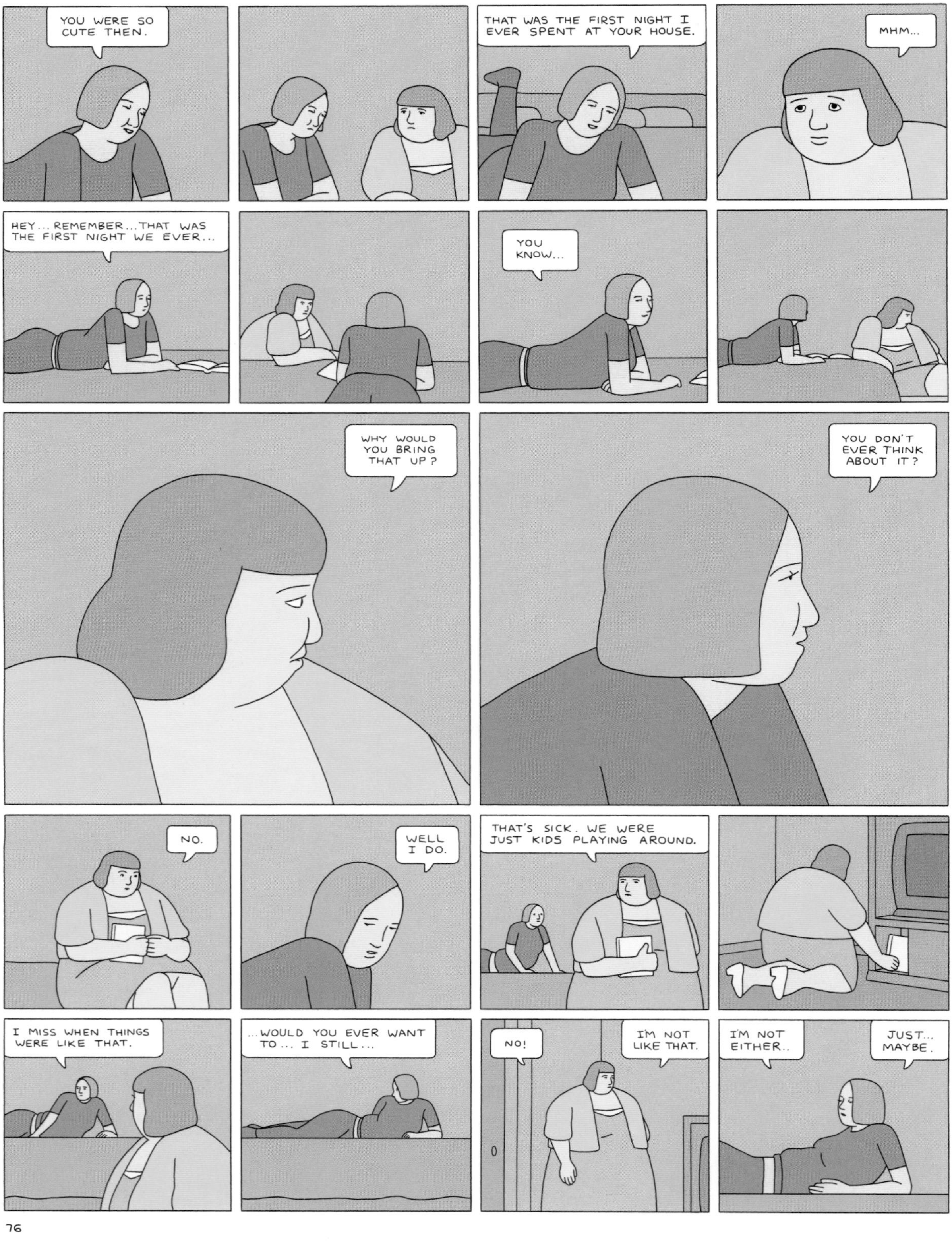
YOU WERE SO CUTE THEN.
THAT WAS THE FIRST NIGHT I EVER SPENT AT YOUR HOUSE.
MHM...
HEY... REMEMBER... THAT WAS THE FIRST NIGHT WE EVER...
YOU KNOW...
WHY WOULD YOU BRING THAT UP?
YOU DON'T EVER THINK ABOUT IT?
NO.
WELL I DO.
THAT'S SICK. WE WERE JUST KIDS PLAYING AROUND.
I MISS WHEN THINGS WERE LIKE THAT.
...WOULD YOU EVER WANT TO... I STILL...
NO!
I'M NOT LIKE THAT.
I'M NOT EITHER..
JUST... MAYBE.

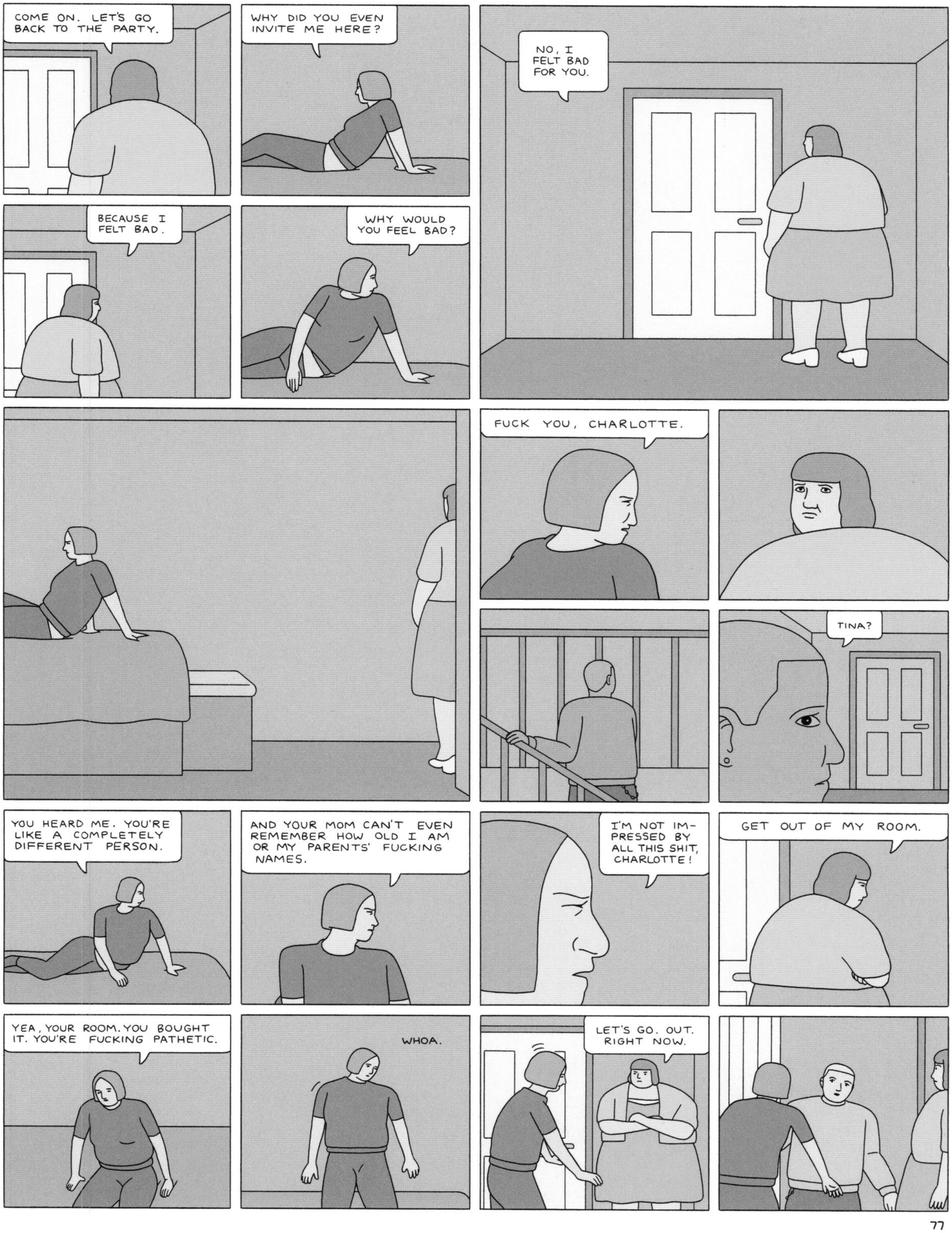
COME ON. LET'S GO BACK TO THE PARTY.
WHY DID YOU EVEN INVITE ME HERE?
BECAUSE I FELT BAD.
WHY WOULD YOU FEEL BAD?
NO, I FELT BAD FOR YOU.
FUCK YOU, CHARLOTTE.
TINA?
YOU HEARD ME. YOU'RE LIKE A COMPLETELY DIFFERENT PERSON.
AND YOUR MOM CAN'T EVEN REMEMBER HOW OLD I AM OR MY PARENTS' FUCKING NAMES.
I'M NOT IMPRESSED BY ALL THIS SHIT, CHARLOTTE!
GET OUT OF MY ROOM.
YEA, YOUR ROOM. YOU BOUGHT IT. YOU'RE FUCKING PATHETIC.
WHOA.
LET'S GO. OUT. RIGHT NOW.

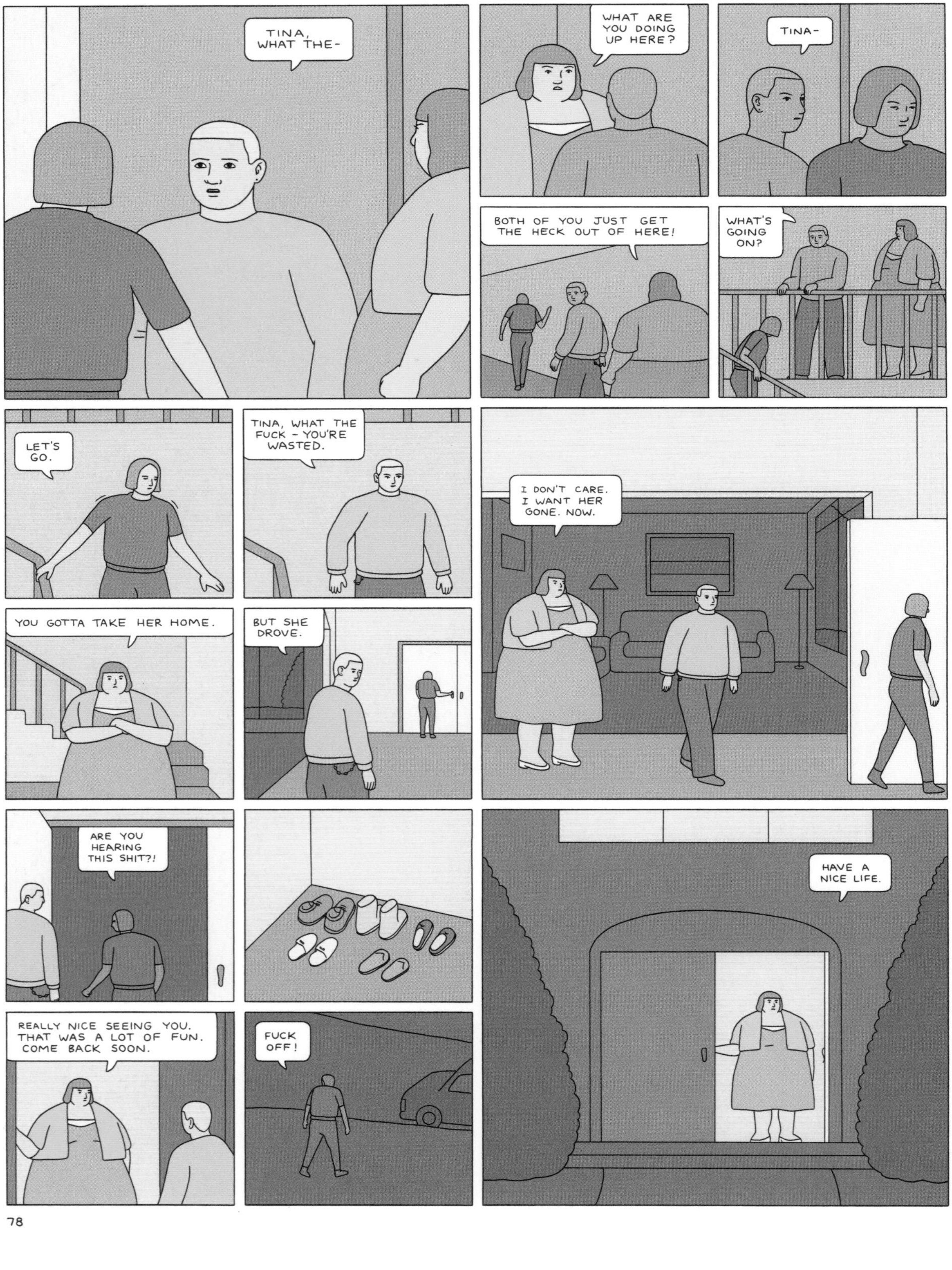
TINA, WHAT THE-
WHAT ARE YOU DOING UP HERE?
TINA-
BOTH OF YOU JUST GET THE HECK OUT OF HERE!
WHAT'S GOING ON?
LET'S GO.
TINA, WHAT THE FUCK - YOU'RE WASTED.
I DON'T CARE. I WANT HER GONE. NOW.
YOU GOTTA TAKE HER HOME.
BUT SHE DROVE.
ARE YOU HEARING THIS SHIT?!
HAVE A NICE LIFE.
REALLY NICE SEEING YOU. THAT WAS A LOT OF FUN. COME BACK SOON.
FUCK OFF!

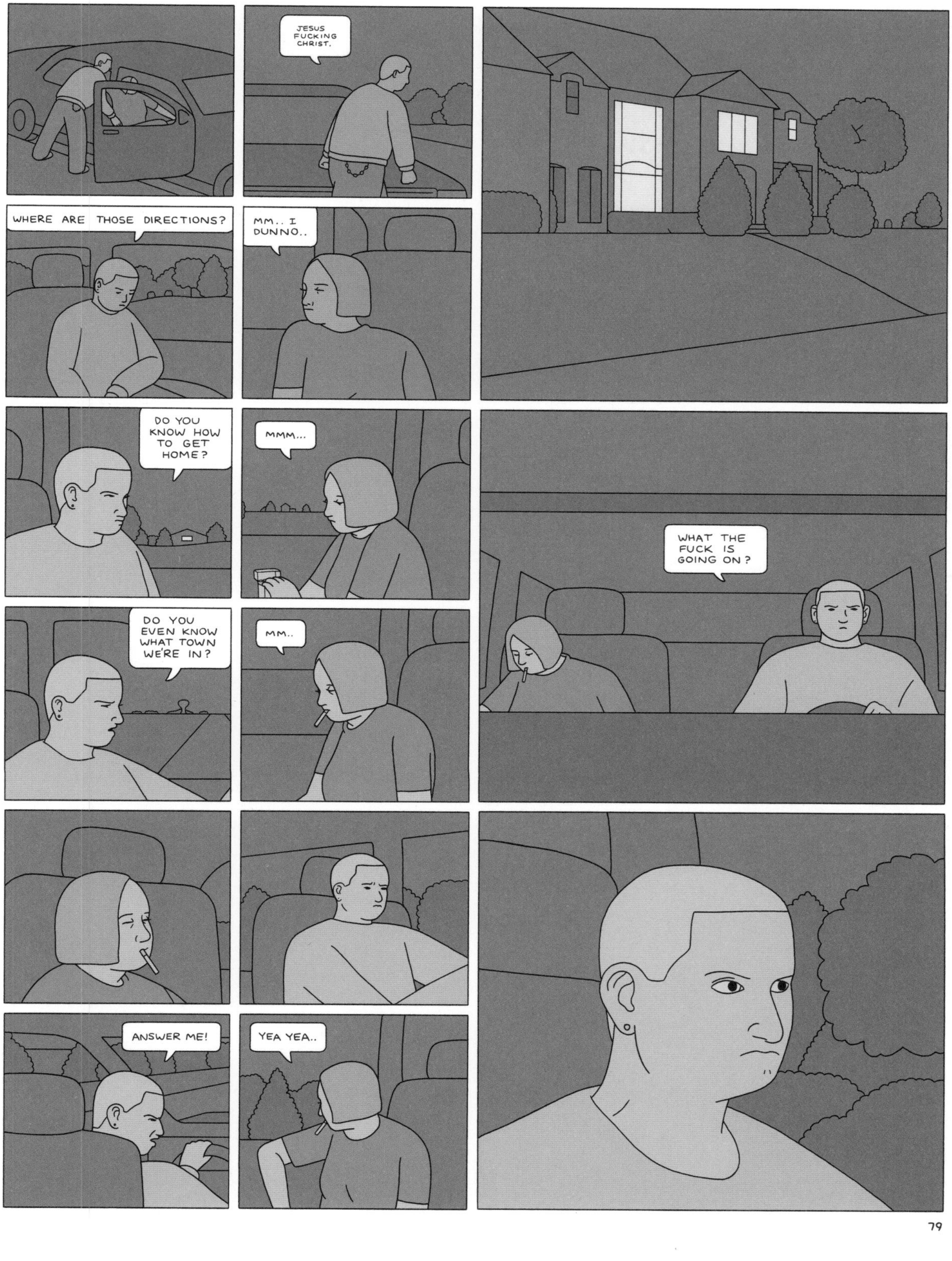
JESUS FUCKING CHRIST.
WHERE ARE THOSE DIRECTIONS?
MM.. I DUNNO..
DO YOU KNOW HOW TO GET HOME?
MMM...
DO YOU EVEN KNOW WHAT TOWN WE'RE IN?
MM..
ANSWER ME!
YEA YEA..
WHAT THE FUCK IS GOING ON?

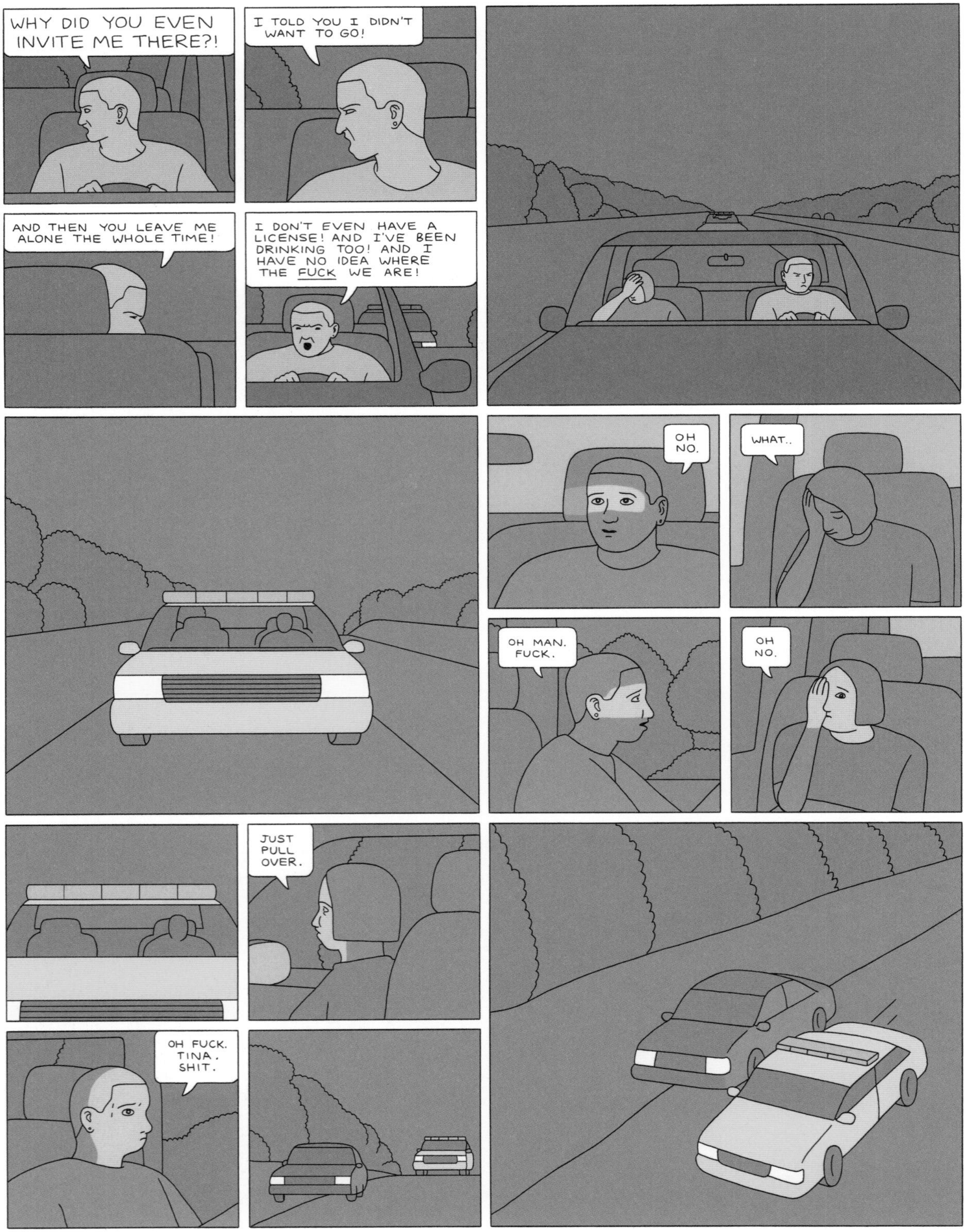
WHY DID YOU EVEN INVITE ME THERE?!
I TOLD YOU I DIDN'T WANT TO GO!
AND THEN YOU LEAVE ME ALONE THE WHOLE TIME!
I DON'T EVEN HAVE A LICENSE! AND I'VE BEEN DRINKING TOO! AND I HAVE NO IDEA WHERE THE FUCK WE ARE!
OH NO.
WHAT..
OH MAN. FUCK.
OH NO.
JUST PULL OVER.
OH FUCK. TINA. SHIT.

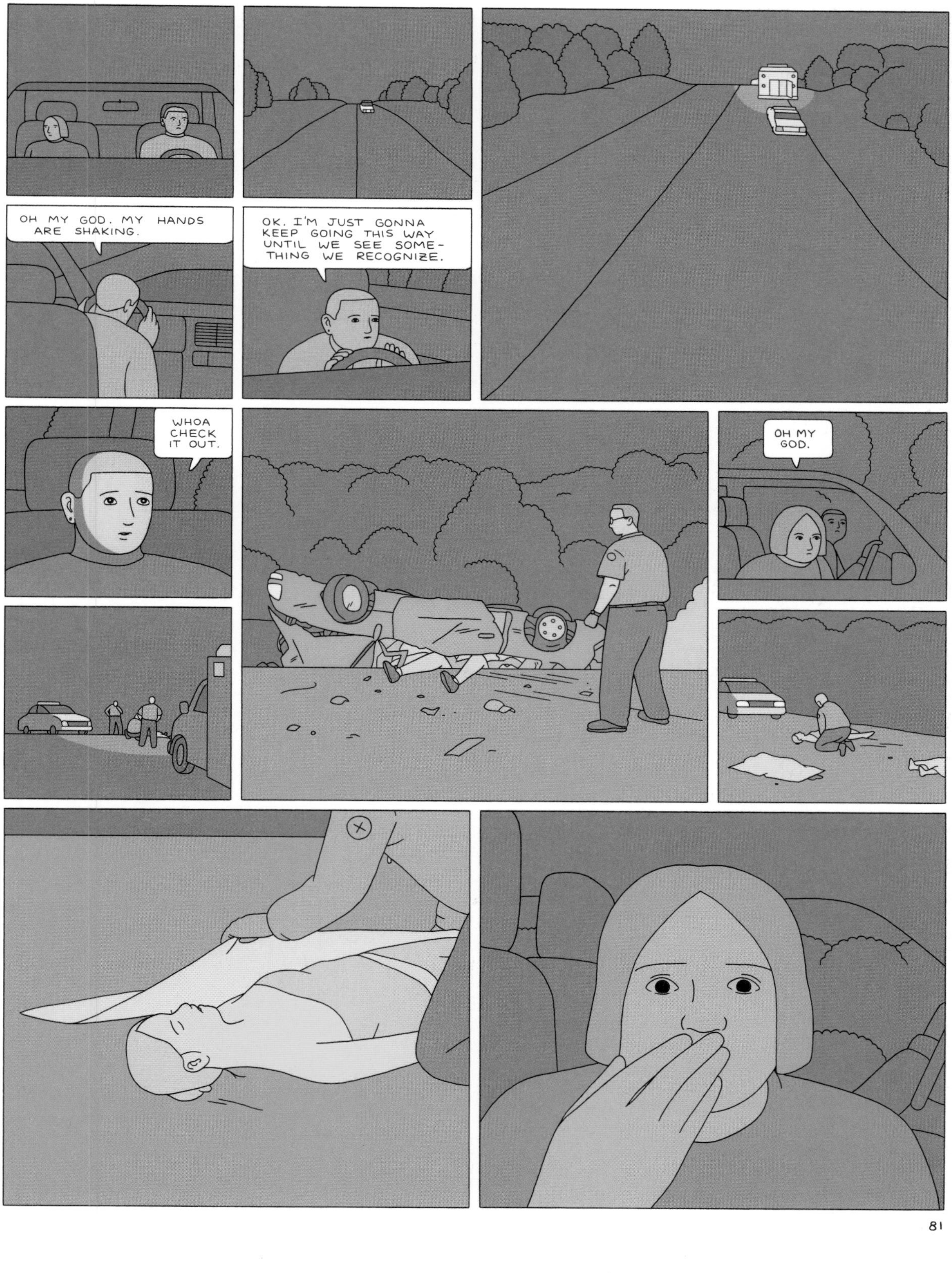
OH MY GOD. MY HANDS ARE SHAKING.
OK. I'M JUST GONNA KEEP GOING THIS WAY UNTIL WE SEE SOME-THING WE RECOGNIZE.
WHOA CHECK IT OUT.
OH MY GOD.

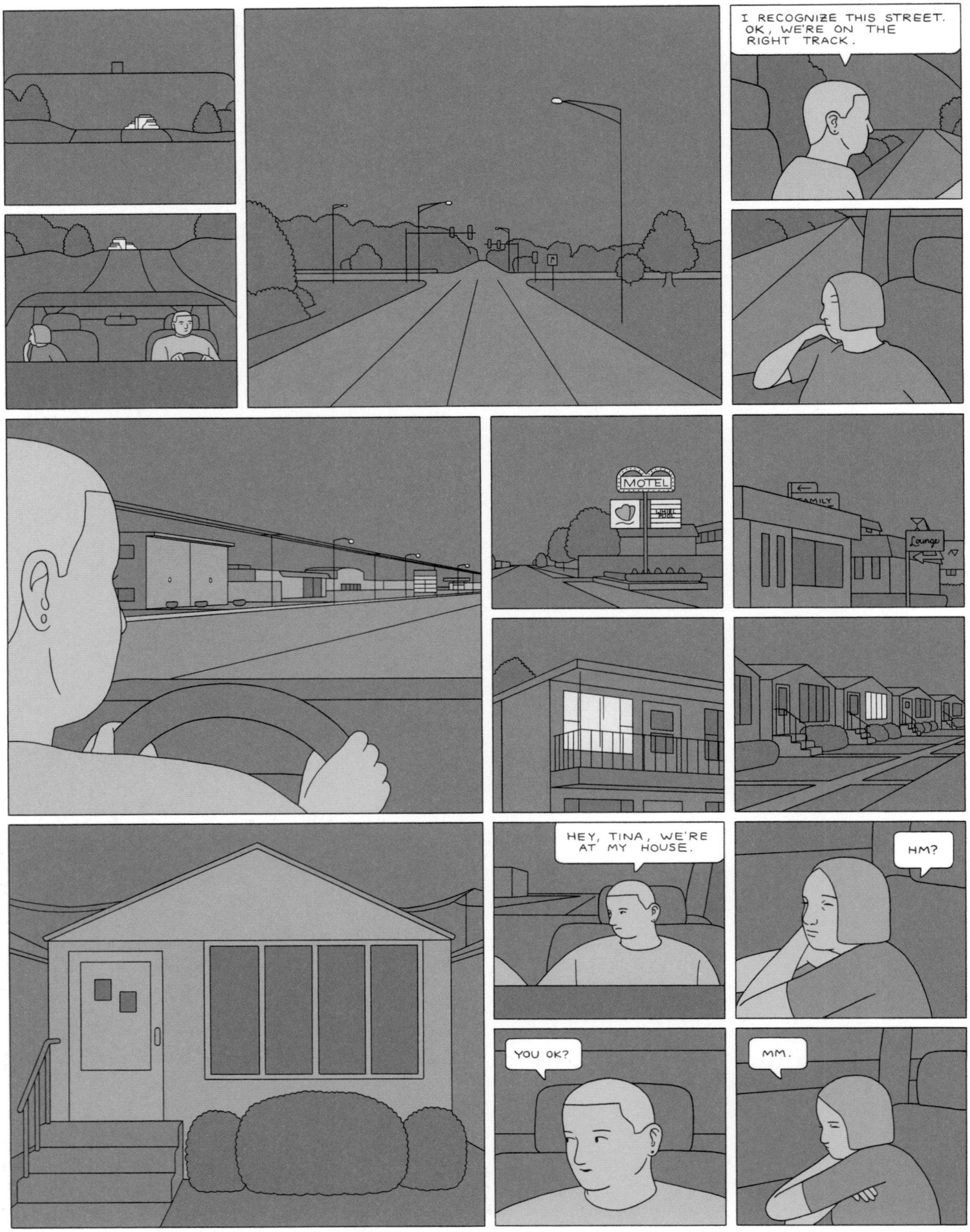
I RECOGNIZE THIS STREET. OK, WE'RE ON THE RIGHT TRACK.
MOTEL
Lounge
HEY, TINA, WE'RE AT MY HOUSE.
HM?
YOU OK?
MM.

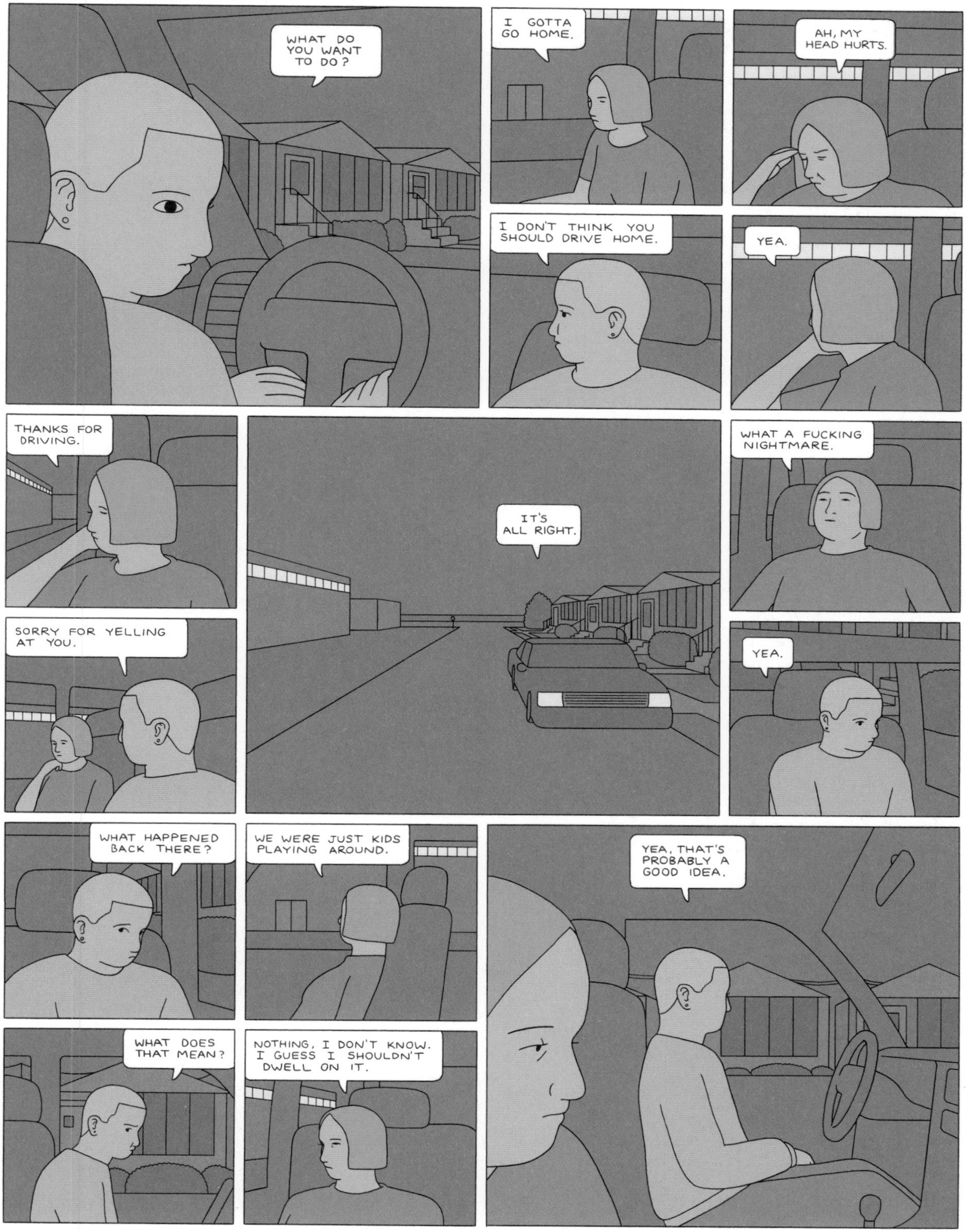
WHAT DO YOU WANT TO DO?
I GOTTA GO HOME.
AH, MY HEAD HURTS.
I DON'T THINK YOU SHOULD DRIVE HOME.
YEA.
THANKS FOR DRIVING.
IT'S ALL RIGHT.
WHAT A FUCKING NIGHTMARE.
SORRY FOR YELLING AT YOU.
YEA.
WHAT HAPPENED BACK THERE?
WE WERE JUST KIDS PLAYING AROUND.
WHAT DOES THAT MEAN?
NOTHING, I DON'T KNOW. I GUESS I SHOULDN'T DWELL ON IT.
YEA, THAT'S PROBABLY A GOOD IDEA.

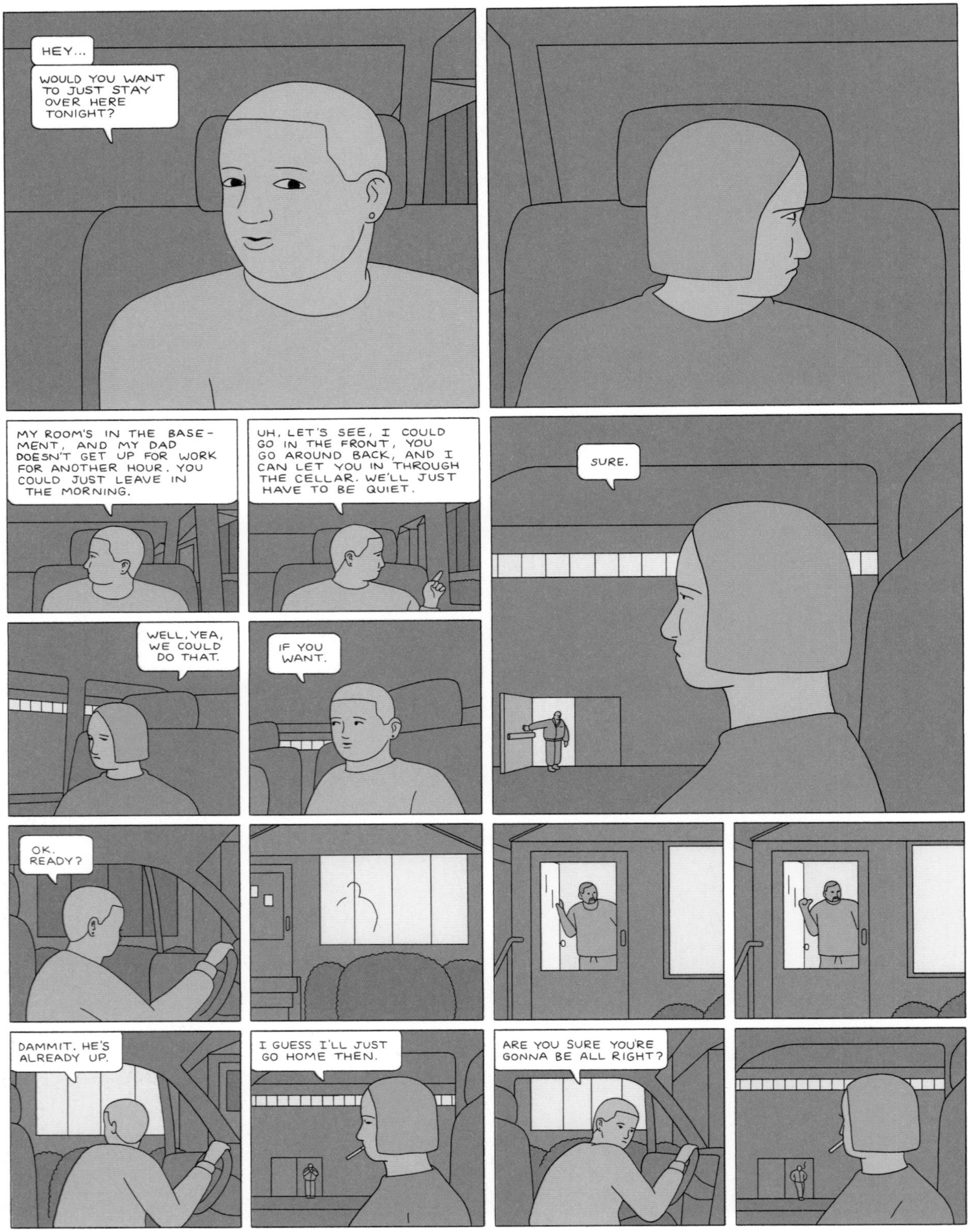
HEY...
WOULD YOU WANT TO JUST STAY OVER HERE TONIGHT?
MY ROOM'S IN THE BASE-MENT, AND MY DAD DOESN'T GET UP FOR WORK FOR ANOTHER HOUR. YOU COULD JUST LEAVE IN THE MORNING.
UH, LET'S SEE, I COULD GO IN THE FRONT, YOU GO AROUND BACK, AND I CAN LET YOU IN THROUGH THE CELLAR. WE'LL JUST HAVE TO BE QUIET.
SURE.
WELL, YEA, WE COULD DO THAT.
IF YOU WANT.
OK. READY?
DAMMIT. HE'S ALREADY UP.
I GUESS I'LL JUST GO HOME THEN.
ARE YOU SURE YOU'RE GONNA BE ALL RIGHT?

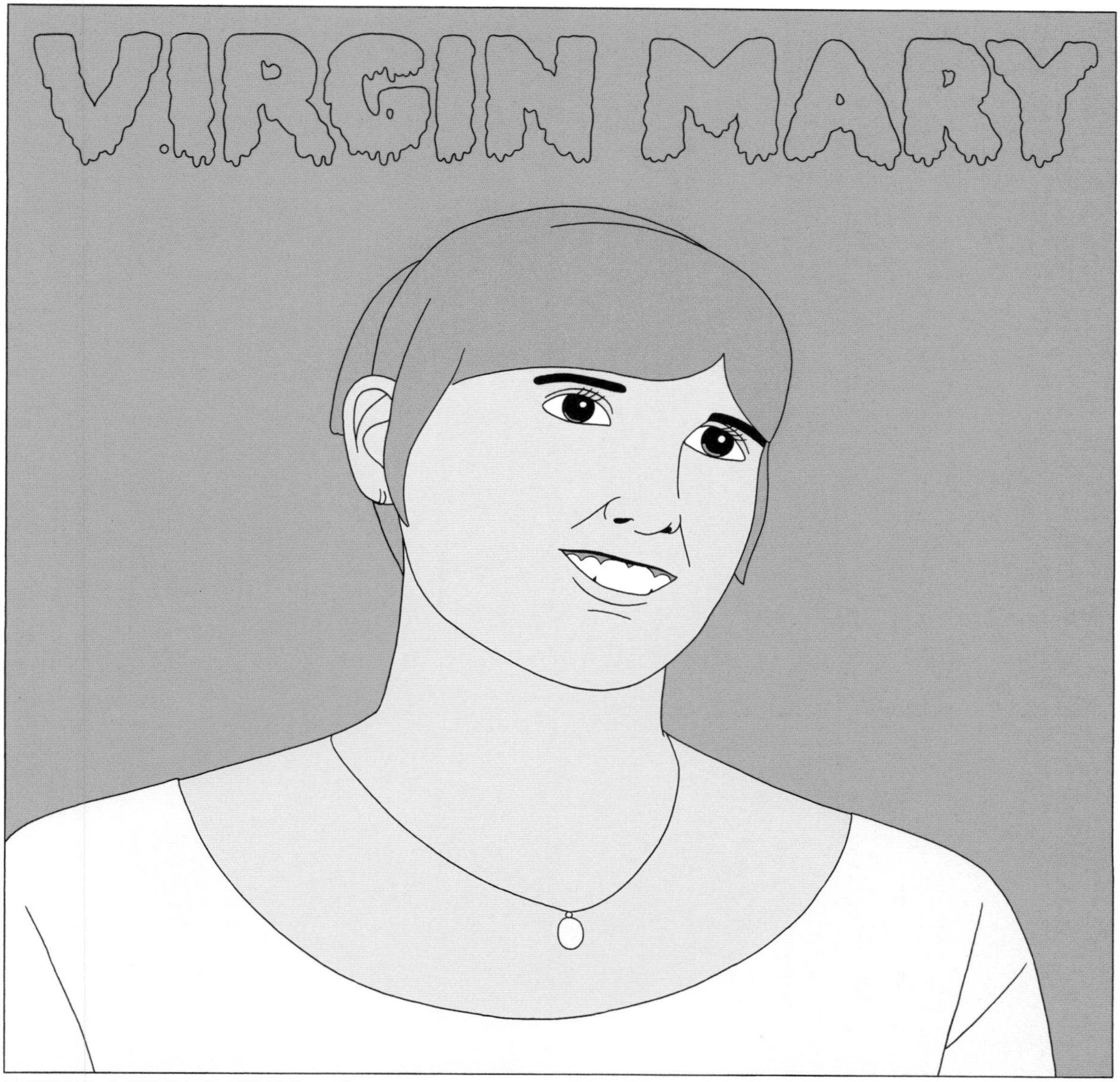
VIRGIN MARY

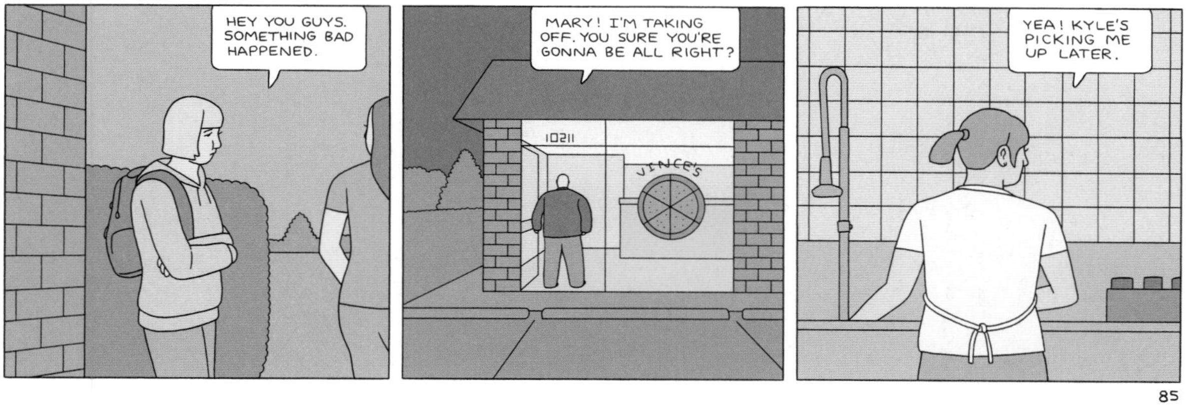
HEY YOU GUYS. SOMETHING BAD HAPPENED.
MARY! I'M TAKING OFF. YOU SURE YOU'RE GONNA BE ALL RIGHT?
10211
VINCE'S
YEA! KYLE'S PICKING ME UP LATER.

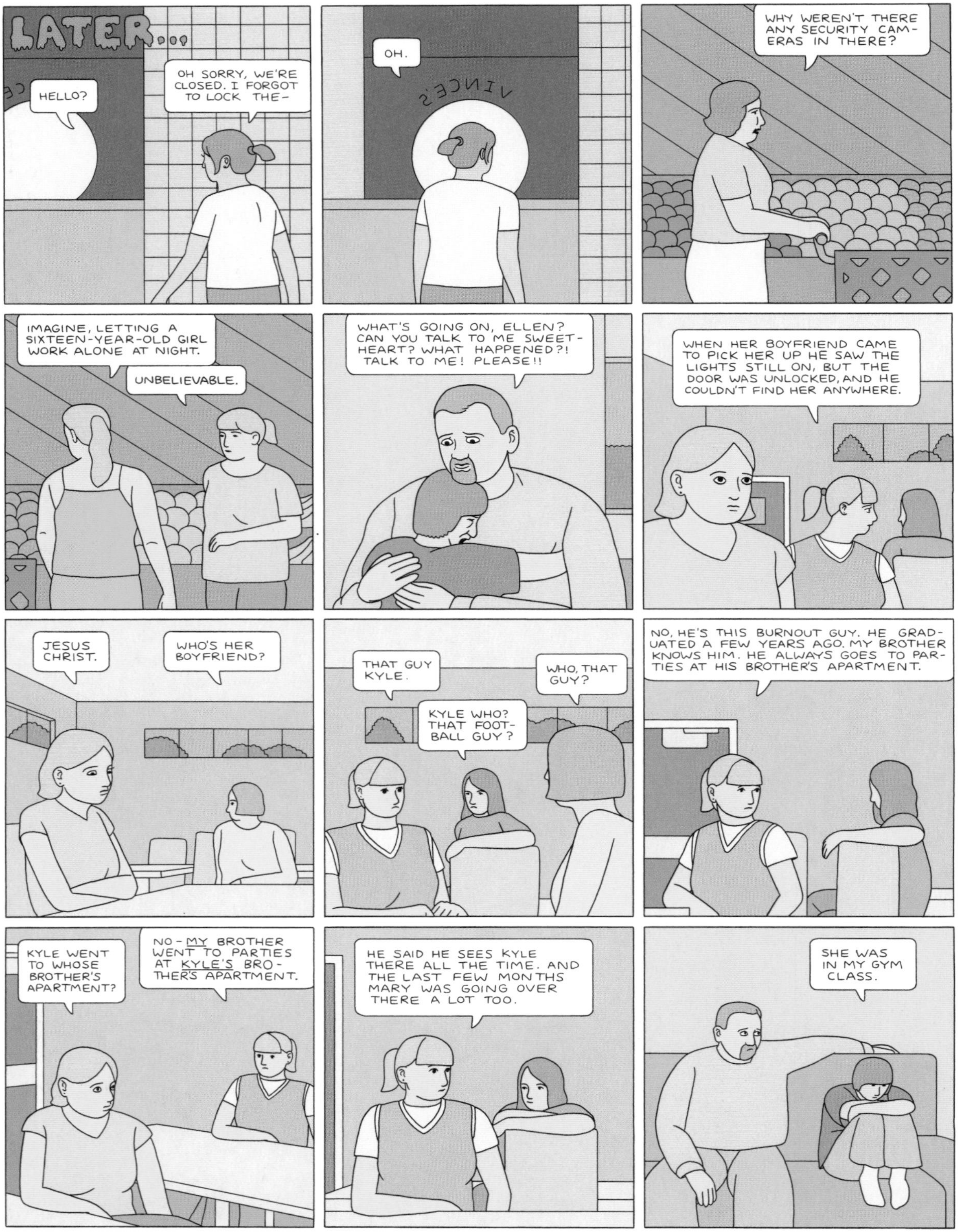
LATER...
HELLO?
OH SORRY, WE'RE CLOSED. I FORGOT TO LOCK THE-
OH.
WHY WEREN'T THERE ANY SECURITY CAMERAS IN THERE?
IMAGINE, LETTING A SIXTEEN-YEAR-OLD GIRL WORK ALONE AT NIGHT.
UNBELIEVABLE.
WHAT'S GOING ON, ELLEN? CAN YOU TALK TO ME SWEETHEART? WHAT HAPPENED?! TALK TO ME! PLEASE!!
WHEN HER BOYFRIEND CAME TO PICK HER UP HE SAW THE LIGHTS STILL ON, BUT THE DOOR WAS UNLOCKED, AND HE COULDN'T FIND HER ANYWHERE.
JESUS CHRIST.
WHO'S HER BOYFRIEND?
THAT GUY KYLE.
WHO, THAT GUY?
KYLE WHO? THAT FOOTBALL GUY?
NO, HE'S THIS BURNOUT GUY. HE GRADUATED A FEW YEARS AGO. MY BROTHER KNOWS HIM. HE ALWAYS GOES TO PARTIES AT HIS BROTHER'S APARTMENT.
KYLE WENT TO WHOSE BROTHER'S APARTMENT?
NO - MY BROTHER WENT TO PARTIES AT KYLE'S BROTHER'S APARTMENT.
HE SAID HE SEES KYLE THERE ALL THE TIME. AND THE LAST FEW MONTHS MARY WAS GOING OVER THERE A LOT TOO.
SHE WAS IN MY GYM CLASS.

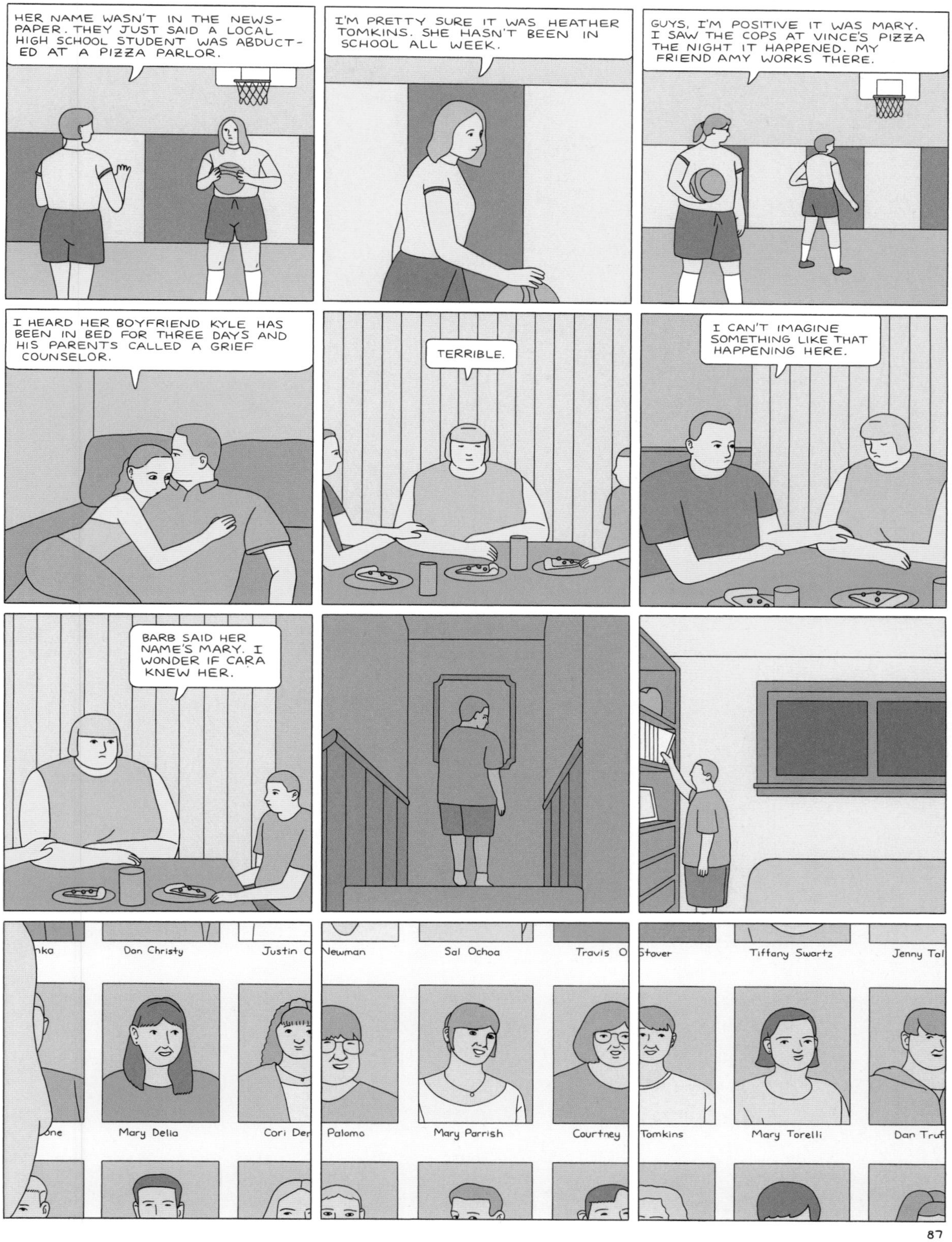
HER NAME WASN'T IN THE NEWSPAPER. THEY JUST SAID A LOCAL HIGH SCHOOL STUDENT WAS ABDUCTED AT A PIZZA PARLOR.
I'M PRETTY SURE IT WAS HEATHER TOMKINS. SHE HASN'T BEEN IN SCHOOL ALL WEEK.
GUYS, I'M POSITIVE IT WAS MARY. I SAW THE COPS AT VINCE'S PIZZA THE NIGHT IT HAPPENED. MY FRIEND AMY WORKS THERE.
I HEARD HER BOYFRIEND KYLE HAS BEEN IN BED FOR THREE DAYS AND HIS PARENTS CALLED A GRIEF COUNSELOR.
TERRIBLE.
I CAN'T IMAGINE SOMETHING LIKE THAT HAPPENING HERE.
BARB SAID HER NAME'S MARY. I WONDER IF CARA KNEW HER.
Dan Christy
Mary Delia
Sal Ochoa
Mary Parrish
Tiffany Swartz
Mary Torelli

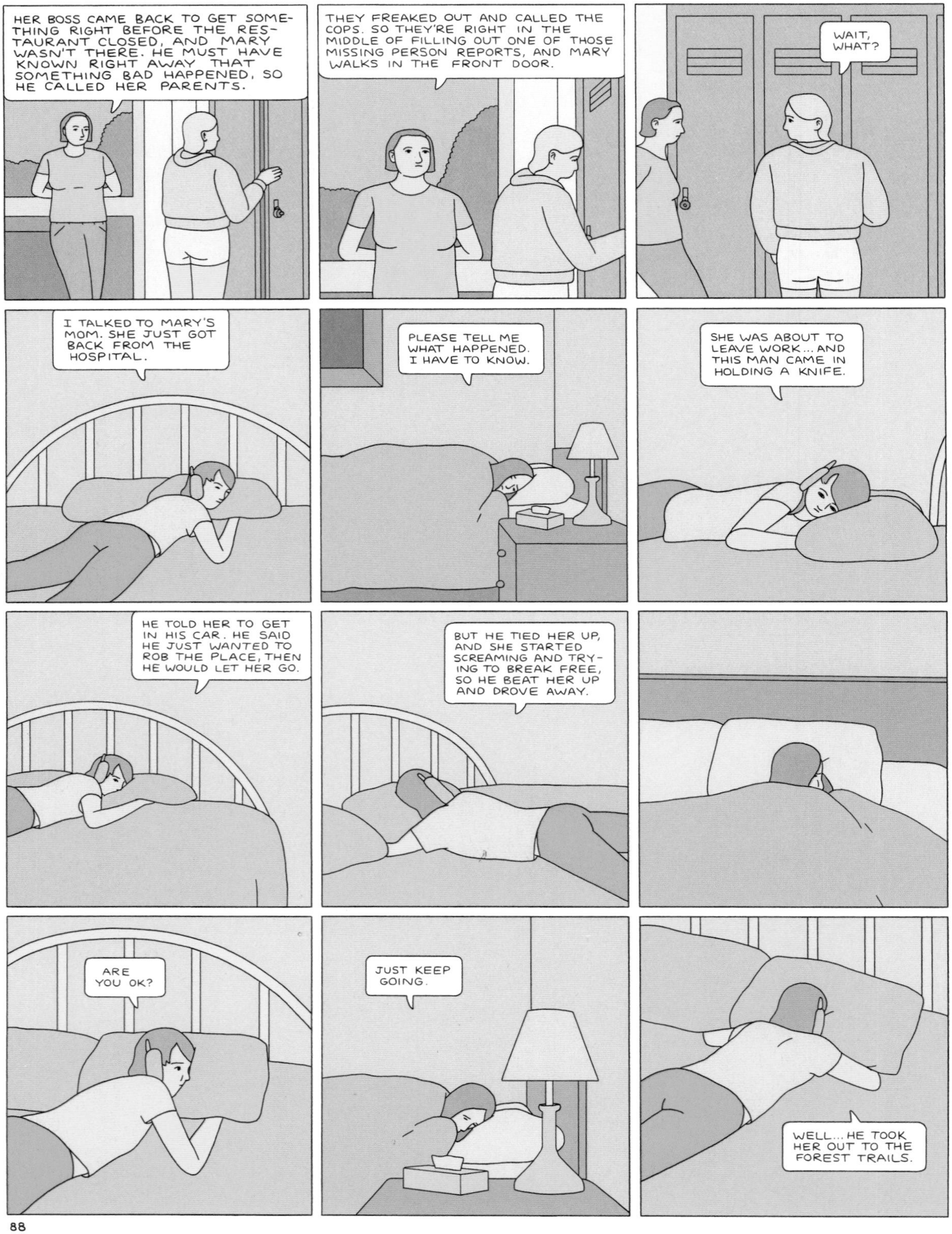
HER BOSS CAME BACK TO GET SOMETHING RIGHT BEFORE THE RESTAURANT CLOSED, AND MARY WASN'T THERE. HE MUST HAVE KNOWN RIGHT AWAY THAT SOMETHING BAD HAPPENED, SO HE CALLED HER PARENTS.
THEY FREAKED OUT AND CALLED THE COPS. SO THEY'RE RIGHT IN THE MIDDLE OF FILLING OUT ONE OF THOSE MISSING PERSON REPORTS, AND MARY WALKS IN THE FRONT DOOR.
WAIT, WHAT?
I TALKED TO MARY'S MOM. SHE JUST GOT BACK FROM THE HOSPITAL.
PLEASE TELL ME WHAT HAPPENED. I HAVE TO KNOW.
SHE WAS ABOUT TO LEAVE WORK... AND THIS MAN CAME IN HOLDING A KNIFE.
HE TOLD HER TO GET IN HIS CAR. HE SAID HE JUST WANTED TO ROB THE PLACE, THEN HE WOULD LET HER GO.
BUT HE TIED HER UP, AND SHE STARTED SCREAMING AND TRYING TO BREAK FREE, SO HE BEAT HER UP AND DROVE AWAY.
ARE YOU OK?
JUST KEEP GOING.
WELL... HE TOOK HER OUT TO THE FOREST TRAILS.

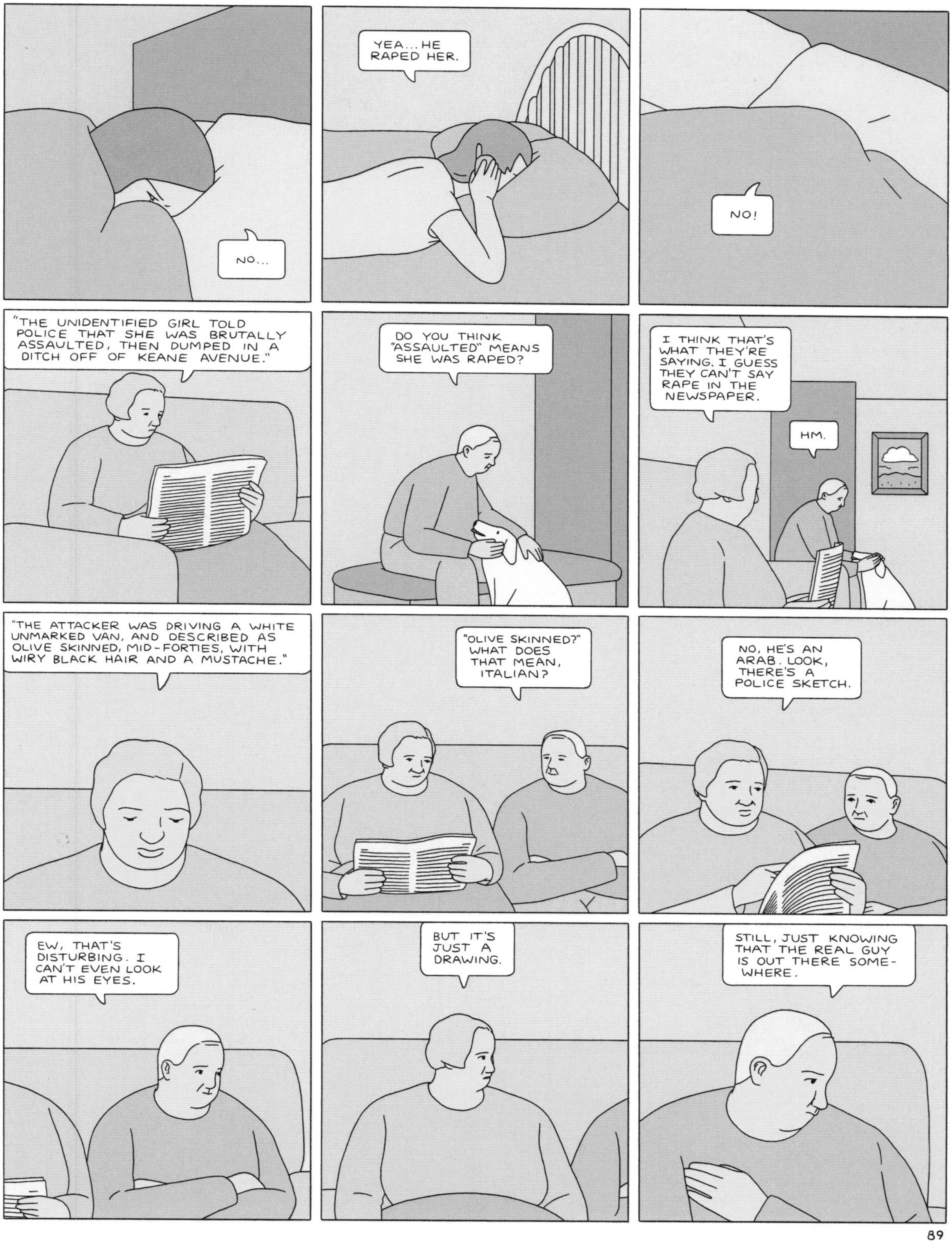
NO...
YEA... HE RAPED HER.
NO!
"THE UNIDENTIFIED GIRL TOLD POLICE THAT SHE WAS BRUTALLY ASSAULTED, THEN DUMPED IN A DITCH OFF OF KEANE AVENUE."
DO YOU THINK "ASSAULTED" MEANS SHE WAS RAPED?
I THINK THAT'S WHAT THEY'RE SAYING. I GUESS THEY CAN'T SAY RAPE IN THE NEWSPAPER.
HM.
"THE ATTACKER WAS DRIVING A WHITE UNMARKED VAN, AND DESCRIBED AS OLIVE SKINNED, MID-FORTIES, WITH WIRY BLACK HAIR AND A MUSTACHE."
"OLIVE SKINNED?" WHAT DOES THAT MEAN, ITALIAN?
NO, HE'S AN ARAB. LOOK, THERE'S A POLICE SKETCH.
EW, THAT'S DISTURBING. I CAN'T EVEN LOOK AT HIS EYES.
BUT IT'S JUST A DRAWING.
STILL, JUST KNOWING THAT THE REAL GUY IS OUT THERE SOME-WHERE.

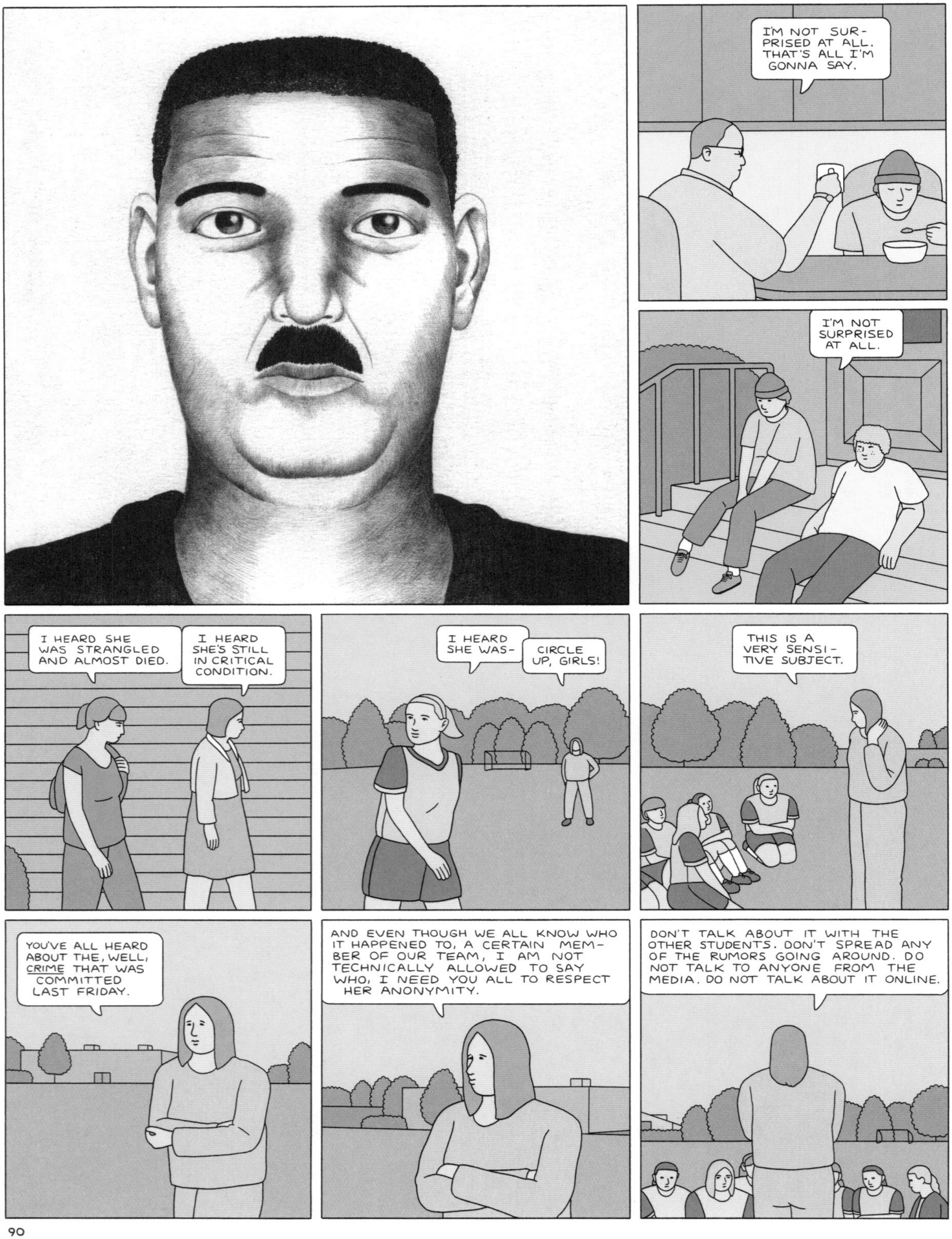
I'M NOT SURPRISED AT ALL. THAT'S ALL I'M GONNA SAY.
I'M NOT SURPRISED AT ALL.
I HEARD SHE WAS STRANGLED AND ALMOST DIED.
I HEARD SHE'S STILL IN CRITICAL CONDITION.
I HEARD SHE WAS-
CIRCLE UP, GIRLS!
THIS IS A VERY SENSITIVE SUBJECT.
YOU'VE ALL HEARD ABOUT THE, WELL, CRIME THAT WAS COMMITTED LAST FRIDAY.
AND EVEN THOUGH WE ALL KNOW WHO IT HAPPENED TO, A CERTAIN MEMBER OF OUR TEAM, I AM NOT TECHNICALLY ALLOWED TO SAY WHO, I NEED YOU ALL TO RESPECT HER ANONYMITY.
DON'T TALK ABOUT IT WITH THE OTHER STUDENTS. DON'T SPREAD ANY OF THE RUMORS GOING AROUND. DO NOT TALK TO ANYONE FROM THE MEDIA. DO NOT TALK ABOUT IT ONLINE.

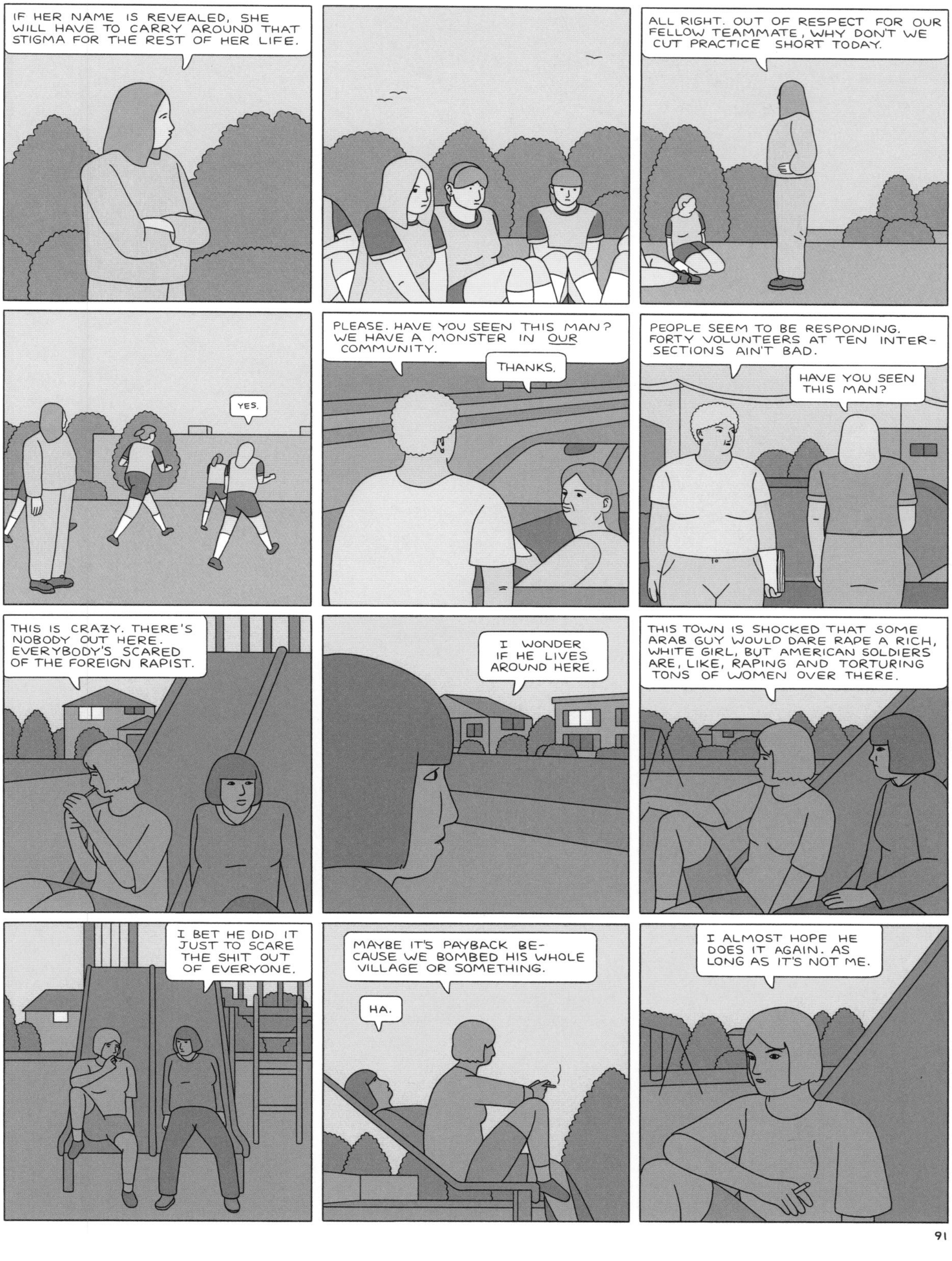
IF HER NAME IS REVEALED, SHE WILL HAVE TO CARRY AROUND THAT STIGMA FOR THE REST OF HER LIFE.
ALL RIGHT. OUT OF RESPECT FOR OUR FELLOW TEAMMATE, WHY DON'T WE CUT PRACTICE SHORT TODAY.
YES.
PLEASE. HAVE YOU SEEN THIS MAN? WE HAVE A MONSTER IN OUR COMMUNITY.
THANKS.
PEOPLE SEEM TO BE RESPONDING. FORTY VOLUNTEERS AT TEN INTERSECTIONS AIN'T BAD.
HAVE YOU SEEN THIS MAN?
THIS IS CRAZY. THERE'S NOBODY OUT HERE. EVERYBODY'S SCARED OF THE FOREIGN RAPIST.
I WONDER IF HE LIVES AROUND HERE.
THIS TOWN IS SHOCKED THAT SOME ARAB GUY WOULD DARE RAPE A RICH, WHITE GIRL, BUT AMERICAN SOLDIERS ARE, LIKE, RAPING AND TORTURING TONS OF WOMEN OVER THERE.
I BET HE DID IT JUST TO SCARE THE SHIT OUT OF EVERYONE.
MAYBE IT'S PAYBACK BECAUSE WE BOMBED HIS WHOLE VILLAGE OR SOMETHING.
HA.
I ALMOST HOPE HE DOES IT AGAIN. AS LONG AS IT'S NOT ME.

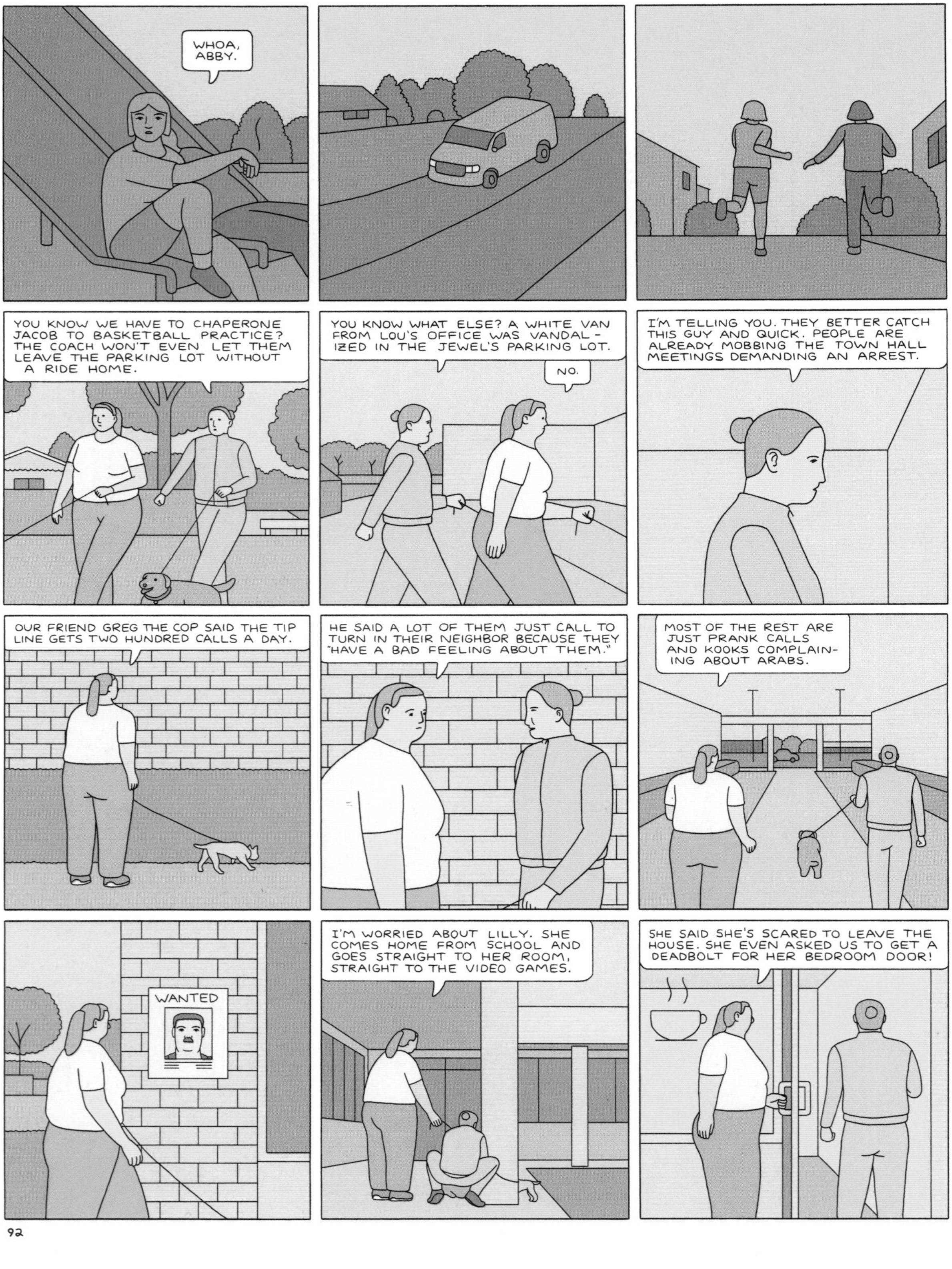
WHOA, ABBY.
YOU KNOW WE HAVE TO CHAPERONE JACOB TO BASKETBALL PRACTICE? THE COACH WON'T EVEN LET THEM LEAVE THE PARKING LOT WITHOUT A RIDE HOME.
YOU KNOW WHAT ELSE? A WHITE VAN FROM LOU'S OFFICE WAS VANDAL-IZED IN THE JEWEL'S PARKING LOT.
NO.
I'M TELLING YOU. THEY BETTER CATCH THIS GUY AND QUICK. PEOPLE ARE ALREADY MOBBING THE TOWN HALL MEETINGS DEMANDING AN ARREST.
OUR FRIEND GREG THE COP SAID THE TIP LINE GETS TWO HUNDRED CALLS A DAY.
HE SAID A LOT OF THEM JUST CALL TO TURN IN THEIR NEIGHBOR BECAUSE THEY "HAVE A BAD FEELING ABOUT THEM."
MOST OF THE REST ARE JUST PRANK CALLS AND KOOKS COMPLAIN-ING ABOUT ARABS.
WANTED
I'M WORRIED ABOUT LILLY. SHE COMES HOME FROM SCHOOL AND GOES STRAIGHT TO HER ROOM, STRAIGHT TO THE VIDEO GAMES.
SHE SAID SHE'S SCARED TO LEAVE THE HOUSE. SHE EVEN ASKED US TO GET A DEADBOLT FOR HER BEDROOM DOOR!

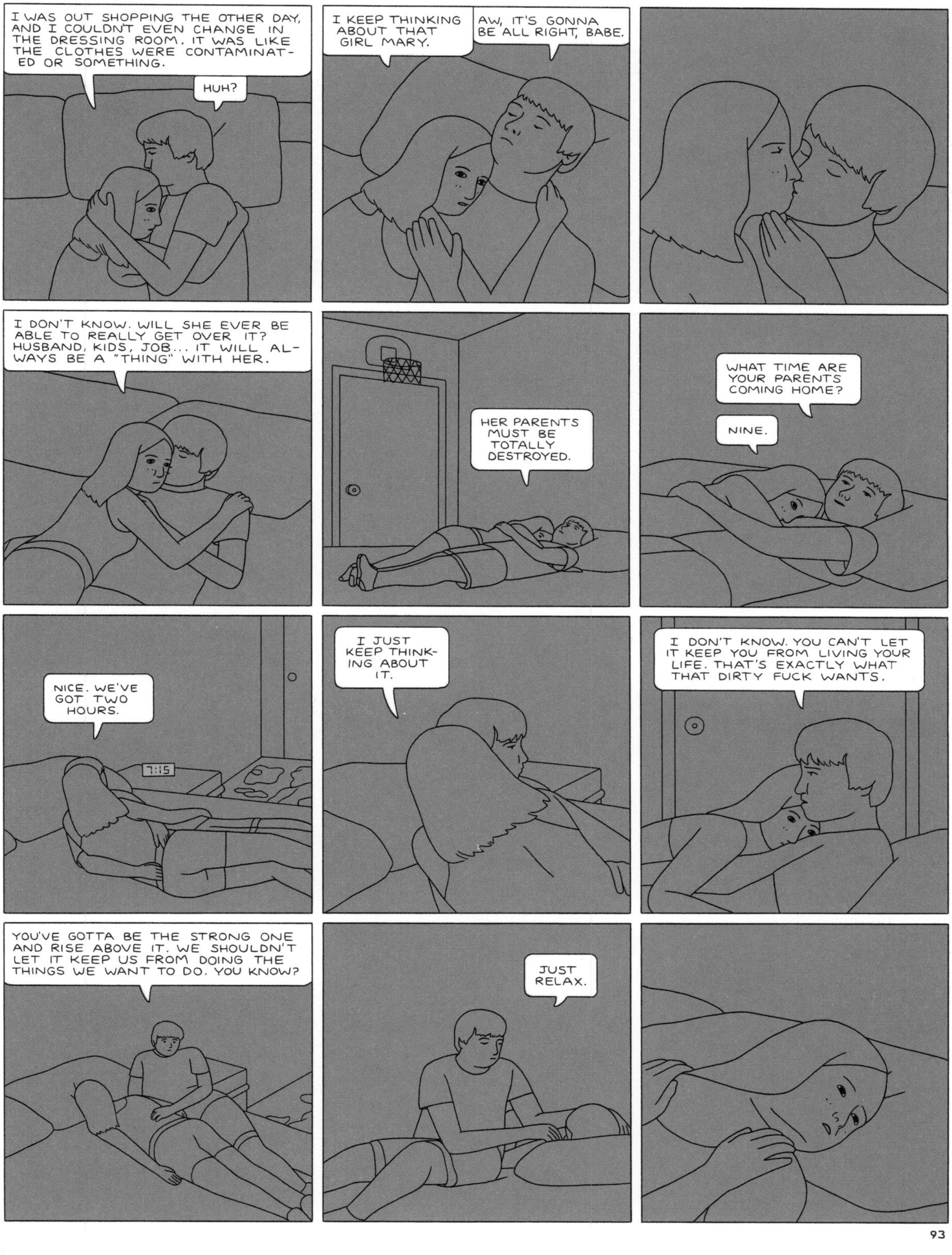

I WAS OUT SHOPPING THE OTHER DAY, AND I COULDN'T EVEN CHANGE IN THE DRESSING ROOM. IT WAS LIKE THE CLOTHES WERE CONTAMINAT-ED OR SOMETHING.
HUH?
I KEEP THINKING ABOUT THAT GIRL MARY.
AW, IT'S GONNA BE ALL RIGHT, BABE.
I DON'T KNOW. WILL SHE EVER BE ABLE TO REALLY GET OVER IT? HUSBAND, KIDS, JOB... IT WILL AL-WAYS BE A "THING" WITH HER.
HER PARENTS MUST BE TOTALLY DESTROYED.
WHAT TIME ARE YOUR PARENTS COMING HOME?
NINE.
NICE. WE'VE GOT TWO HOURS.
7:15
I JUST KEEP THINK-ING ABOUT IT.
I DON'T KNOW. YOU CAN'T LET IT KEEP YOU FROM LIVING YOUR LIFE. THAT'S EXACTLY WHAT THAT DIRTY FUCK WANTS.
YOU'VE GOTTA BE THE STRONG ONE AND RISE ABOVE IT. WE SHOULDN'T LET IT KEEP US FROM DOING THE THINGS WE WANT TO DO. YOU KNOW?
JUST RELAX.

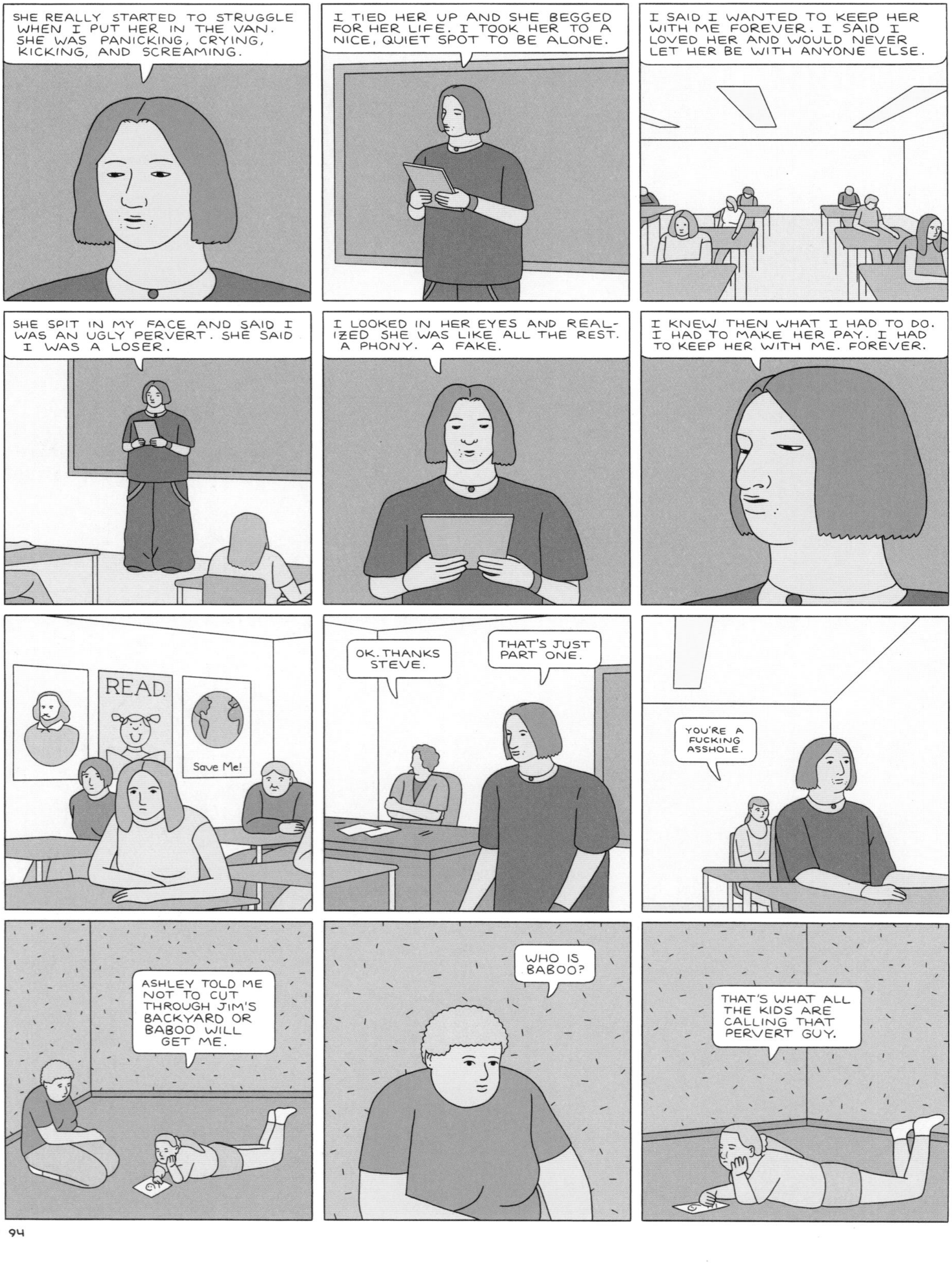
SHE REALLY STARTED TO STRUGGLE WHEN I PUT HER IN THE VAN. SHE WAS PANICKING, CRYING, KICKING, AND SCREAMING.
I TIED HER UP AND SHE BEGGED FOR HER LIFE. I TOOK HER TO A NICE, QUIET SPOT TO BE ALONE.
I SAID I WANTED TO KEEP HER WITH ME FOREVER. I SAID I LOVED HER AND WOULD NEVER LET HER BE WITH ANYONE ELSE.
SHE SPIT IN MY FACE AND SAID I WAS AN UGLY PERVERT. SHE SAID I WAS A LOSER.
I LOOKED IN HER EYES AND REAL-IZED SHE WAS LIKE ALL THE REST. A PHONY. A FAKE.
I KNEW THEN WHAT I HAD TO DO. I HAD TO MAKE HER PAY. I HAD TO KEEP HER WITH ME. FOREVER.
READ.
Save Me!
OK. THANKS STEVE.
THAT'S JUST PART ONE.
YOU'RE A FUCKING ASSHOLE.
ASHLEY TOLD ME NOT TO CUT THROUGH JIM'S BACKYARD OR BABOO WILL GET ME.
WHO IS BABOO?
THAT'S WHAT ALL THE KIDS ARE CALLING THAT PERVERT GUY.

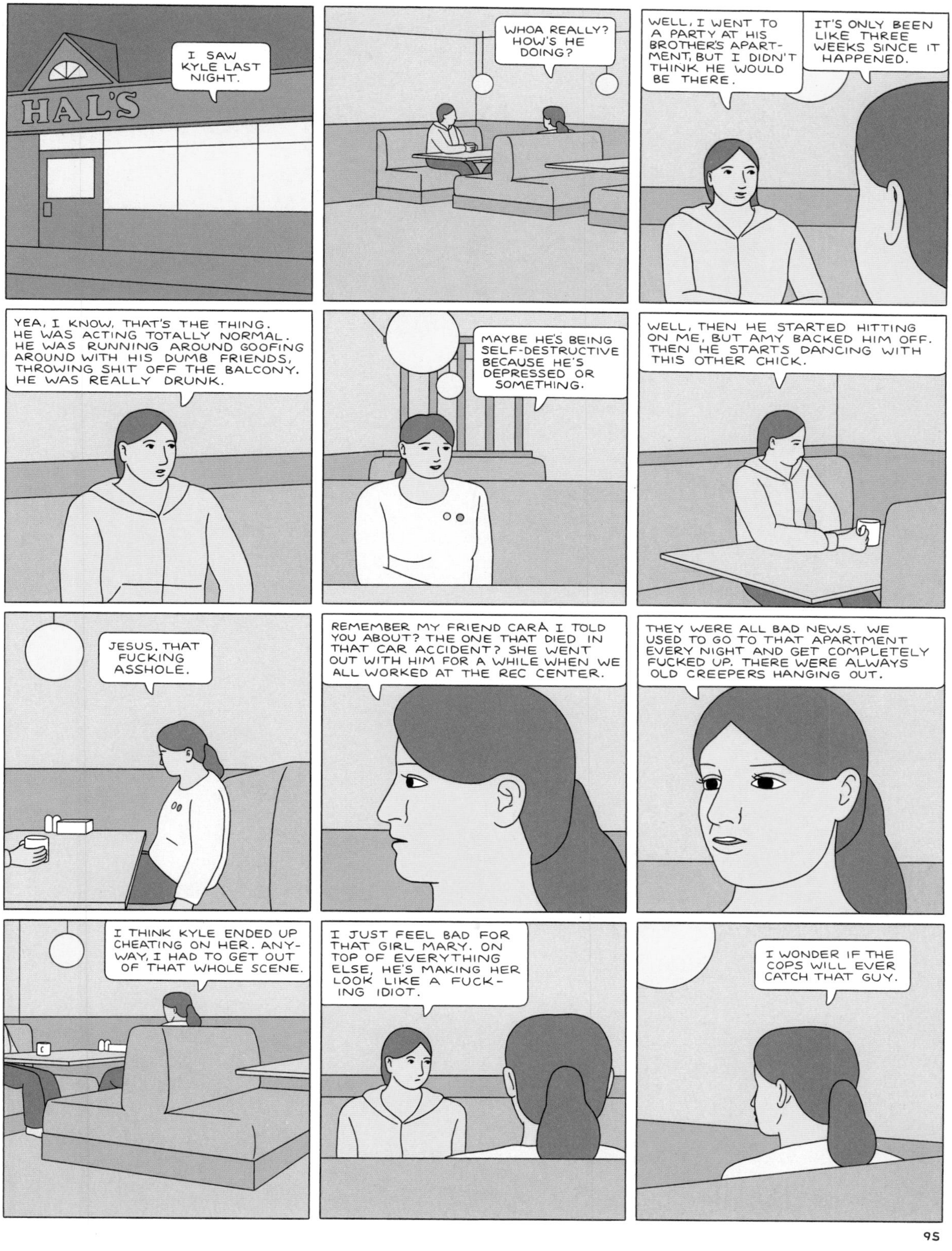
HAL'S
I SAW KYLE LAST NIGHT.
WHOA REALLY? HOW'S HE DOING?
WELL, I WENT TO A PARTY AT HIS BROTHER'S APARTMENT, BUT I DIDN'T THINK HE WOULD BE THERE.
IT'S ONLY BEEN LIKE THREE WEEKS SINCE IT HAPPENED.
YEA, I KNOW, THAT'S THE THING. HE WAS ACTING TOTALLY NORMAL. HE WAS RUNNING AROUND GOOFING AROUND WITH HIS DUMB FRIENDS, THROWING SHIT OFF THE BALCONY. HE WAS REALLY DRUNK.
MAYBE HE'S BEING SELF-DESTRUCTIVE BECAUSE HE'S DEPRESSED OR SOMETHING.
WELL, THEN HE STARTED HITTING ON ME, BUT AMY BACKED HIM OFF. THEN HE STARTS DANCING WITH THIS OTHER CHICK.
JESUS, THAT FUCKING ASSHOLE.
REMEMBER MY FRIEND CARA I TOLD YOU ABOUT? THE ONE THAT DIED IN THAT CAR ACCIDENT? SHE WENT OUT WITH HIM FOR A WHILE WHEN WE ALL WORKED AT THE REC CENTER.
THEY WERE ALL BAD NEWS. WE USED TO GO TO THAT APARTMENT EVERY NIGHT AND GET COMPLETELY FUCKED UP. THERE WERE ALWAYS OLD CREEPERS HANGING OUT.
I THINK KYLE ENDED UP CHEATING ON HER. ANYWAY, I HAD TO GET OUT OF THAT WHOLE SCENE.
I JUST FEEL BAD FOR THAT GIRL MARY. ON TOP OF EVERYTHING ELSE, HE'S MAKING HER LOOK LIKE A FUCKING IDIOT.
I WONDER IF THE COPS WILL EVER CATCH THAT GUY.

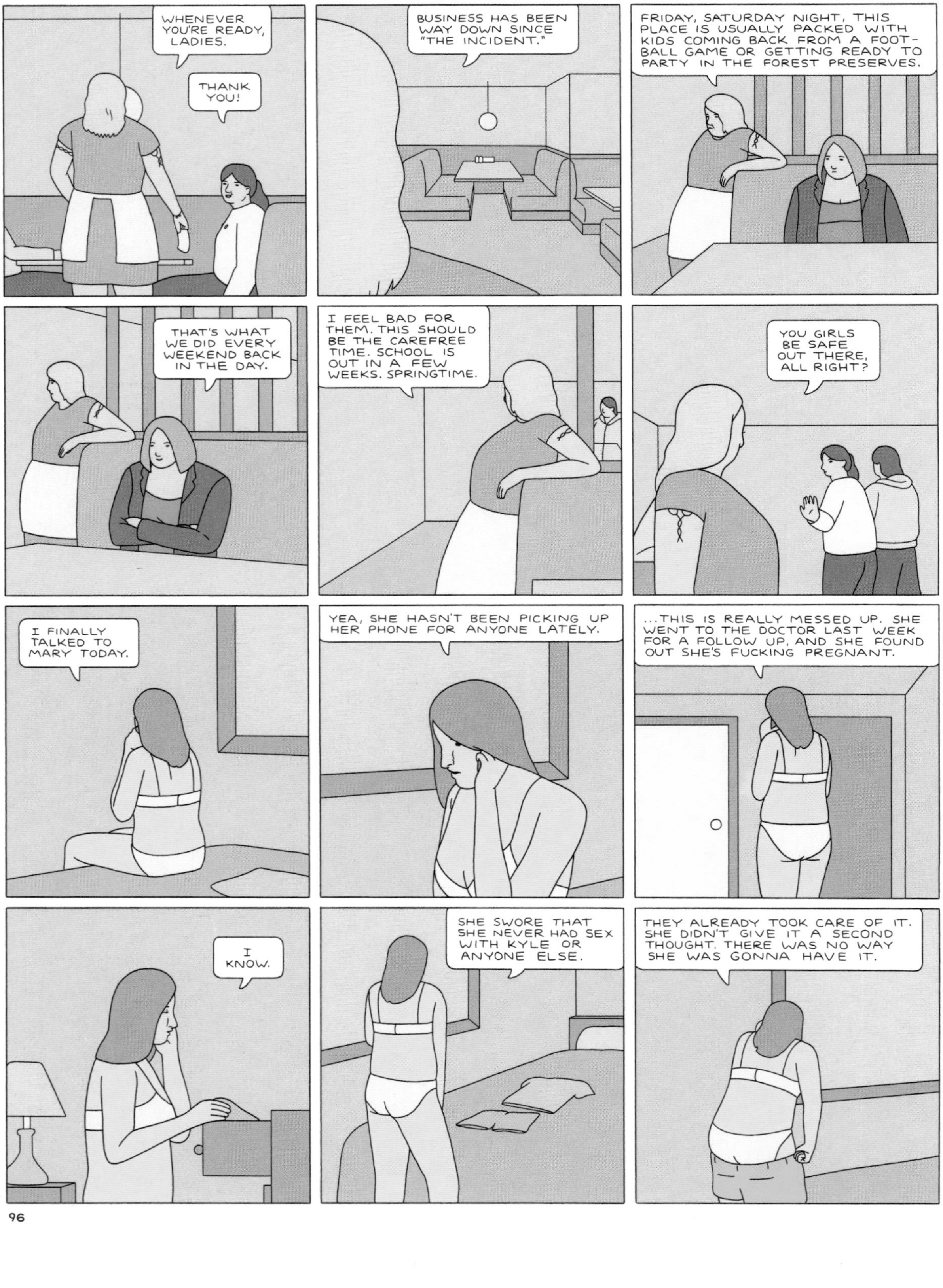
WHENEVER YOU'RE READY, LADIES.
THANK YOU!
BUSINESS HAS BEEN WAY DOWN SINCE "THE INCIDENT."
FRIDAY, SATURDAY NIGHT, THIS PLACE IS USUALLY PACKED WITH KIDS COMING BACK FROM A FOOT-BALL GAME OR GETTING READY TO PARTY IN THE FOREST PRESERVES.
THAT'S WHAT WE DID EVERY WEEKEND BACK IN THE DAY.
I FEEL BAD FOR THEM. THIS SHOULD BE THE CAREFREE TIME. SCHOOL IS OUT IN A FEW WEEKS. SPRINGTIME.
YOU GIRLS BE SAFE OUT THERE, ALL RIGHT?
I FINALLY TALKED TO MARY TODAY.
YEA, SHE HASN'T BEEN PICKING UP HER PHONE FOR ANYONE LATELY.
...THIS IS REALLY MESSED UP. SHE WENT TO THE DOCTOR LAST WEEK FOR A FOLLOW UP, AND SHE FOUND OUT SHE'S FUCKING PREGNANT.
I KNOW.
SHE SWORE THAT SHE NEVER HAD SEX WITH KYLE OR ANYONE ELSE.
THEY ALREADY TOOK CARE OF IT. SHE DIDN'T GIVE IT A SECOND THOUGHT. THERE WAS NO WAY SHE WAS GONNA HAVE IT.

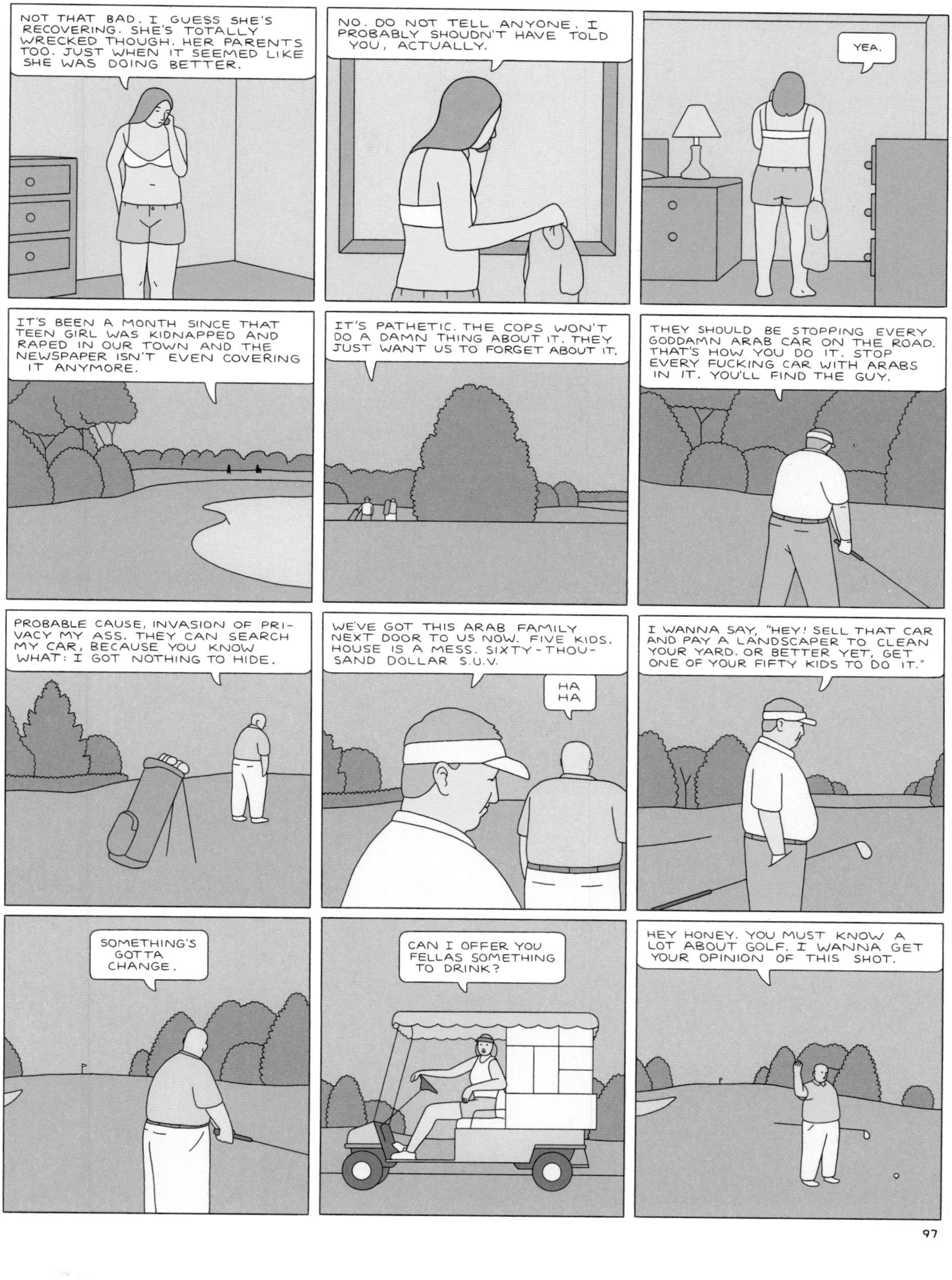
NOT THAT BAD. I GUESS SHE'S RECOVERING. SHE'S TOTALLY WRECKED THOUGH. HER PARENTS TOO. JUST WHEN IT SEEMED LIKE SHE WAS DOING BETTER.
NO. DO NOT TELL ANYONE. I PROBABLY SHOUDN'T HAVE TOLD YOU, ACTUALLY.
YEA.
IT'S BEEN A MONTH SINCE THAT TEEN GIRL WAS KIDNAPPED AND RAPED IN OUR TOWN AND THE NEWSPAPER ISN'T EVEN COVERING IT ANYMORE.
IT'S PATHETIC. THE COPS WON'T DO A DAMN THING ABOUT IT. THEY JUST WANT US TO FORGET ABOUT IT.
THEY SHOULD BE STOPPING EVERY GODDAMN ARAB CAR ON THE ROAD. THAT'S HOW YOU DO IT. STOP EVERY FUCKING CAR WITH ARABS IN IT. YOU'LL FIND THE GUY.
PROBABLE CAUSE, INVASION OF PRIVACY MY ASS. THEY CAN SEARCH MY CAR, BECAUSE YOU KNOW WHAT: I GOT NOTHING TO HIDE.
WE'VE GOT THIS ARAB FAMILY NEXT DOOR TO US NOW. FIVE KIDS. HOUSE IS A MESS. SIXTY-THOUSAND DOLLAR S.U.V.
HA HA
I WANNA SAY, "HEY! SELL THAT CAR AND PAY A LANDSCAPER TO CLEAN YOUR YARD. OR BETTER YET, GET ONE OF YOUR FIFTY KIDS TO DO IT."
SOMETHING'S GOTTA CHANGE.
CAN I OFFER YOU FELLAS SOMETHING TO DRINK?
HEY HONEY. YOU MUST KNOW A LOT ABOUT GOLF. I WANNA GET YOUR OPINION OF THIS SHOT.

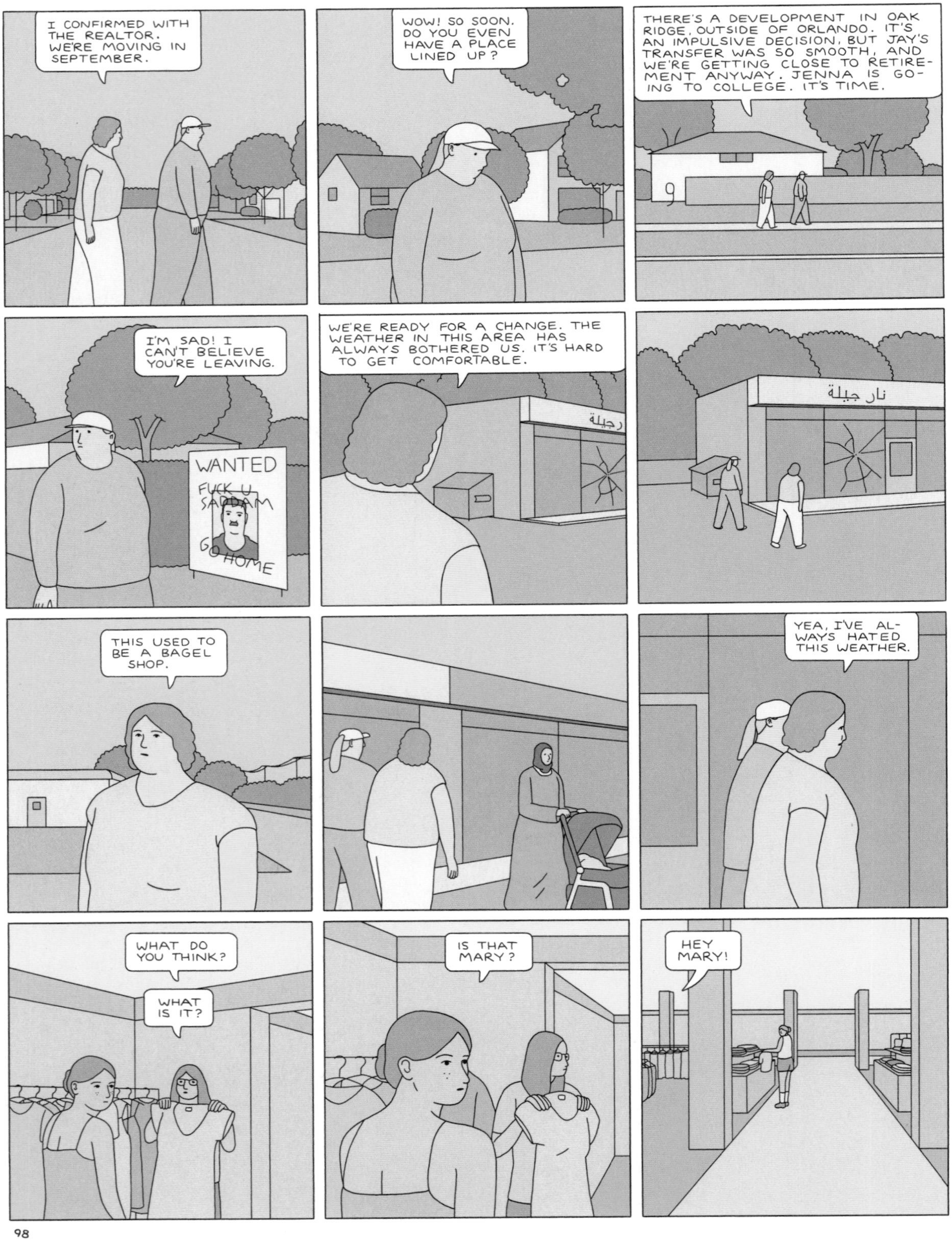
I CONFIRMED WITH THE REALTOR. WE'RE MOVING IN SEPTEMBER.
WOW! SO SOON. DO YOU EVEN HAVE A PLACE LINED UP?
THERE'S A DEVELOPMENT IN OAK RIDGE, OUTSIDE OF ORLANDO. IT'S AN IMPULSIVE DECISION, BUT JAY'S TRANSFER WAS SO SMOOTH, AND WE'RE GETTING CLOSE TO RETIREMENT ANYWAY. JENNA IS GOING TO COLLEGE. IT'S TIME.
I'M SAD! I CAN'T BELIEVE YOU'RE LEAVING.
WANTED
FUCK U SADDAM
GO HOME
WE'RE READY FOR A CHANGE. THE WEATHER IN THIS AREA HAS ALWAYS BOTHERED US. IT'S HARD TO GET COMFORTABLE.
نار جيلة
THIS USED TO BE A BAGEL SHOP.
YEA, I'VE ALWAYS HATED THIS WEATHER.
WHAT DO YOU THINK?
WHAT IS IT?
IS THAT MARY?
HEY MARY!

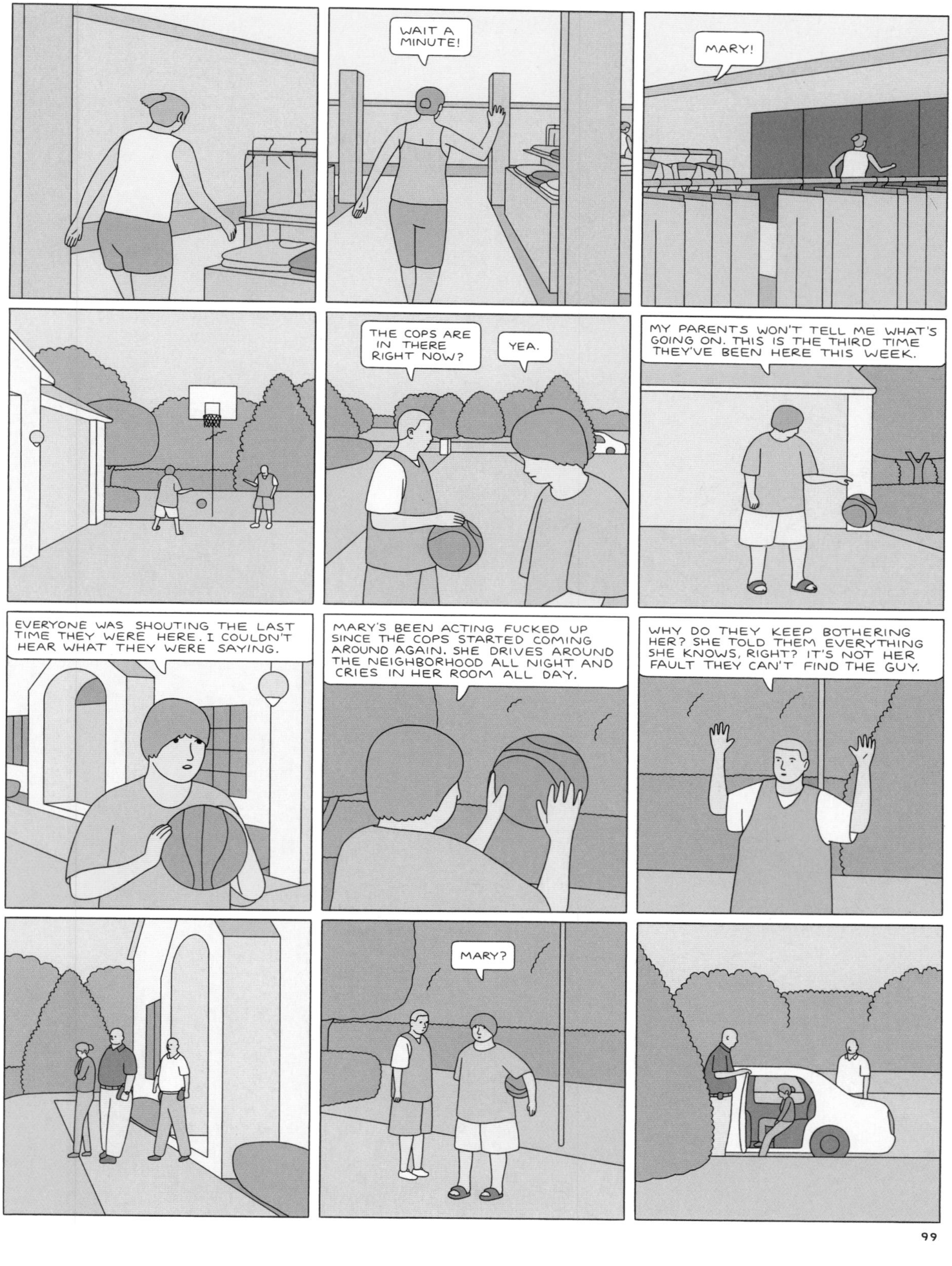
WAIT A MINUTE!
MARY!
THE COPS ARE IN THERE RIGHT NOW?
YEA.
MY PARENTS WON'T TELL ME WHAT'S GOING ON. THIS IS THE THIRD TIME THEY'VE BEEN HERE THIS WEEK.
EVERYONE WAS SHOUTING THE LAST TIME THEY WERE HERE. I COULDN'T HEAR WHAT THEY WERE SAYING.
MARY'S BEEN ACTING FUCKED UP SINCE THE COPS STARTED COMING AROUND AGAIN. SHE DRIVES AROUND THE NEIGHBORHOOD ALL NIGHT AND CRIES IN HER ROOM ALL DAY.
WHY DO THEY KEEP BOTHERING HER? SHE TOLD THEM EVERYTHING SHE KNOWS, RIGHT? IT'S NOT HER FAULT THEY CAN'T FIND THE GUY.
MARY?

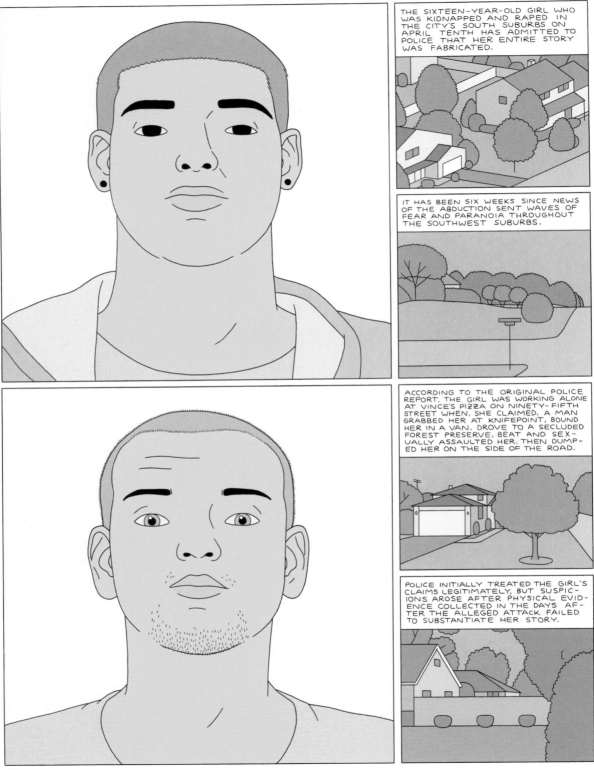

THE SIXTEEN-YEAR-OLD GIRL WHO WAS KIDNAPPED AND RAPED IN THE CITY'S SOUTH SUBURBS ON APRIL TENTH HAS ADMITTED TO POLICE THAT HER ENTIRE STORY WAS FABRICATED.

IT HAS BEEN SIX WEEKS SINCE NEWS OF THE ABDUCTION SENT WAVES OF FEAR AND PARANOIA THROUGHOUT THE SOUTHWEST SUBURBS.

ACCORDING TO THE ORIGINAL POLICE REPORT, THE GIRL WAS WORKING ALONE AT VINCE'S PIZZA ON NINETY-FIFTH STREET WHEN, SHE CLAIMED, A MAN GRABBED HER AT KNIFEPOINT, BOUND HER IN A VAN, DROVE TO A SECLUDED FOREST PRESERVE, BEAT AND SEXUALLY ASSAULTED HER, THEN DUMPED HER ON THE SIDE OF THE ROAD.

POLICE INITIALLY TREATED THE GIRL'S CLAIMS LEGITIMATELY, BUT SUSPICIONS AROSE AFTER PHYSICAL EVIDENCE COLLECTED IN THE DAYS AFTER THE ALLEGED ATTACK FAILED TO SUBSTANTIATE HER STORY.

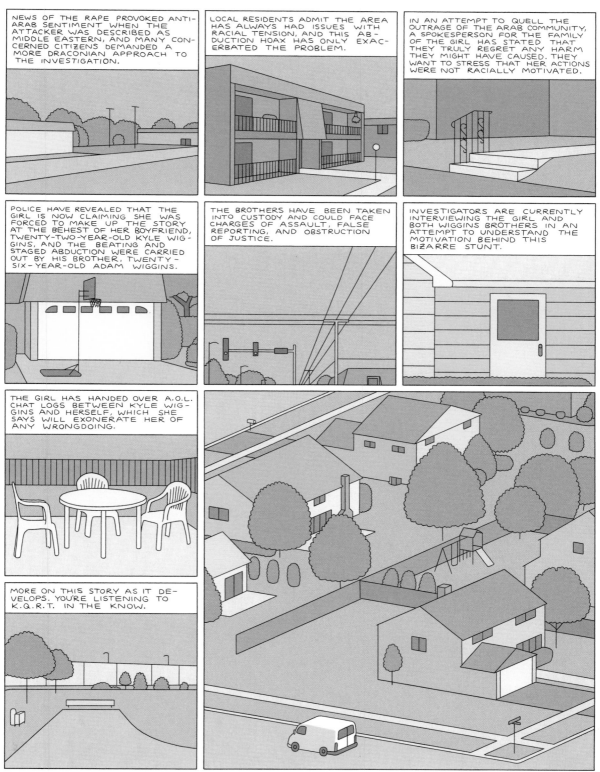

NEWS OF THE RAPE PROVOKED ANTI-ARAB SENTIMENT WHEN THE ATTACKER WAS DESCRIBED AS MIDDLE EASTERN, AND MANY CONCERNED CITIZENS DEMANDED A MORE DRACONIAN APPROACH TO THE INVESTIGATION.

LOCAL RESIDENTS ADMIT THE AREA HAS ALWAYS HAD ISSUES WITH RACIAL TENSION, AND THIS ABDUCTION HOAX HAS ONLY EXACERBATED THE PROBLEM.

IN AN ATTEMPT TO QUELL THE OUTRAGE OF THE ARAB COMMUNITY, A SPOKESPERSON FOR THE FAMILY OF THE GIRL HAS STATED THAT THEY TRULY REGRET ANY HARM THEY MIGHT HAVE CAUSED. THEY WANT TO STRESS THAT HER ACTIONS WERE NOT RACIALLY MOTIVATED.

POLICE HAVE REVEALED THAT THE GIRL IS NOW CLAIMING SHE WAS FORCED TO MAKE UP THE STORY AT THE BEHEST OF HER BOYFRIEND, TWENTY-TWO-YEAR-OLD KYLE WIGGINS, AND THE BEATING AND STAGED ABDUCTION WERE CARRIED OUT BY HIS BROTHER, TWENTY-SIX-YEAR-OLD ADAM WIGGINS.

THE BROTHERS HAVE BEEN TAKEN INTO CUSTODY AND COULD FACE CHARGES OF ASSAULT, FALSE REPORTING, AND OBSTRUCTION OF JUSTICE.

INVESTIGATORS ARE CURRENTLY INTERVIEWING THE GIRL AND BOTH WIGGINS BROTHERS IN AN ATTEMPT TO UNDERSTAND THE MOTIVATION BEHIND THIS BIZARRE STUNT.

THE GIRL HAS HANDED OVER A.O.L. CHAT LOGS BETWEEN KYLE WIGGINS AND HERSELF, WHICH SHE SAYS WILL EXONERATE HER OF ANY WRONGDOING.

MORE ON THIS STORY AS IT DEVELOPS. YOU'RE LISTENING TO K.Q.R.T. IN THE KNOW.

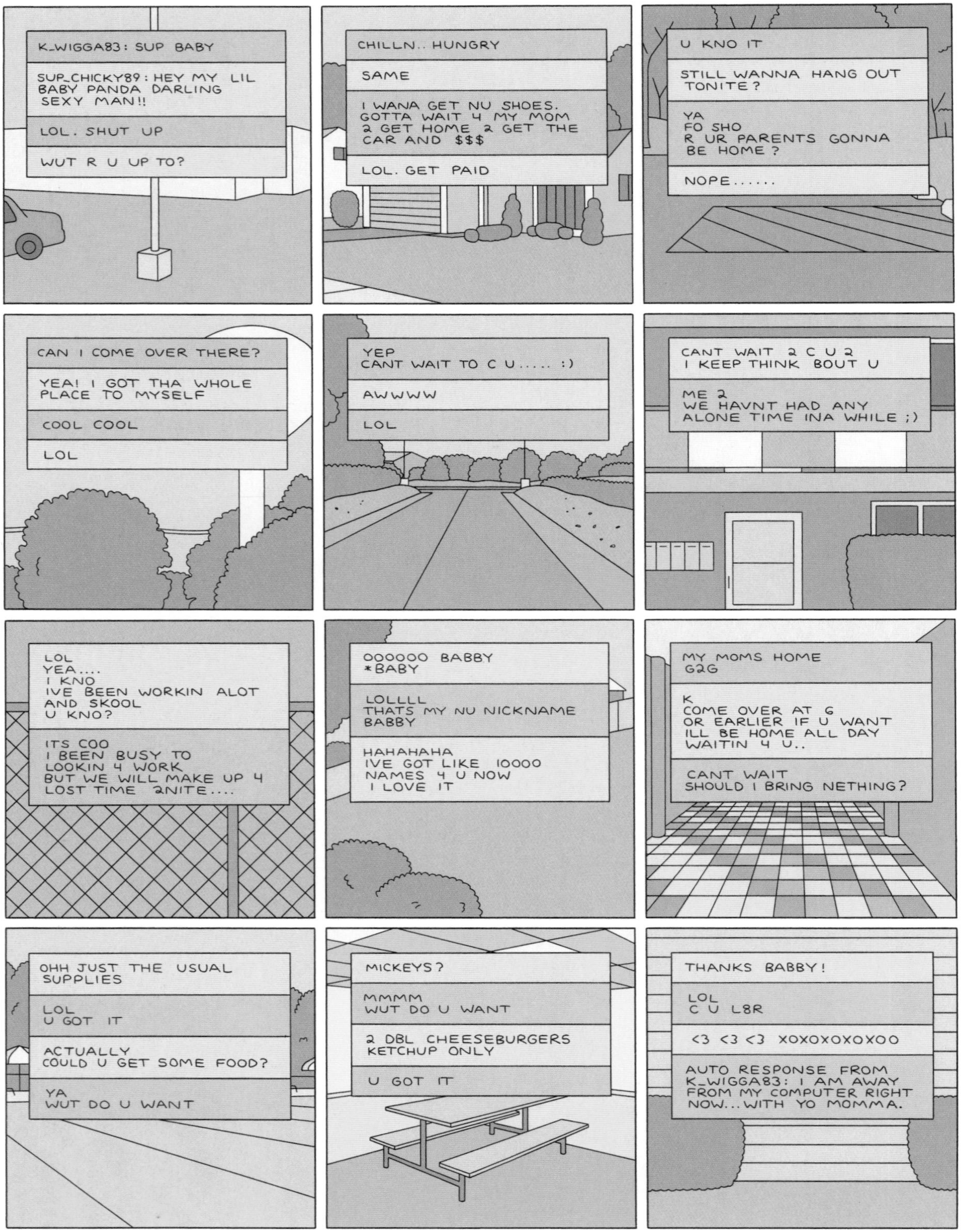
K_WIGGA83: SUP BABY
SUP_CHICKY89: HEY MY LIL BABY PANDA DARLING SEXY MAN!!
LOL. SHUT UP
WUT R U UP TO?
CHILLN.. HUNGRY
SAME
I WANA GET NU SHOES. GOTTA WAIT 4 MY MOM 2 GET HOME 2 GET THE CAR AND $$$
LOL. GET PAID
U KNO IT
STILL WANNA HANG OUT TONITE?
YA FO SHO R UR PARENTS GONNA BE HOME?
NOPE......
CAN I COME OVER THERE?
YEA! I GOT THA WHOLE PLACE TO MYSELF
COOL COOL
LOL
YEP CANT WAIT TO C U..... :)
AWWWW
LOL
CANT WAIT 2 C U 2 I KEEP THINK BOUT U
ME 2 WE HAVNT HAD ANY ALONE TIME INA WHILE ;)
LOL YEA.... I KNO IVE BEEN WORKIN ALOT AND SKOOL U KNO?
ITS COO I BEEN BUSY TO LOOKIN 4 WORK BUT WE WILL MAKE UP 4 LOST TIME 2NITE....
OOOOOO BABBY *BABY
LOLLLL THATS MY NU NICKNAME BABBY
HAHAHAHA IVE GOT LIKE 10000 NAMES 4 U NOW I LOVE IT
MY MOMS HOME G2G
K COME OVER AT 6 OR EARLIER IF U WANT ILL BE HOME ALL DAY WAITIN 4 U..
CANT WAIT SHOULD I BRING NETHING?
OHH JUST THE USUAL SUPPLIES
LOL U GOT IT
ACTUALLY COULD U GET SOME FOOD?
YA WUT DO U WANT
MICKEYS?
MMMM WUT DO U WANT
2 DBL CHEESEBURGERS KETCHUP ONLY
U GOT IT
THANKS BABBY!
LOL C U L8R
<3 <3 <3 XOXOXOXOXOO
AUTO RESPONSE FROM K_WIGGA83: I AM AWAY FROM MY COMPUTER RIGHT NOW... WITH YO MOMMA.

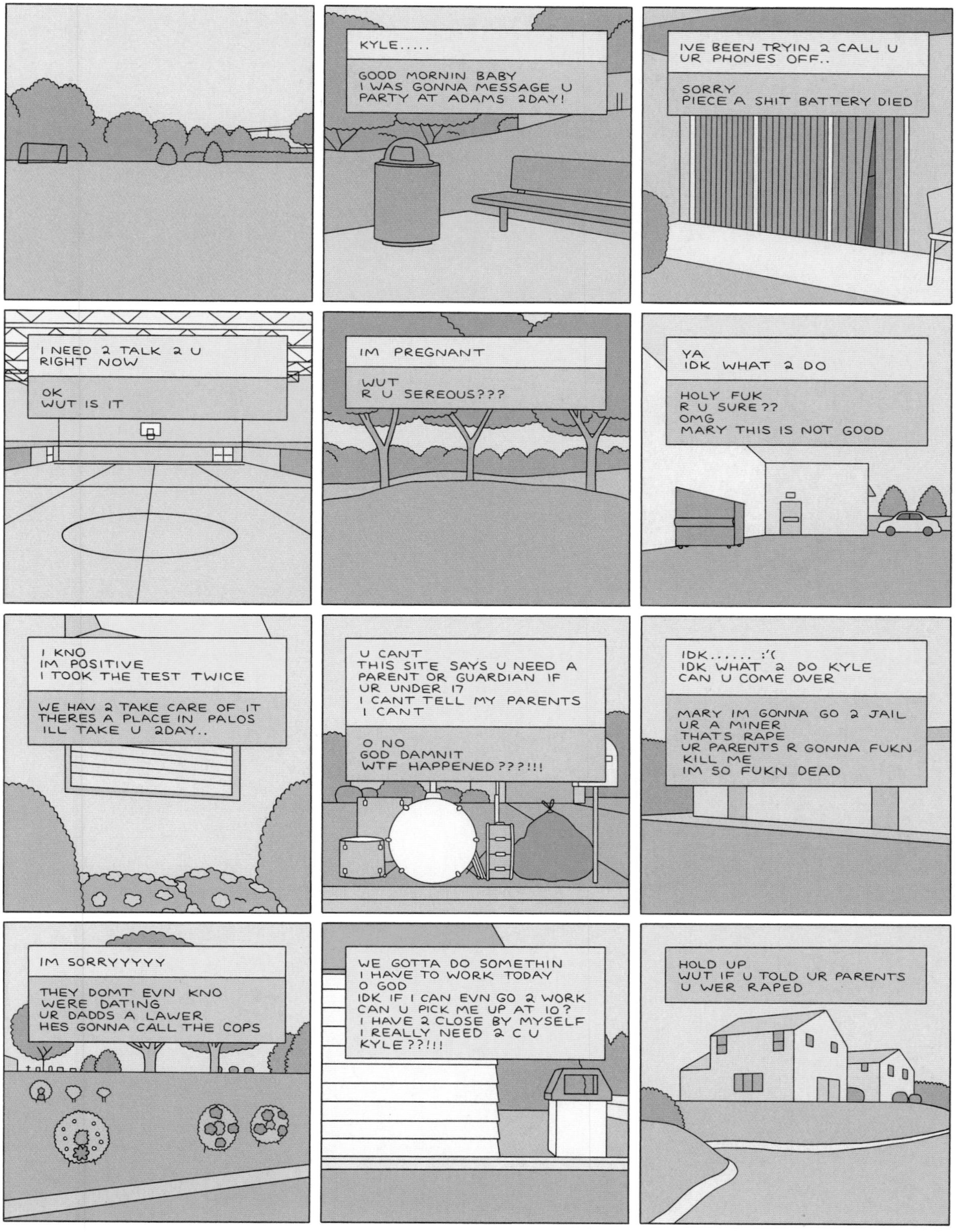
KYLE.....
GOOD MORNIN BABY
I WAS GONNA MESSAGE U
PARTY AT ADAMS 2DAY!
IVE BEEN TRYIN 2 CALL U
UR PHONES OFF..
SORRY
PIECE A SHIT BATTERY DIED
I NEED 2 TALK 2 U
RIGHT NOW
OK
WUT IS IT
IM PREGNANT
WUT
R U SEREOUS???
YA
IDK WHAT 2 DO
HOLY FUK
R U SURE??
OMG
MARY THIS IS NOT GOOD
I KNO
IM POSITIVE
I TOOK THE TEST TWICE
WE HAV 2 TAKE CARE OF IT
THERES A PLACE IN PALOS
ILL TAKE U 2DAY..
U CANT
THIS SITE SAYS U NEED A
PARENT OR GUARDIAN IF
UR UNDER 17
I CANT TELL MY PARENTS
I CANT
O NO
GOD DAMNIT
WTF HAPPENED???!!!
IDK...... :'(
IDK WHAT 2 DO KYLE
CAN U COME OVER
MARY IM GONNA GO 2 JAIL
UR A MINER
THATS RAPE
UR PARENTS R GONNA FUKN
KILL ME
IM SO FUKN DEAD
IM SORRYYYYY
THEY DOMT EVN KNO
WERE DATING
UR DADDS A LAWER
HES GONNA CALL THE COPS
WE GOTTA DO SOMETHIN
I HAVE TO WORK TODAY
O GOD
IDK IF I CAN EVN GO 2 WORK
CAN U PICK ME UP AT 10?
I HAVE 2 CLOSE BY MYSELF
I REALLY NEED 2 C U
KYLE??!!!
HOLD UP
WUT IF U TOLD UR PARENTS
U WER RAPED

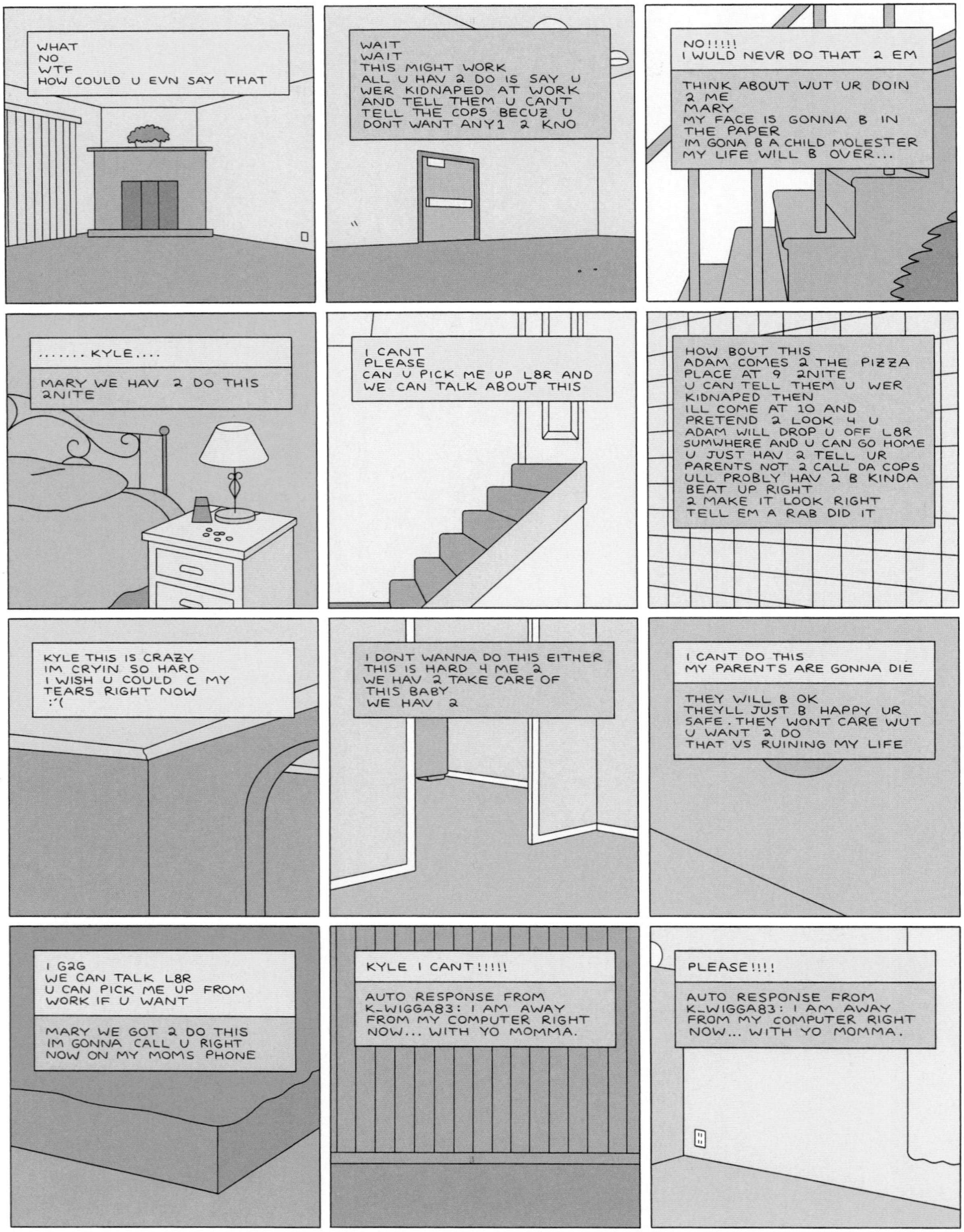
WHAT
NO
WTF
HOW COULD U EVN SAY THAT
WAIT
WAIT
THIS MIGHT WORK
ALL U HAV 2 DO IS SAY U WER KIDNAPED AT WORK AND TELL THEM U CANT TELL THE COPS BECUZ U DONT WANT ANY1 2 KNO
NO!!!!!
I WULD NEVR DO THAT 2 EM
THINK ABOUT WUT UR DOIN 2 ME
MARY
MY FACE IS GONNA B IN THE PAPER
IM GONA B A CHILD MOLESTER
MY LIFE WILL B OVER...
.......KYLE....
MARY WE HAV 2 DO THIS 2NITE
I CANT
PLEASE
CAN U PICK ME UP L8R AND WE CAN TALK ABOUT THIS
HOW BOUT THIS
ADAM COMES 2 THE PIZZA PLACE AT 9 2NITE
U CAN TELL THEM U WER KIDNAPED THEN
ILL COME AT 10 AND PRETEND 2 LOOK 4 U
ADAM WILL DROP U OFF L8R SUMWHERE AND U CAN GO HOME
U JUST HAV 2 TELL UR PARENTS NOT 2 CALL DA COPS
ULL PROBLY HAV 2 B KINDA BEAT UP RIGHT
2 MAKE IT LOOK RIGHT
TELL EM A RAB DID IT
KYLE THIS IS CRAZY
IM CRYIN SO HARD
I WISH U COULD C MY TEARS RIGHT NOW
:'(
I DONT WANNA DO THIS EITHER
THIS IS HARD 4 ME 2
WE HAV 2 TAKE CARE OF THIS BABY
WE HAV 2
I CANT DO THIS
MY PARENTS ARE GONNA DIE
THEY WILL B OK
THEYLL JUST B HAPPY UR SAFE. THEY WONT CARE WUT U WANT 2 DO
THAT VS RUINING MY LIFE
I G2G
WE CAN TALK L8R
U CAN PICK ME UP FROM WORK IF U WANT
MARY WE GOT 2 DO THIS
IM GONNA CALL U RIGHT NOW ON MY MOMS PHONE
KYLE I CANT!!!!!
AUTO RESPONSE FROM K_WIGGA83: I AM AWAY FROM MY COMPUTER RIGHT NOW... WITH YO MOMMA.
PLEASE!!!!
AUTO RESPONSE FROM K_WIGGA83: I AM AWAY FROM MY COMPUTER RIGHT NOW... WITH YO MOMMA.

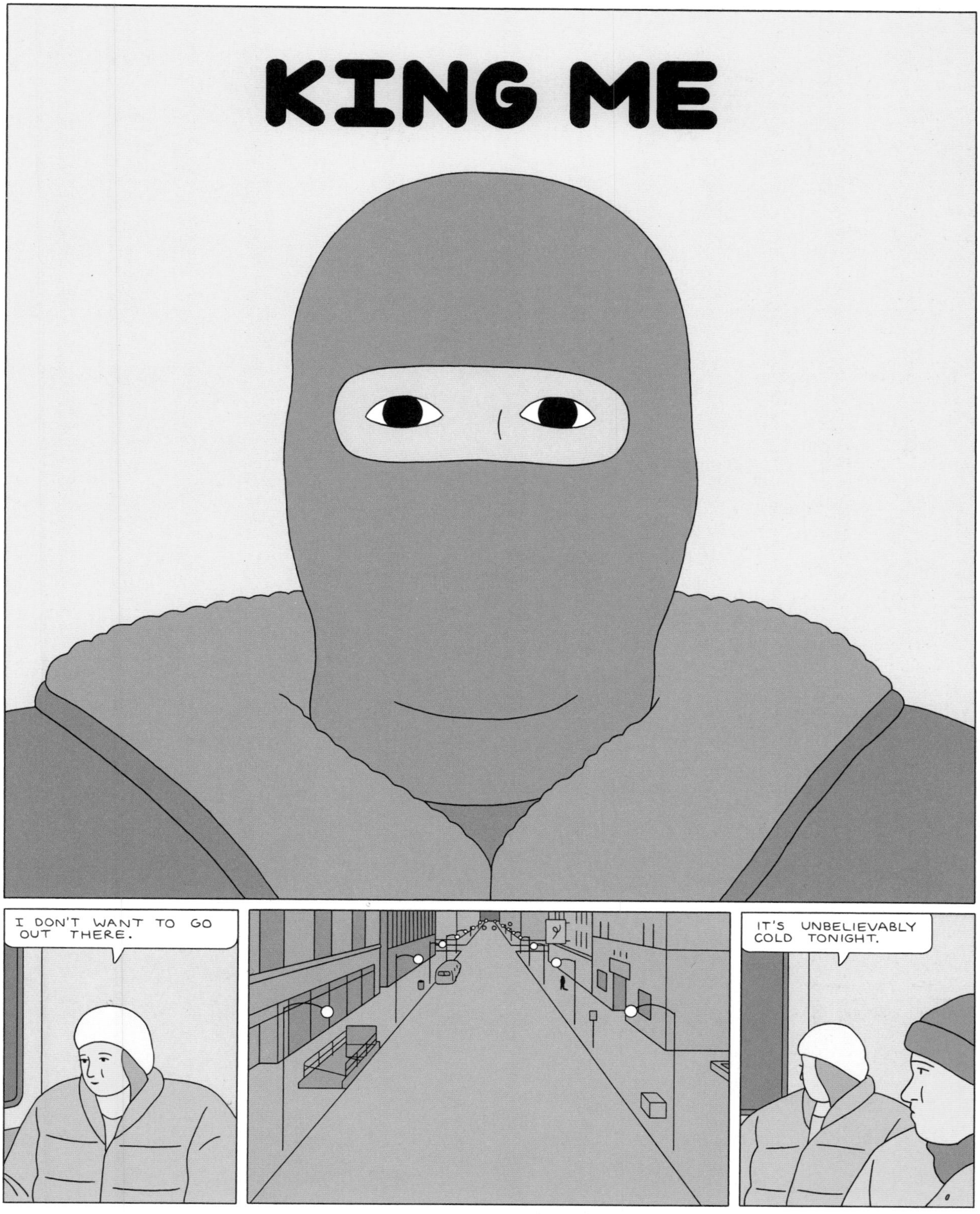
KING ME
I DON'T WANT TO GO OUT THERE.
IT'S UNBELIEVABLY COLD TONIGHT.

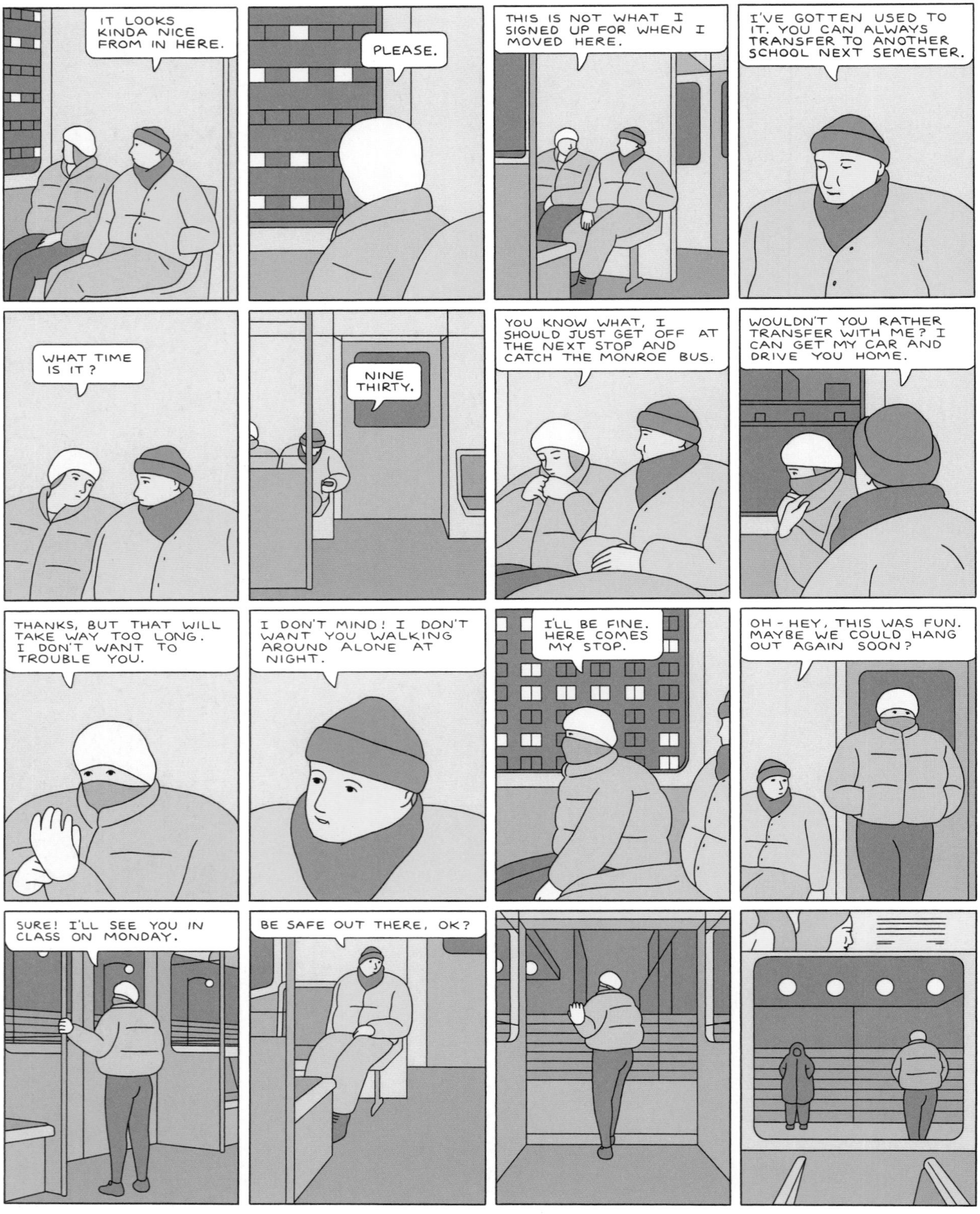
IT LOOKS KINDA NICE FROM IN HERE.
PLEASE.
THIS IS NOT WHAT I SIGNED UP FOR WHEN I MOVED HERE.
I'VE GOTTEN USED TO IT. YOU CAN ALWAYS TRANSFER TO ANOTHER SCHOOL NEXT SEMESTER.
WHAT TIME IS IT?
NINE THIRTY.
YOU KNOW WHAT, I SHOULD JUST GET OFF AT THE NEXT STOP AND CATCH THE MONROE BUS.
WOULDN'T YOU RATHER TRANSFER WITH ME? I CAN GET MY CAR AND DRIVE YOU HOME.
THANKS, BUT THAT WILL TAKE WAY TOO LONG. I DON'T WANT TO TROUBLE YOU.
I DON'T MIND! I DON'T WANT YOU WALKING AROUND ALONE AT NIGHT.
I'LL BE FINE. HERE COMES MY STOP.
OH - HEY, THIS WAS FUN. MAYBE WE COULD HANG OUT AGAIN SOON?
SURE! I'LL SEE YOU IN CLASS ON MONDAY.
BE SAFE OUT THERE, OK?

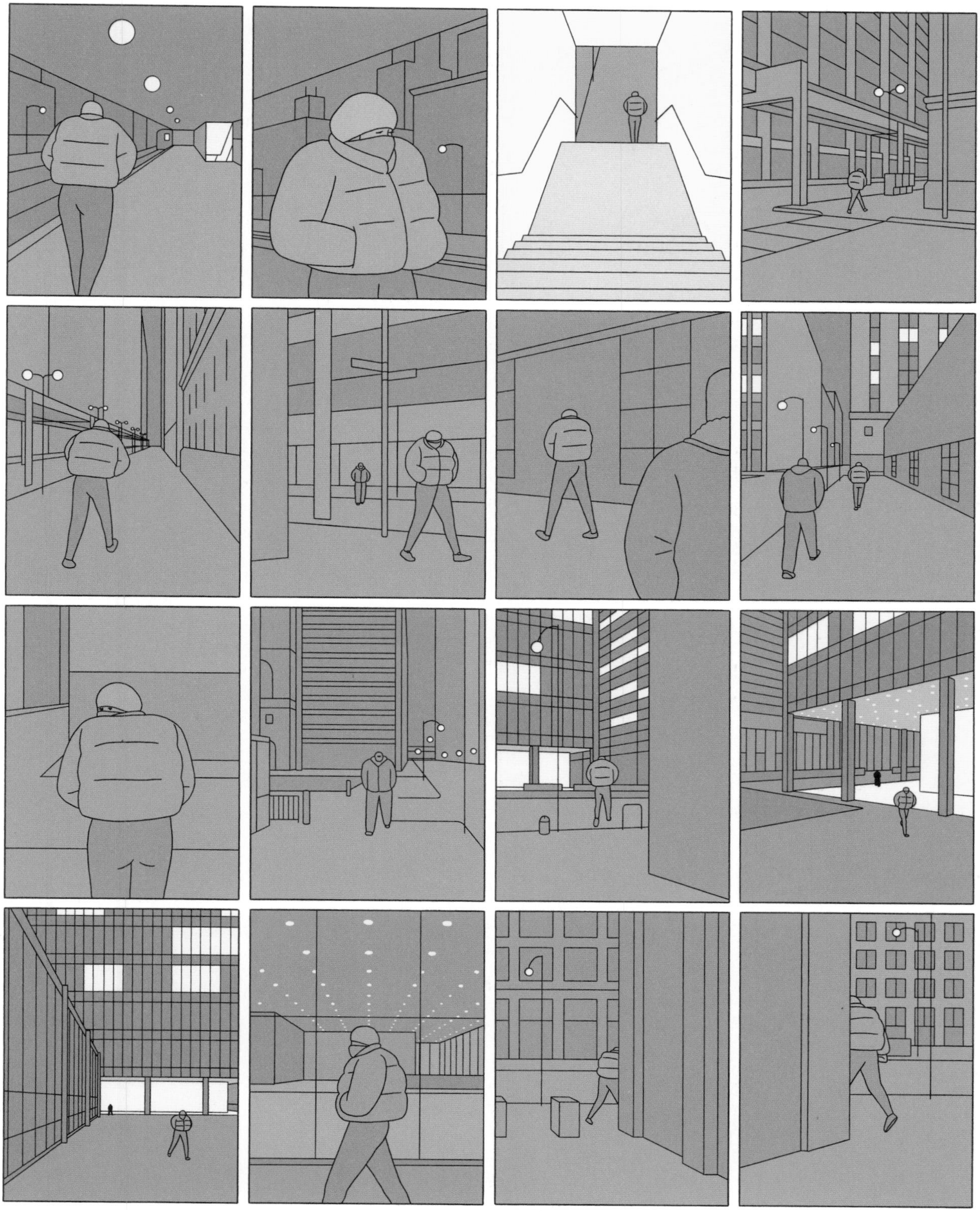

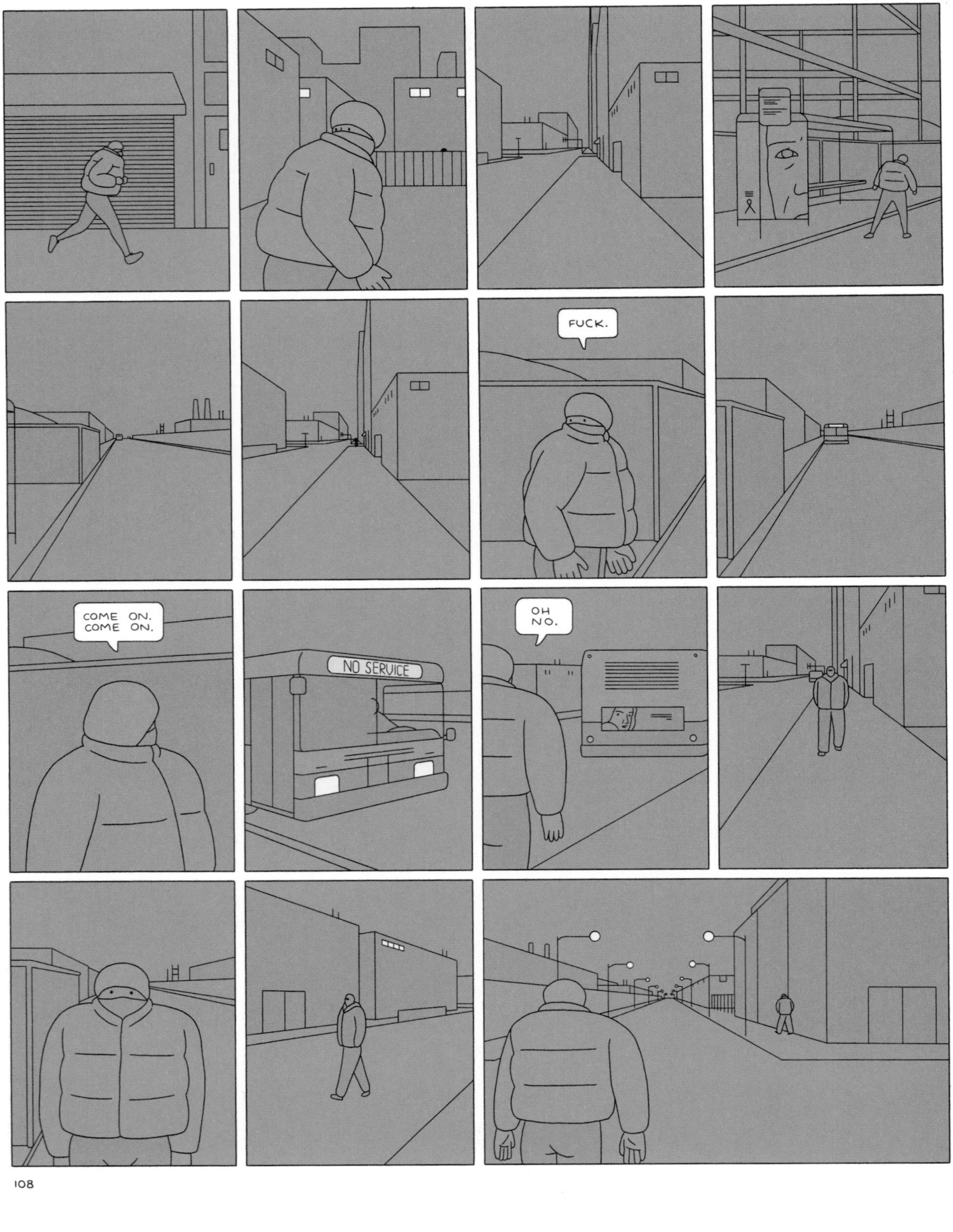
FUCK.
COME ON. COME ON.
NO SERVICE
OH NO.

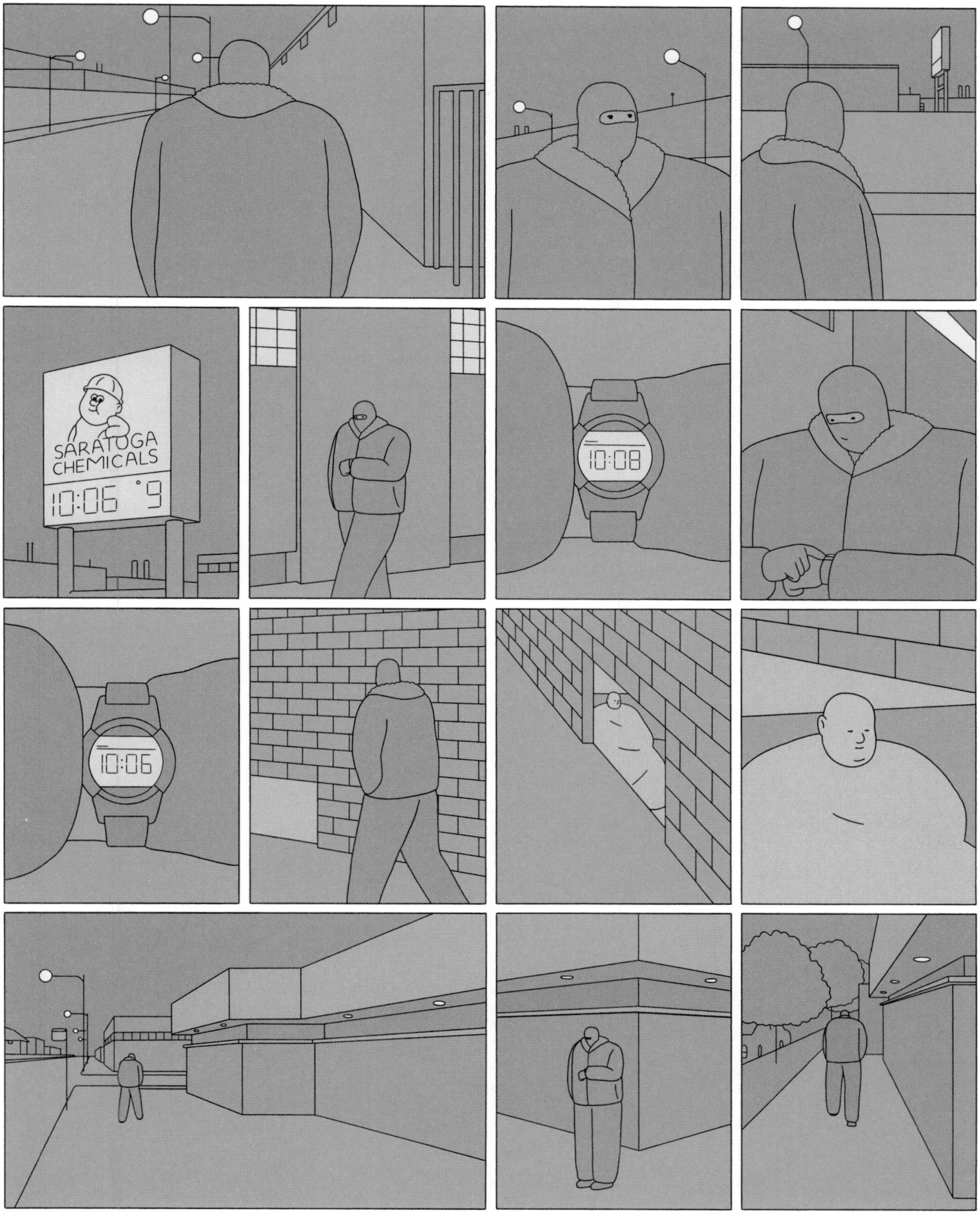
SARATOGA
CHEMICALS
10:06 °9
10:08
10:06

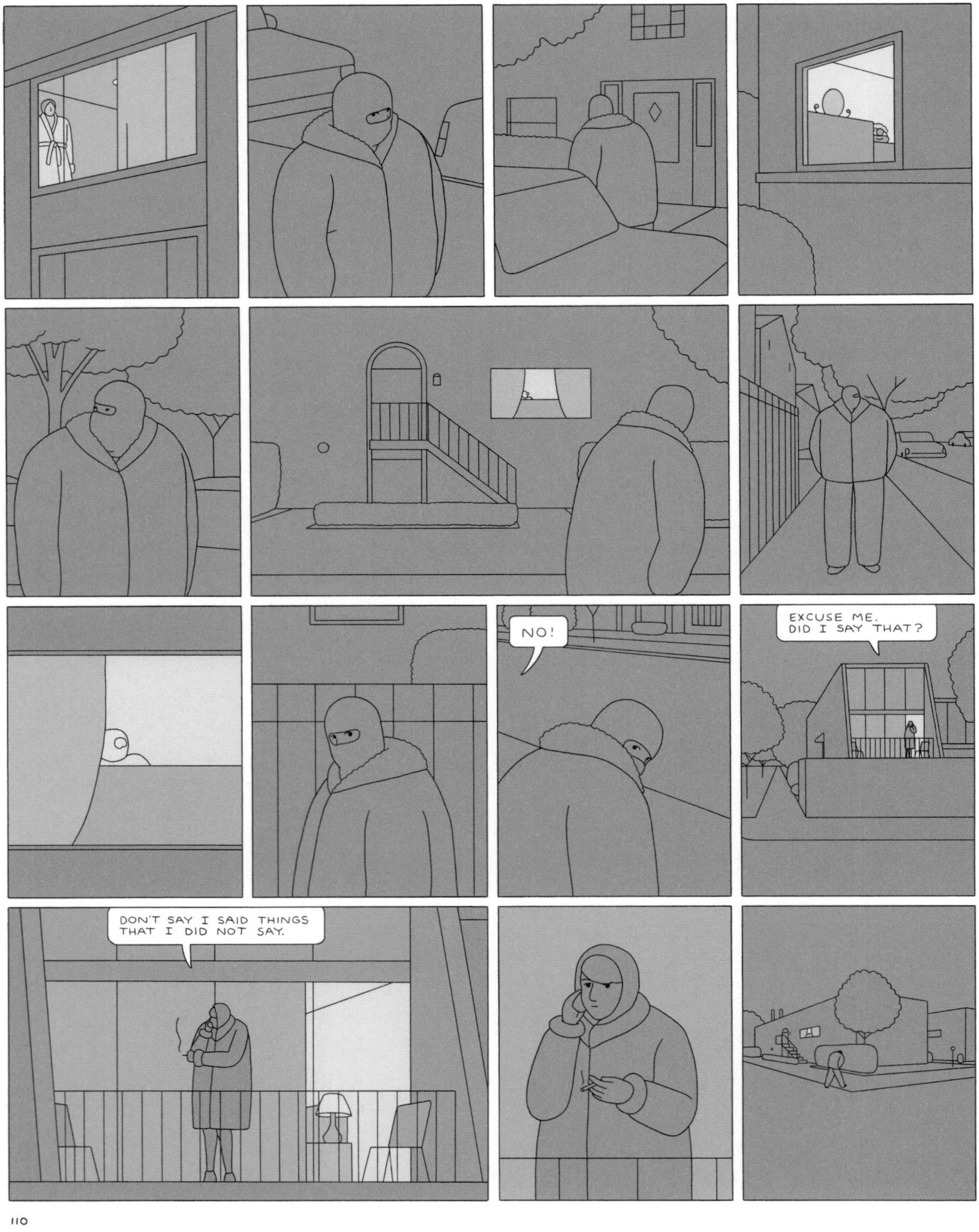
NO!
EXCUSE ME. DID I SAY THAT?
DON'T SAY I SAID THINGS THAT I DID NOT SAY.

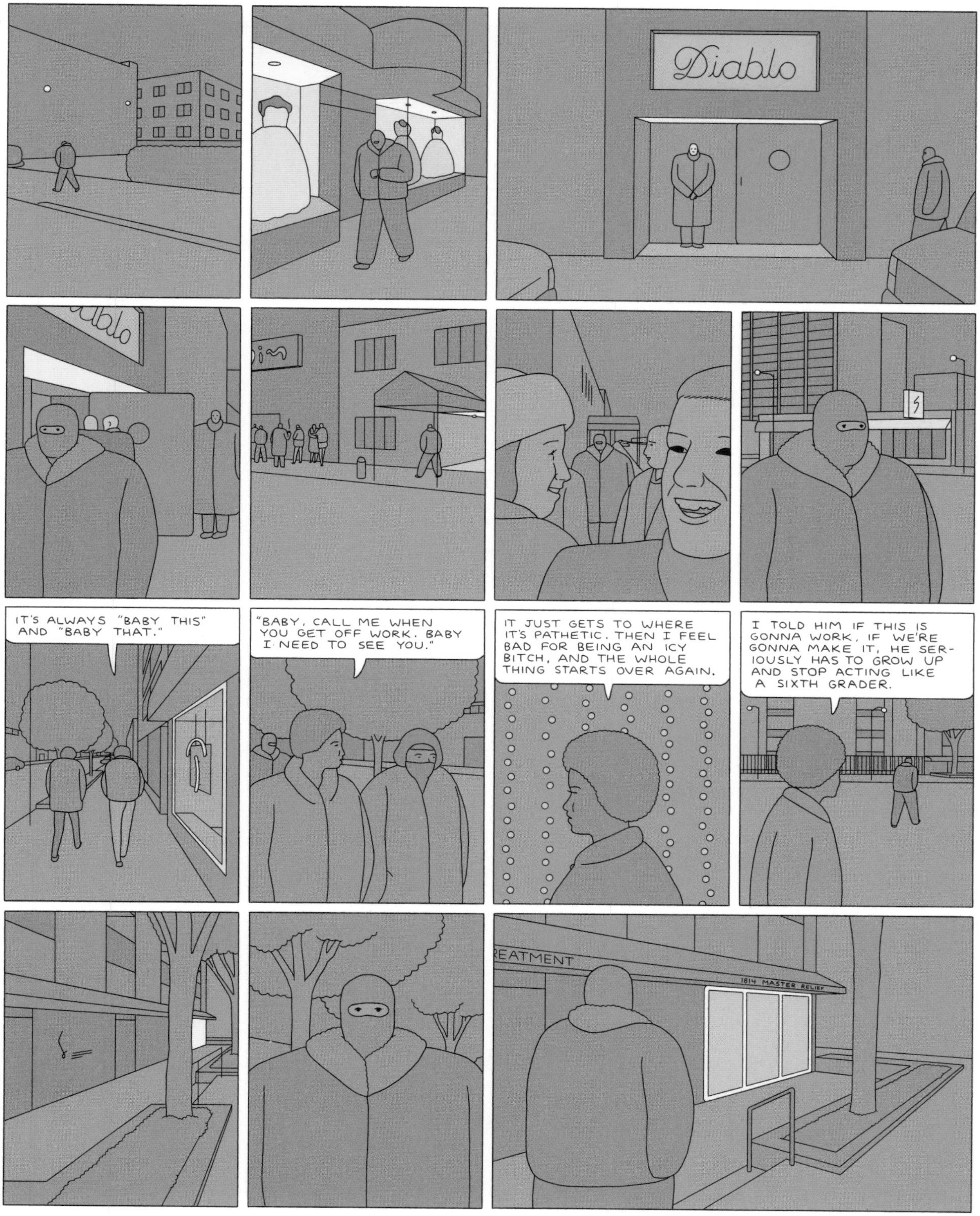
Diablo
IT'S ALWAYS "BABY THIS" AND "BABY THAT."
"BABY, CALL ME WHEN YOU GET OFF WORK. BABY I NEED TO SEE YOU."
IT JUST GETS TO WHERE IT'S PATHETIC. THEN I FEEL BAD FOR BEING AN ICY BITCH, AND THE WHOLE THING STARTS OVER AGAIN.
I TOLD HIM IF THIS IS GONNA WORK, IF WE'RE GONNA MAKE IT, HE SERIOUSLY HAS TO GROW UP AND STOP ACTING LIKE A SIXTH GRADER.
REATMENT
1814 MASTER RELIEF

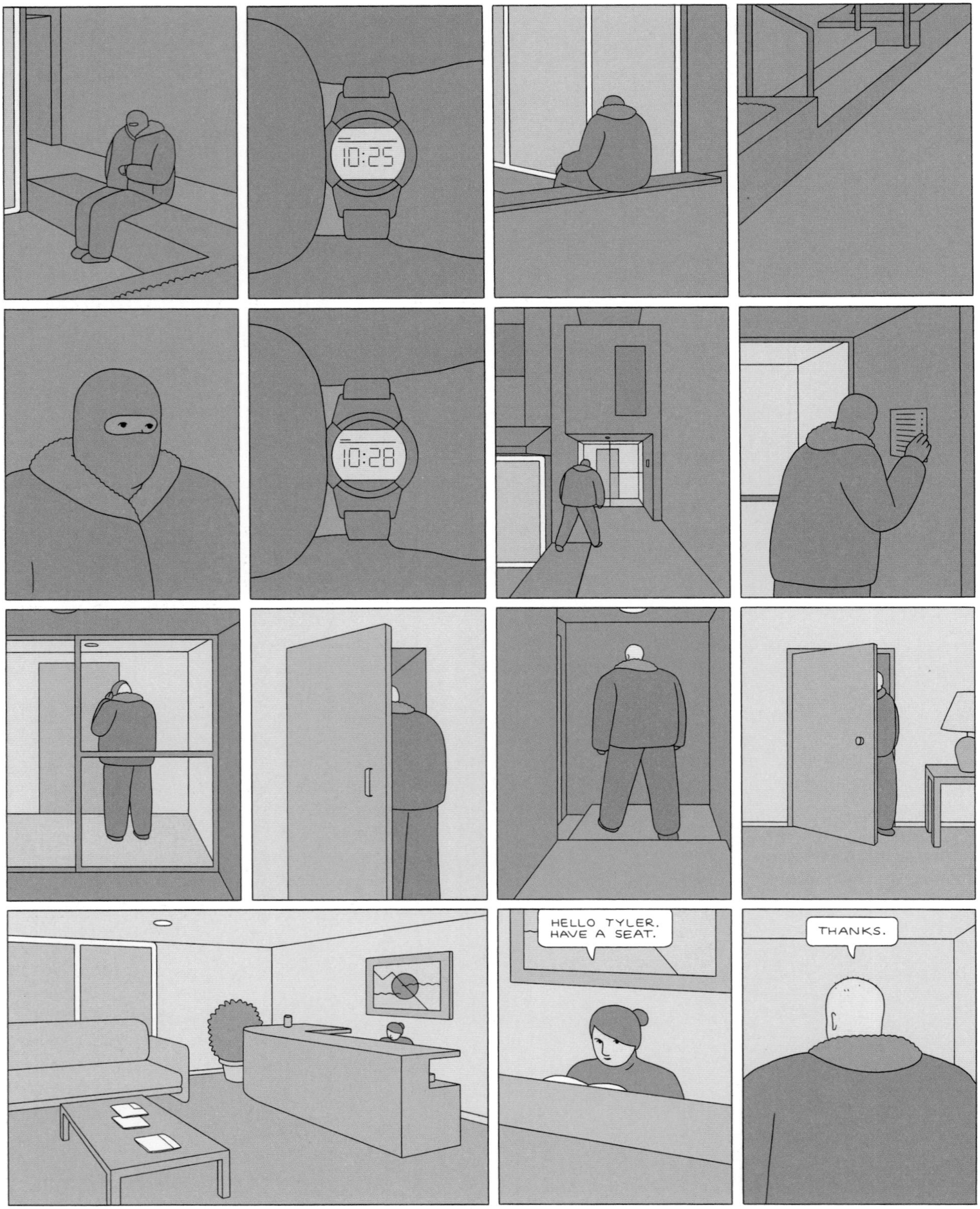
10:25
10:28
HELLO TYLER.
HAVE A SEAT.
THANKS.

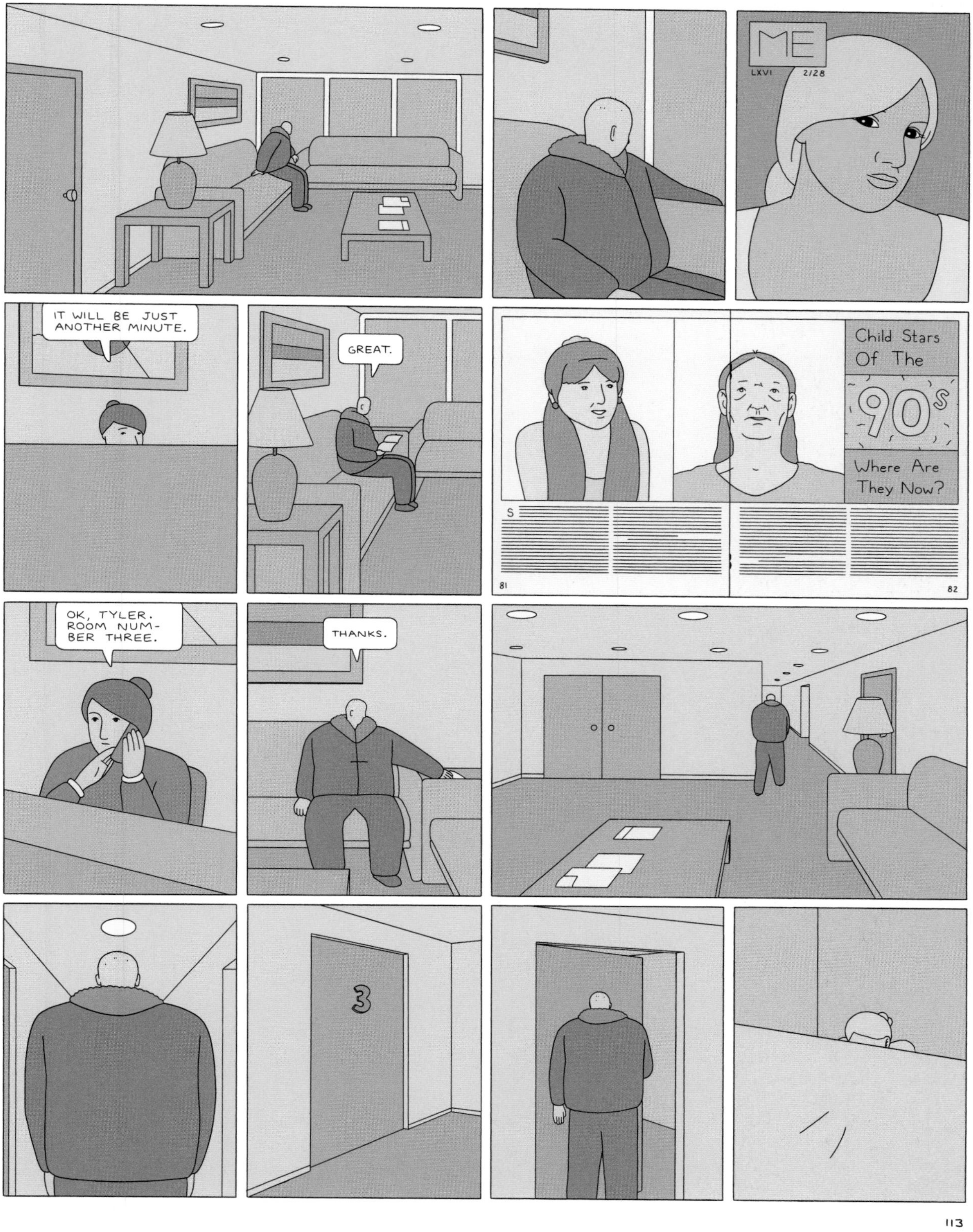
ME
LXVI
2/28
IT WILL BE JUST ANOTHER MINUTE.
GREAT.
Child Stars Of The 90s
Where Are They Now?
81
82
OK, TYLER. ROOM NUMBER THREE.
THANKS.
3

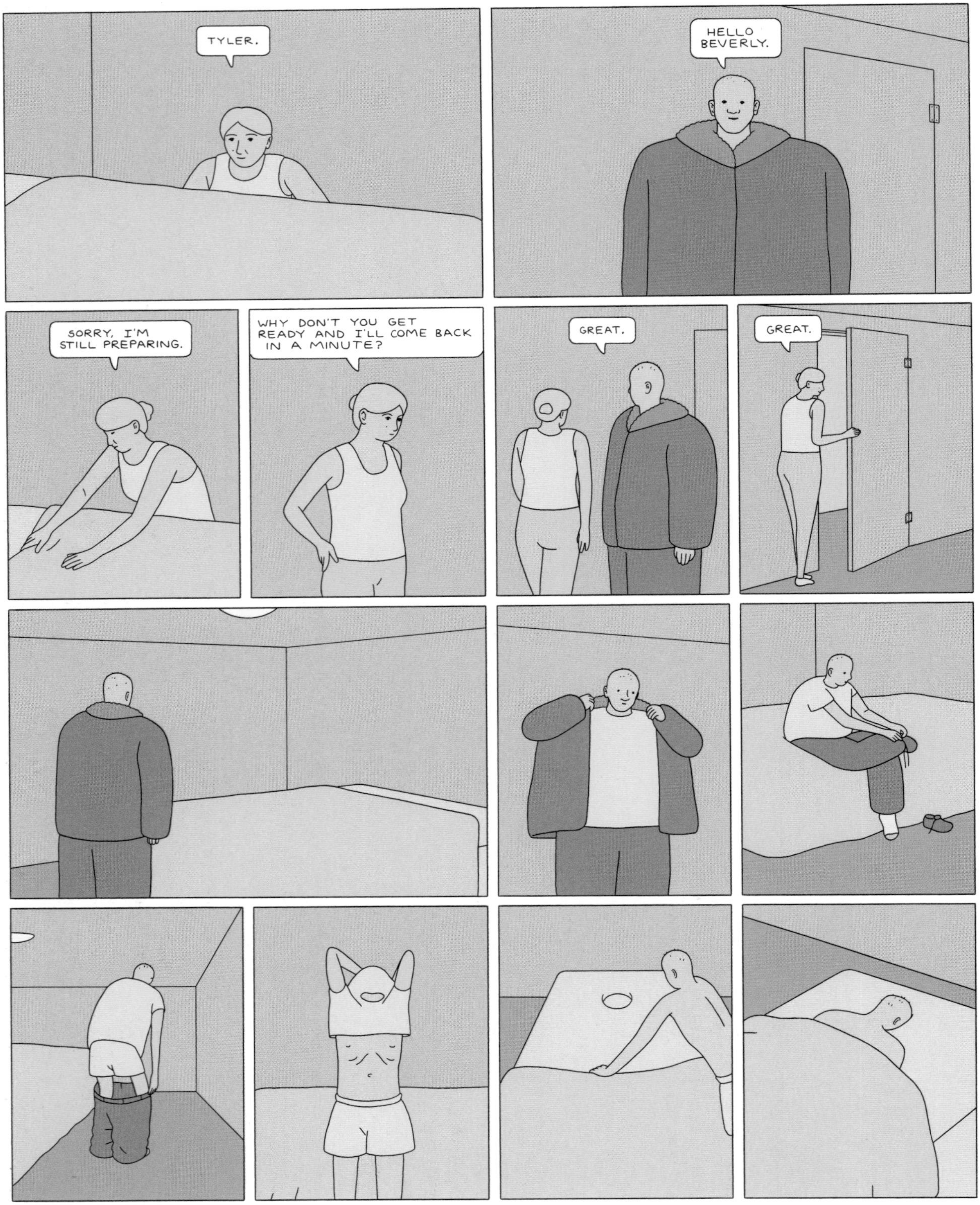
TYLER.
HELLO BEVERLY.
SORRY, I'M STILL PREPARING.
WHY DON'T YOU GET READY AND I'LL COME BACK IN A MINUTE?
GREAT.
GREAT.

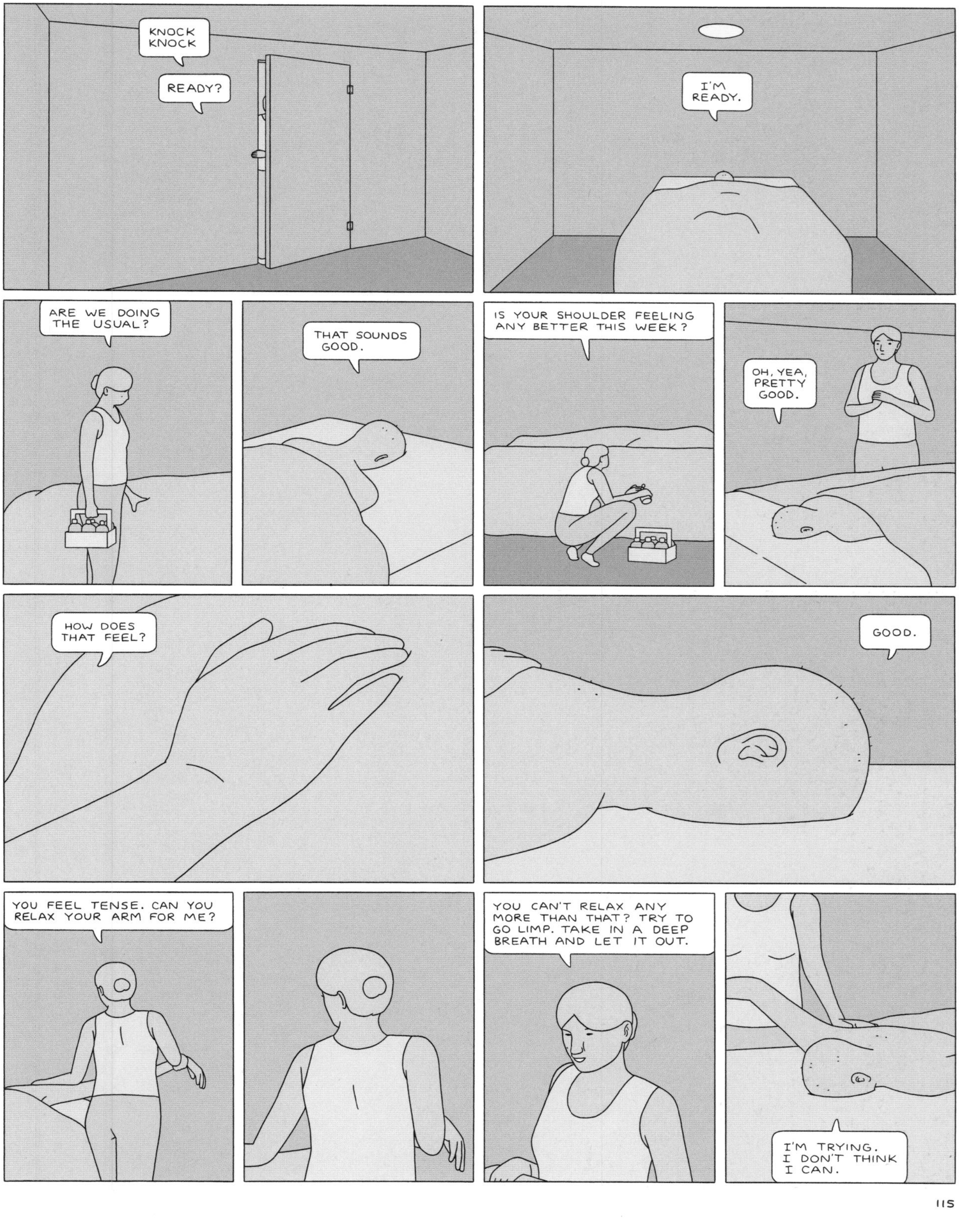
KNOCK KNOCK
READY?
I'M READY.
ARE WE DOING THE USUAL?
THAT SOUNDS GOOD.
IS YOUR SHOULDER FEELING ANY BETTER THIS WEEK?
OH, YEA, PRETTY GOOD.
HOW DOES THAT FEEL?
GOOD.
YOU FEEL TENSE. CAN YOU RELAX YOUR ARM FOR ME?
YOU CAN'T RELAX ANY MORE THAN THAT? TRY TO GO LIMP. TAKE IN A DEEP BREATH AND LET IT OUT.
I'M TRYING. I DON'T THINK I CAN.

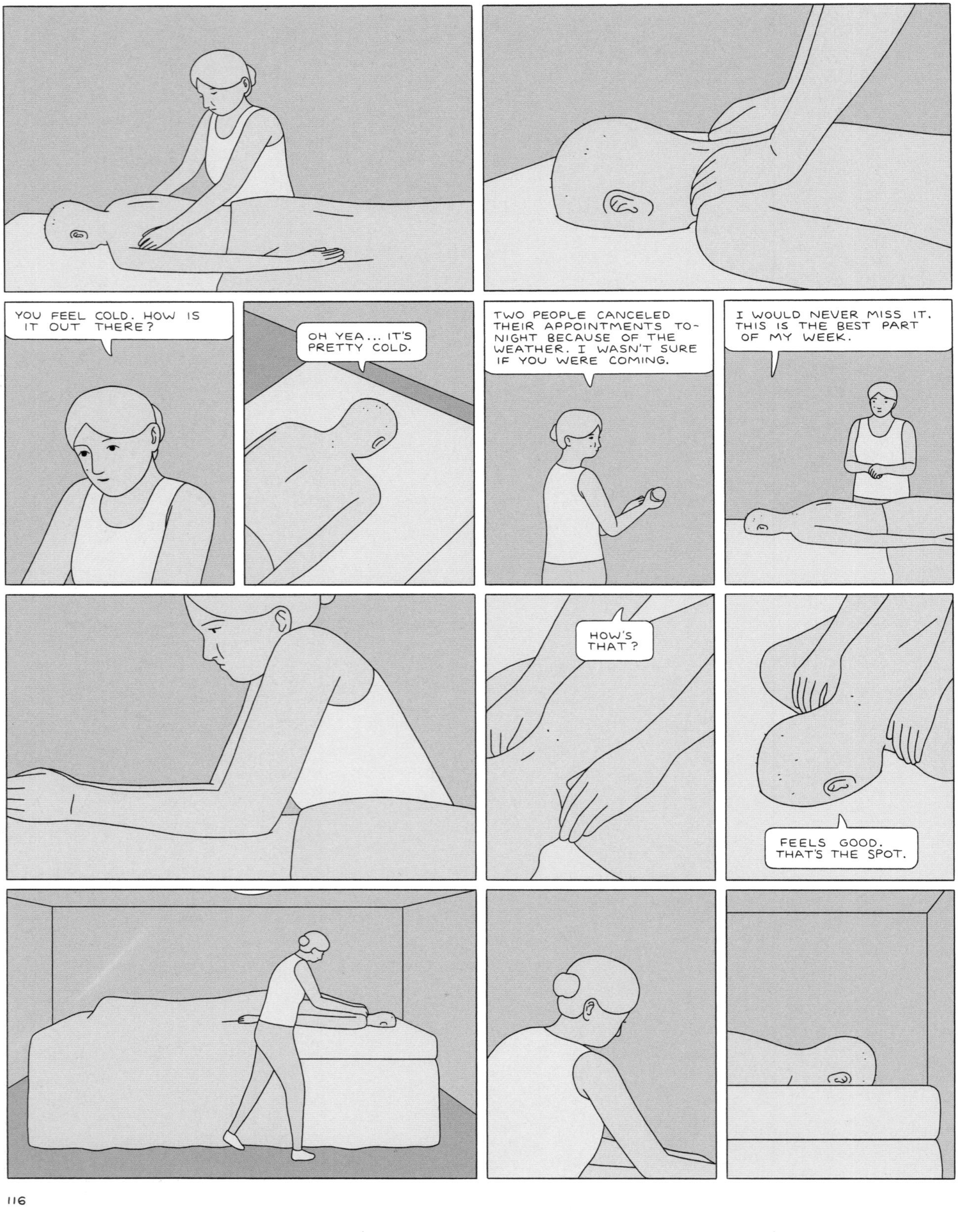

YOU FEEL COLD. HOW IS IT OUT THERE?
OH YEA... IT'S PRETTY COLD.
TWO PEOPLE CANCELED THEIR APPOINTMENTS TO-NIGHT BECAUSE OF THE WEATHER. I WASN'T SURE IF YOU WERE COMING.
I WOULD NEVER MISS IT. THIS IS THE BEST PART OF MY WEEK.
HOW'S THAT?
FEELS GOOD. THAT'S THE SPOT.

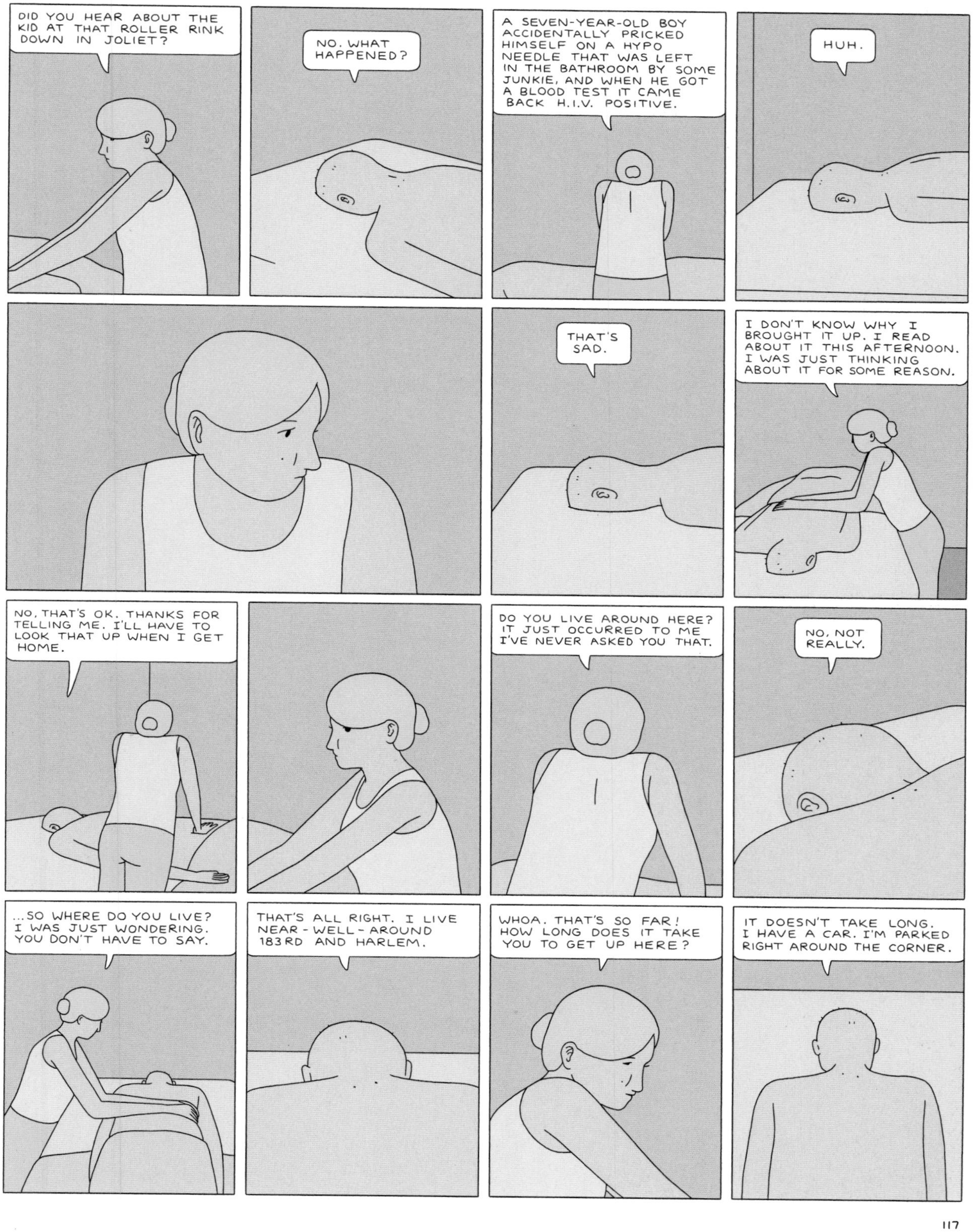
DID YOU HEAR ABOUT THE KID AT THAT ROLLER RINK DOWN IN JOLIET?
NO. WHAT HAPPENED?
A SEVEN-YEAR-OLD BOY ACCIDENTALLY PRICKED HIMSELF ON A HYPO NEEDLE THAT WAS LEFT IN THE BATHROOM BY SOME JUNKIE, AND WHEN HE GOT A BLOOD TEST IT CAME BACK H.I.V. POSITIVE.
HUH.
THAT'S SAD.
I DON'T KNOW WHY I BROUGHT IT UP. I READ ABOUT IT THIS AFTERNOON. I WAS JUST THINKING ABOUT IT FOR SOME REASON.
NO, THAT'S OK. THANKS FOR TELLING ME. I'LL HAVE TO LOOK THAT UP WHEN I GET HOME.
DO YOU LIVE AROUND HERE? IT JUST OCCURRED TO ME I'VE NEVER ASKED YOU THAT.
NO, NOT REALLY.
...SO WHERE DO YOU LIVE? I WAS JUST WONDERING. YOU DON'T HAVE TO SAY.
THAT'S ALL RIGHT. I LIVE NEAR - WELL - AROUND 183RD AND HARLEM.
WHOA. THAT'S SO FAR! HOW LONG DOES IT TAKE YOU TO GET UP HERE?
IT DOESN'T TAKE LONG. I HAVE A CAR. I'M PARKED RIGHT AROUND THE CORNER.

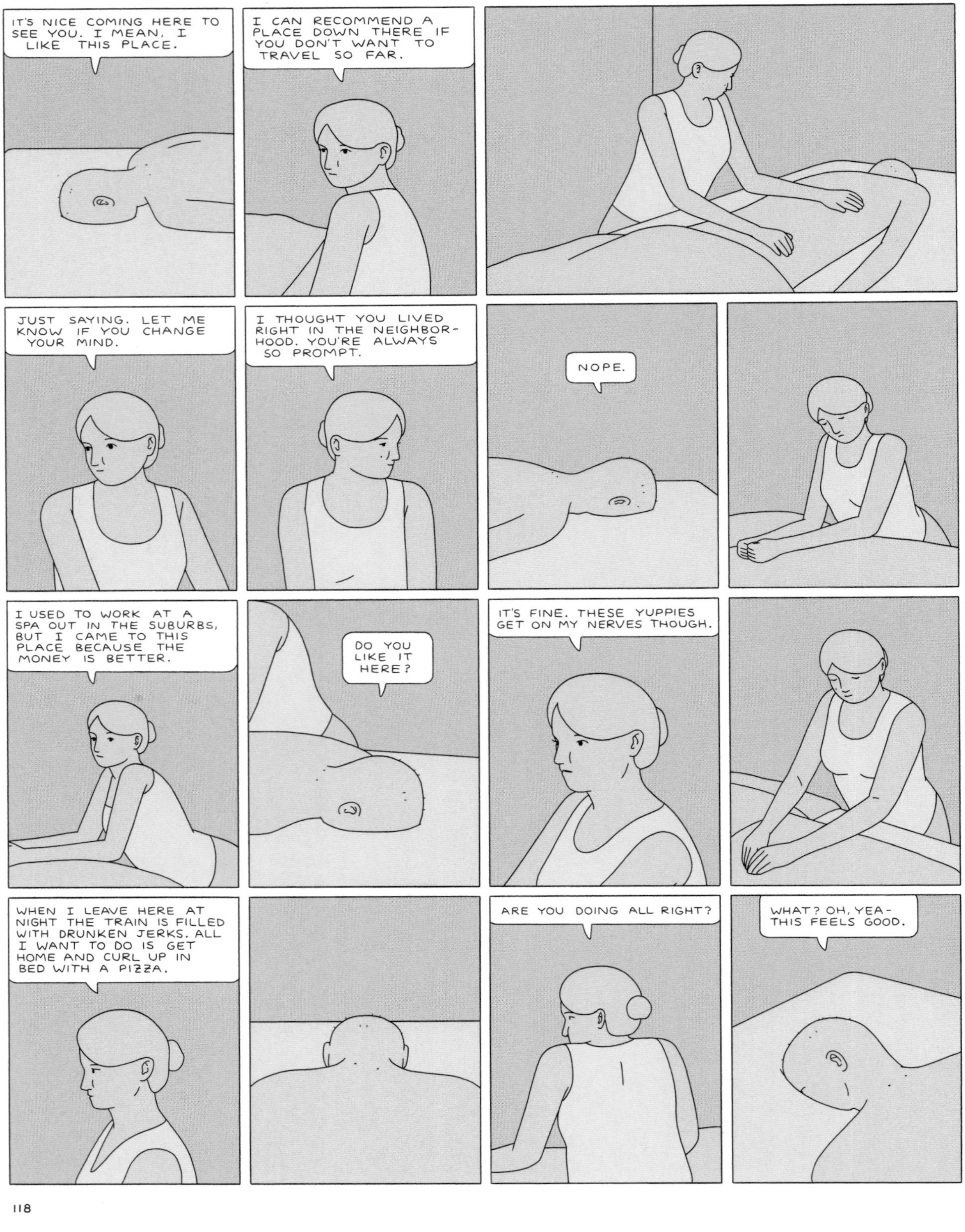
IT'S NICE COMING HERE TO SEE YOU. I MEAN, I LIKE THIS PLACE.
I CAN RECOMMEND A PLACE DOWN THERE IF YOU DON'T WANT TO TRAVEL SO FAR.
JUST SAYING. LET ME KNOW IF YOU CHANGE YOUR MIND.
I THOUGHT YOU LIVED RIGHT IN THE NEIGHBOR-HOOD. YOU'RE ALWAYS SO PROMPT.
NOPE.
I USED TO WORK AT A SPA OUT IN THE SUBURBS, BUT I CAME TO THIS PLACE BECAUSE THE MONEY IS BETTER.
DO YOU LIKE IT HERE?
IT'S FINE. THESE YUPPIES GET ON MY NERVES THOUGH.
WHEN I LEAVE HERE AT NIGHT THE TRAIN IS FILLED WITH DRUNKEN JERKS. ALL I WANT TO DO IS GET HOME AND CURL UP IN BED WITH A PIZZA.
ARE YOU DOING ALL RIGHT?
WHAT? OH, YEA-THIS FEELS GOOD.

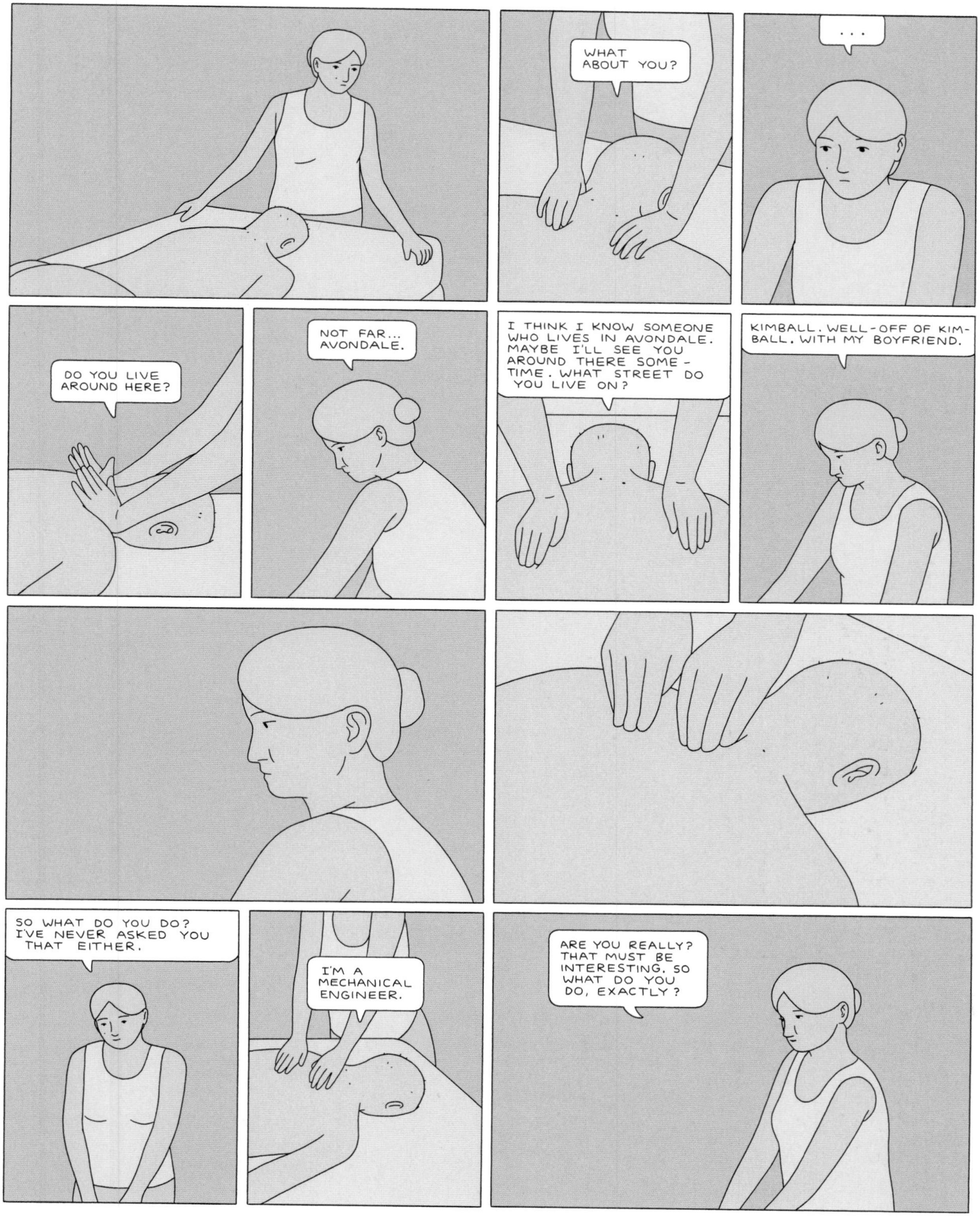
WHAT ABOUT YOU?
. . .
DO YOU LIVE AROUND HERE?
NOT FAR... AVONDALE.
I THINK I KNOW SOMEONE WHO LIVES IN AVONDALE. MAYBE I'LL SEE YOU AROUND THERE SOME-TIME. WHAT STREET DO YOU LIVE ON?
KIMBALL. WELL-OFF OF KIM-BALL. WITH MY BOYFRIEND.
SO WHAT DO YOU DO? I'VE NEVER ASKED YOU THAT EITHER.
I'M A MECHANICAL ENGINEER.
ARE YOU REALLY? THAT MUST BE INTERESTING. SO WHAT DO YOU DO, EXACTLY?

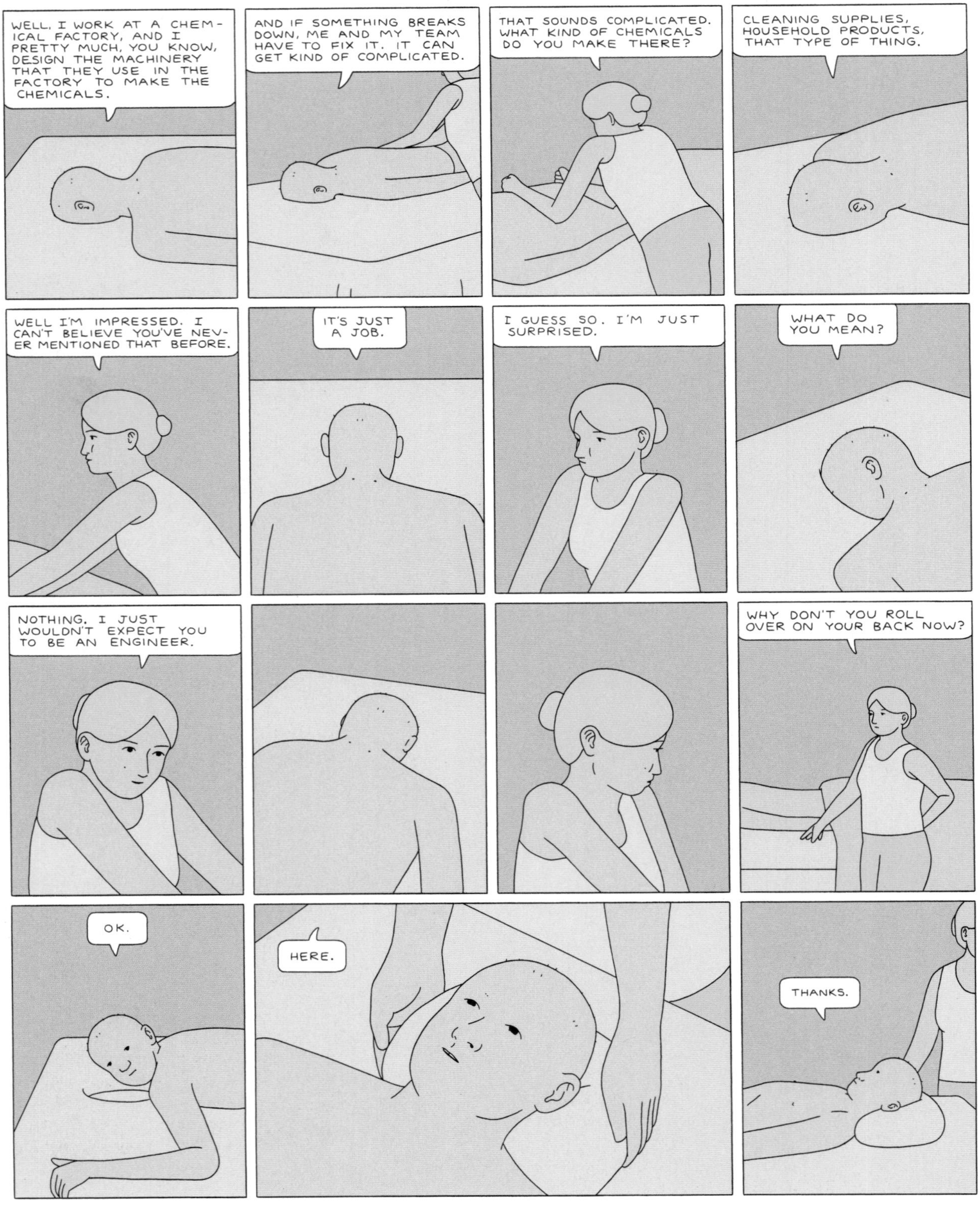
WELL, I WORK AT A CHEMICAL FACTORY, AND I PRETTY MUCH, YOU KNOW, DESIGN THE MACHINERY THAT THEY USE IN THE FACTORY TO MAKE THE CHEMICALS.
AND IF SOMETHING BREAKS DOWN, ME AND MY TEAM HAVE TO FIX IT. IT CAN GET KIND OF COMPLICATED.
THAT SOUNDS COMPLICATED. WHAT KIND OF CHEMICALS DO YOU MAKE THERE?
CLEANING SUPPLIES, HOUSEHOLD PRODUCTS, THAT TYPE OF THING.
WELL I'M IMPRESSED. I CAN'T BELIEVE YOU'VE NEVER MENTIONED THAT BEFORE.
IT'S JUST A JOB.
I GUESS SO. I'M JUST SURPRISED.
WHAT DO YOU MEAN?
NOTHING. I JUST WOULDN'T EXPECT YOU TO BE AN ENGINEER.
WHY DON'T YOU ROLL OVER ON YOUR BACK NOW?
OK.
HERE.
THANKS.

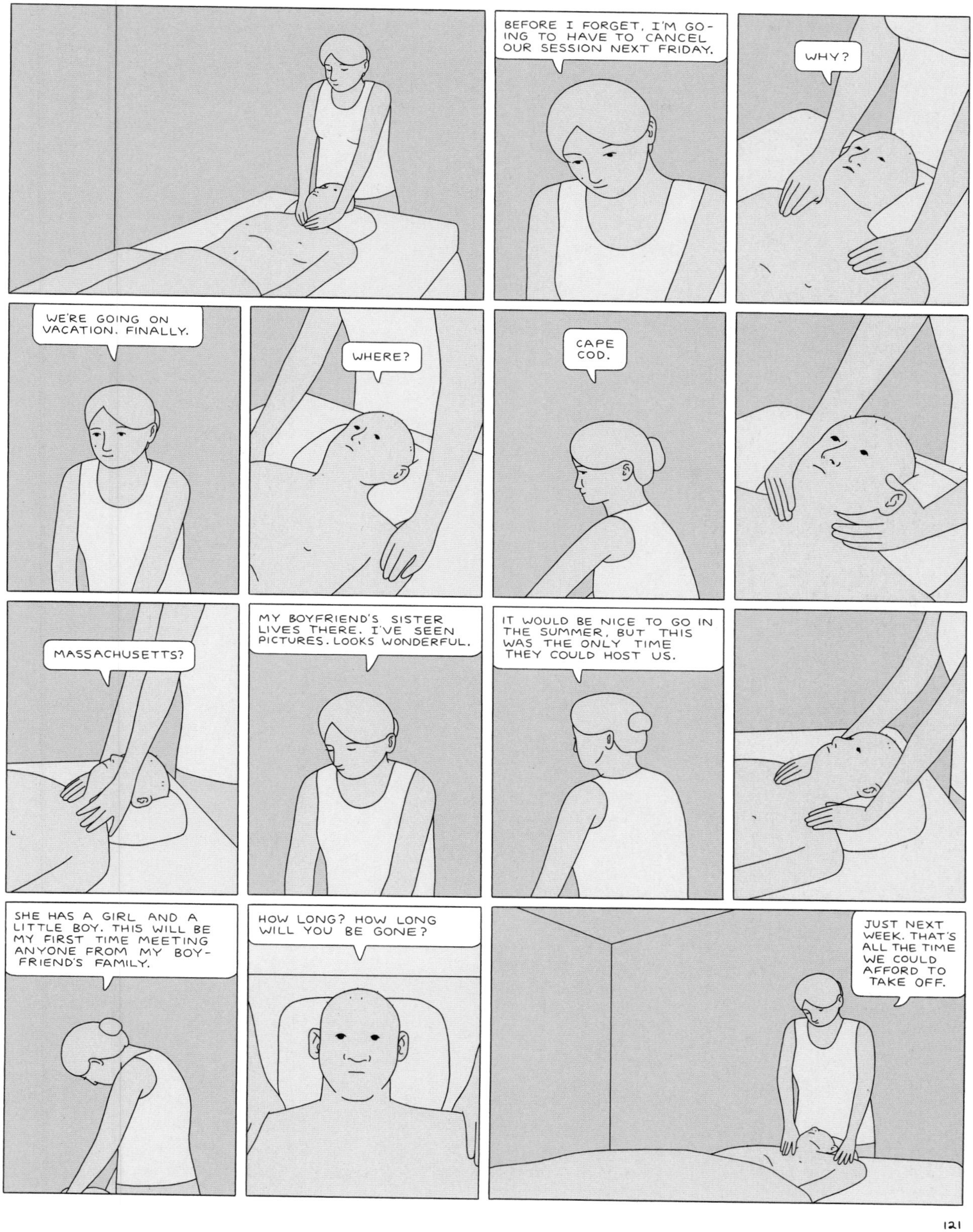
BEFORE I FORGET, I'M GOING TO HAVE TO CANCEL OUR SESSION NEXT FRIDAY.
WHY?
WE'RE GOING ON VACATION. FINALLY.
WHERE?
CAPE COD.
MASSACHUSETTS?
MY BOYFRIEND'S SISTER LIVES THERE. I'VE SEEN PICTURES. LOOKS WONDERFUL.
IT WOULD BE NICE TO GO IN THE SUMMER, BUT THIS WAS THE ONLY TIME THEY COULD HOST US.
SHE HAS A GIRL AND A LITTLE BOY. THIS WILL BE MY FIRST TIME MEETING ANYONE FROM MY BOYFRIEND'S FAMILY.
HOW LONG? HOW LONG WILL YOU BE GONE?
JUST NEXT WEEK. THAT'S ALL THE TIME WE COULD AFFORD TO TAKE OFF.

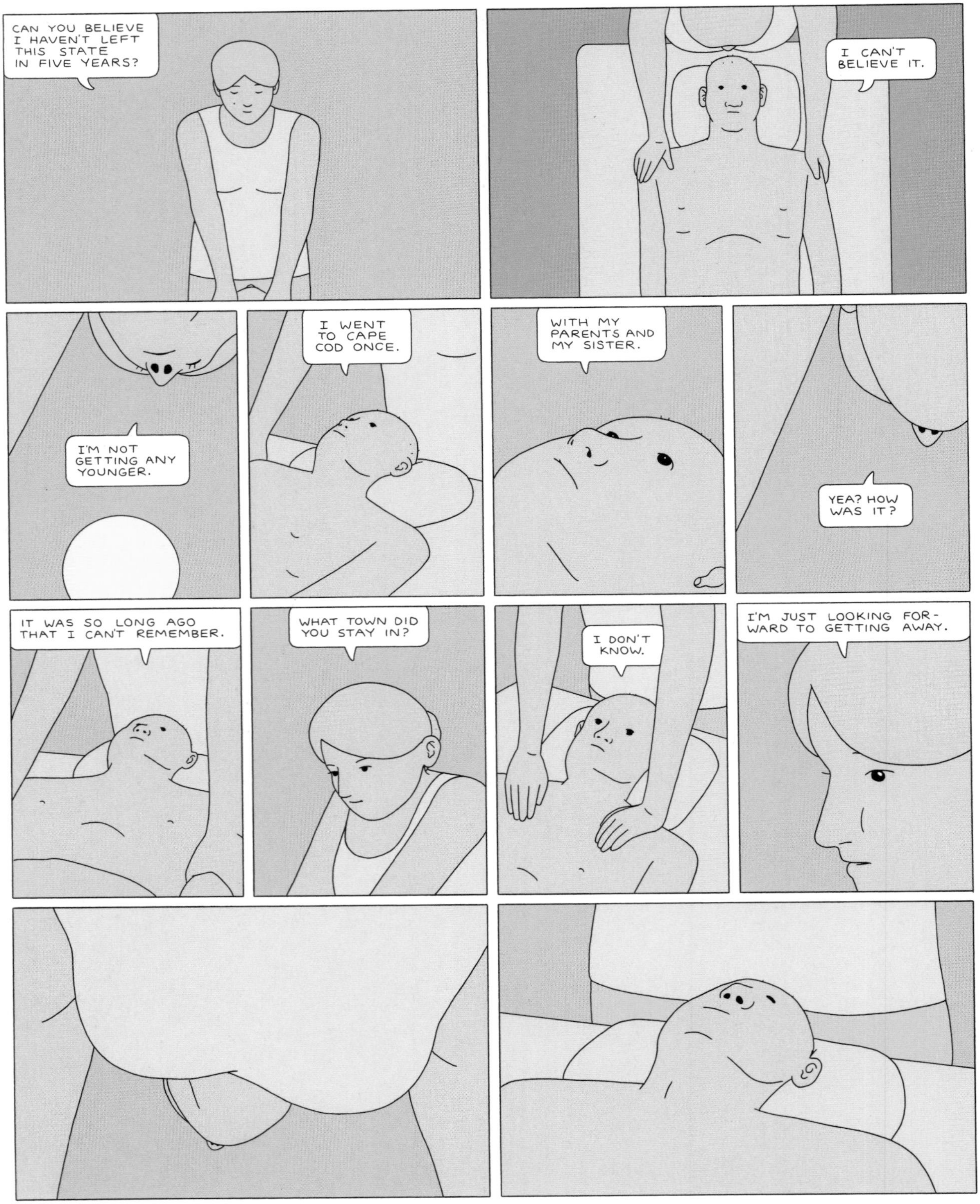
CAN YOU BELIEVE I HAVEN'T LEFT THIS STATE IN FIVE YEARS?
I CAN'T BELIEVE IT.
I'M NOT GETTING ANY YOUNGER.
I WENT TO CAPE COD ONCE.
WITH MY PARENTS AND MY SISTER.
YEA? HOW WAS IT?
IT WAS SO LONG AGO THAT I CAN'T REMEMBER.
WHAT TOWN DID YOU STAY IN?
I DON'T KNOW.
I'M JUST LOOKING FOR-WARD TO GETTING AWAY.

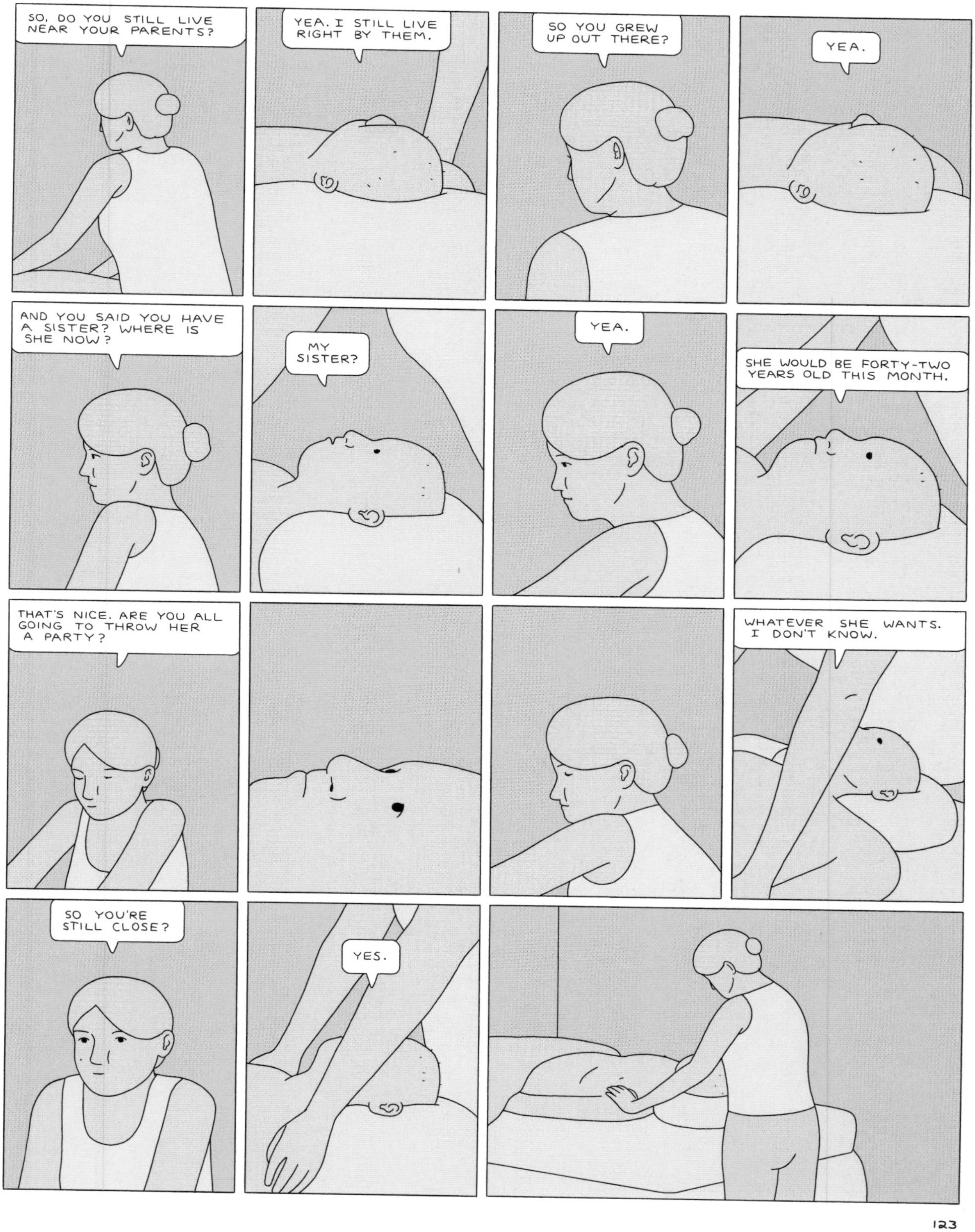
SO, DO YOU STILL LIVE NEAR YOUR PARENTS?
YEA. I STILL LIVE RIGHT BY THEM.
SO YOU GREW UP OUT THERE?
YEA.
AND YOU SAID YOU HAVE A SISTER? WHERE IS SHE NOW?
MY SISTER?
YEA.
SHE WOULD BE FORTY-TWO YEARS OLD THIS MONTH.
THAT'S NICE. ARE YOU ALL GOING TO THROW HER A PARTY?
WHATEVER SHE WANTS. I DON'T KNOW.
SO YOU'RE STILL CLOSE?
YES.

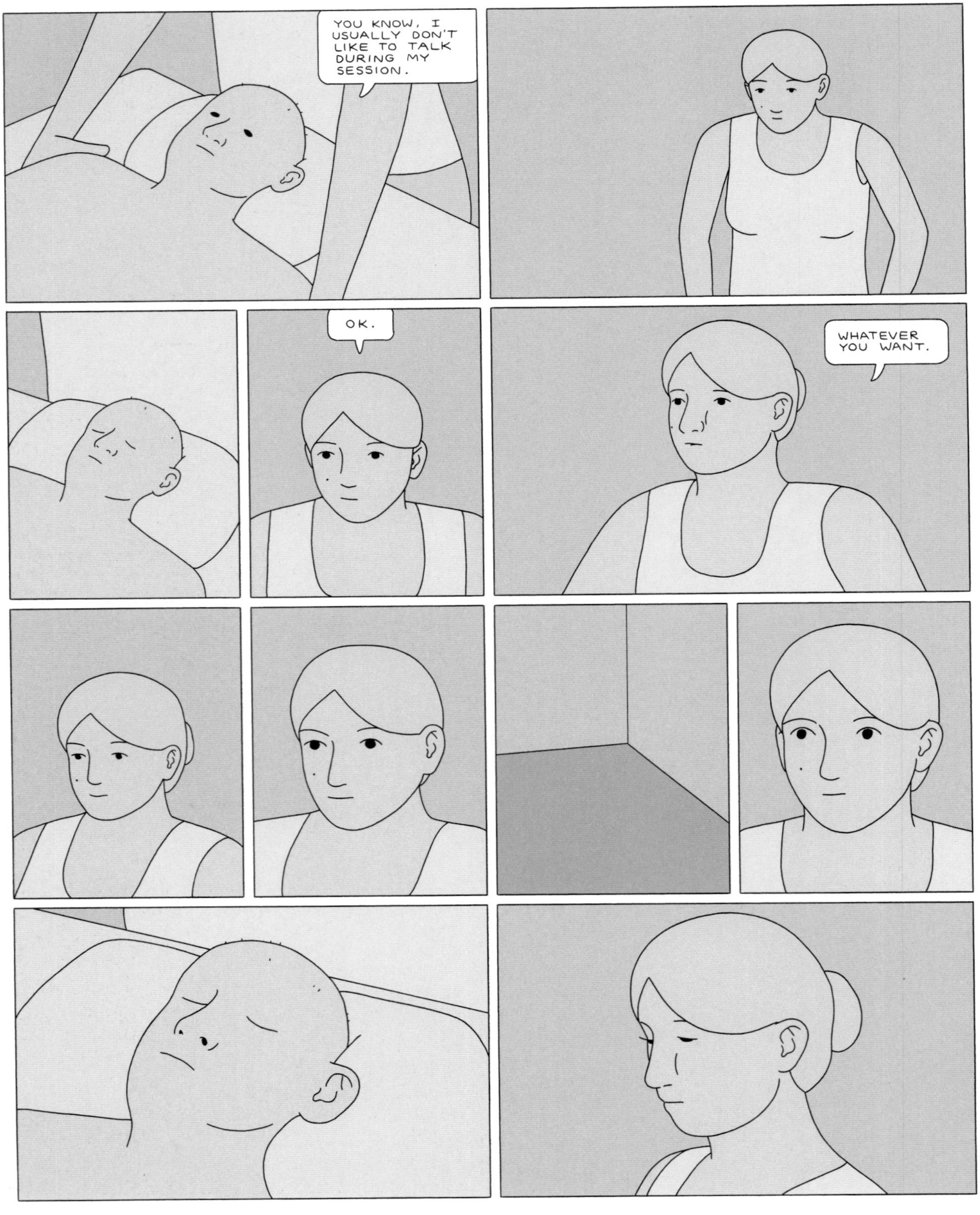
YOU KNOW, I USUALLY DON'T LIKE TO TALK DURING MY SESSION.
OK.
WHATEVER YOU WANT.

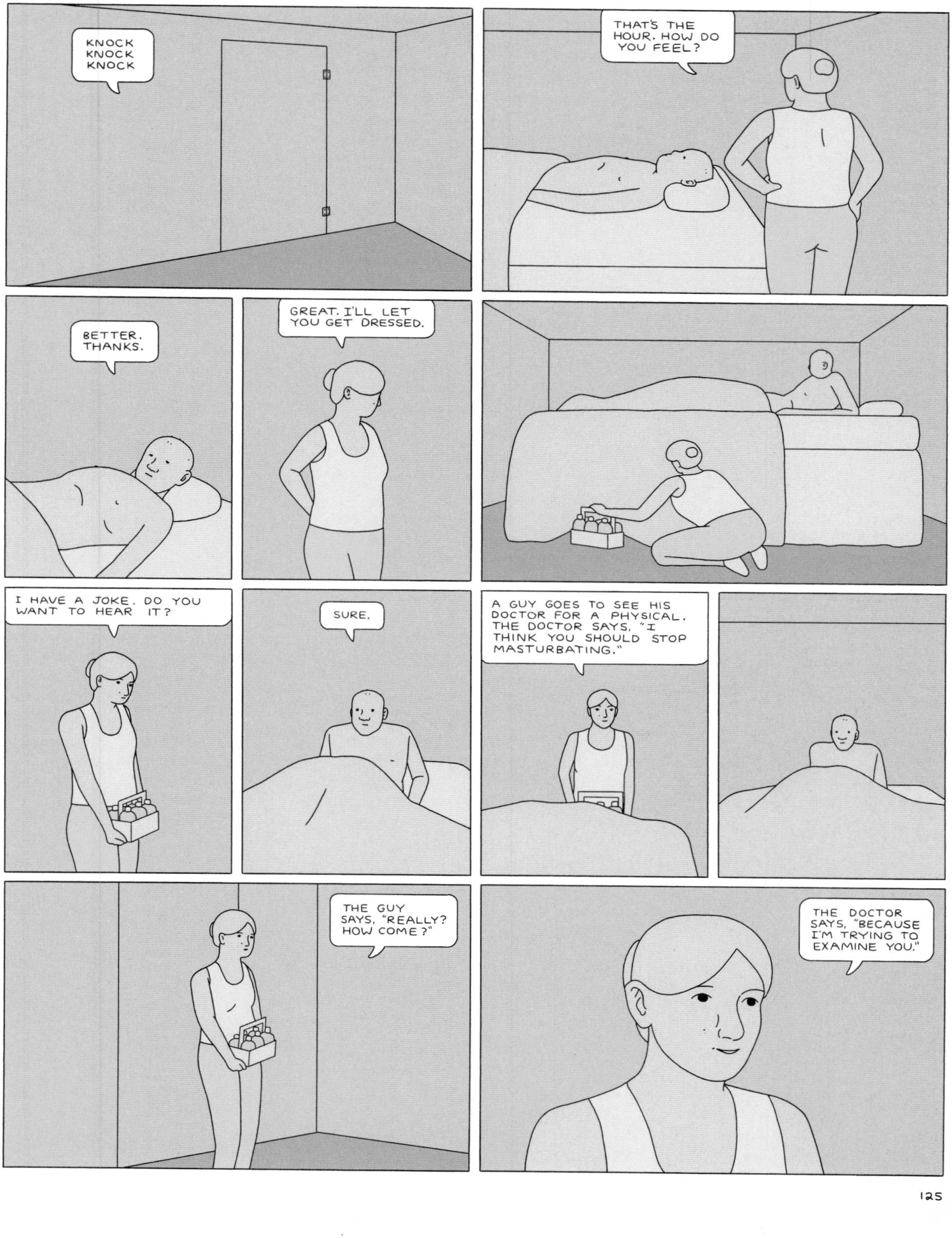
KNOCK KNOCK KNOCK
THAT'S THE HOUR. HOW DO YOU FEEL?
BETTER. THANKS.
GREAT. I'LL LET YOU GET DRESSED.
I HAVE A JOKE. DO YOU WANT TO HEAR IT?
SURE.
A GUY GOES TO SEE HIS DOCTOR FOR A PHYSICAL. THE DOCTOR SAYS, "I THINK YOU SHOULD STOP MASTURBATING."
THE GUY SAYS, "REALLY? HOW COME?"
THE DOCTOR SAYS, "BECAUSE I'M TRYING TO EXAMINE YOU."

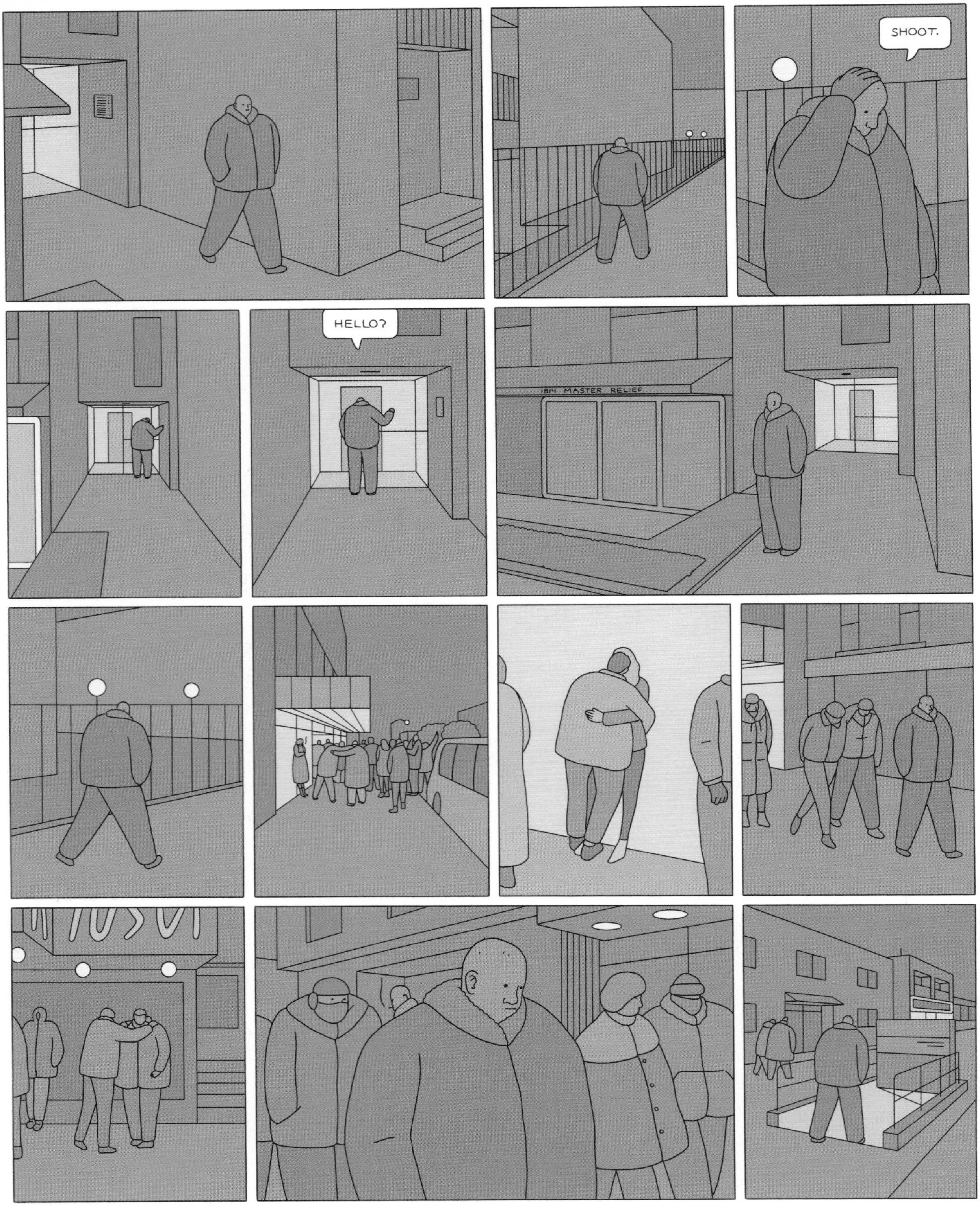
SHOOT.
HELLO?
1814 MASTER RELIEF

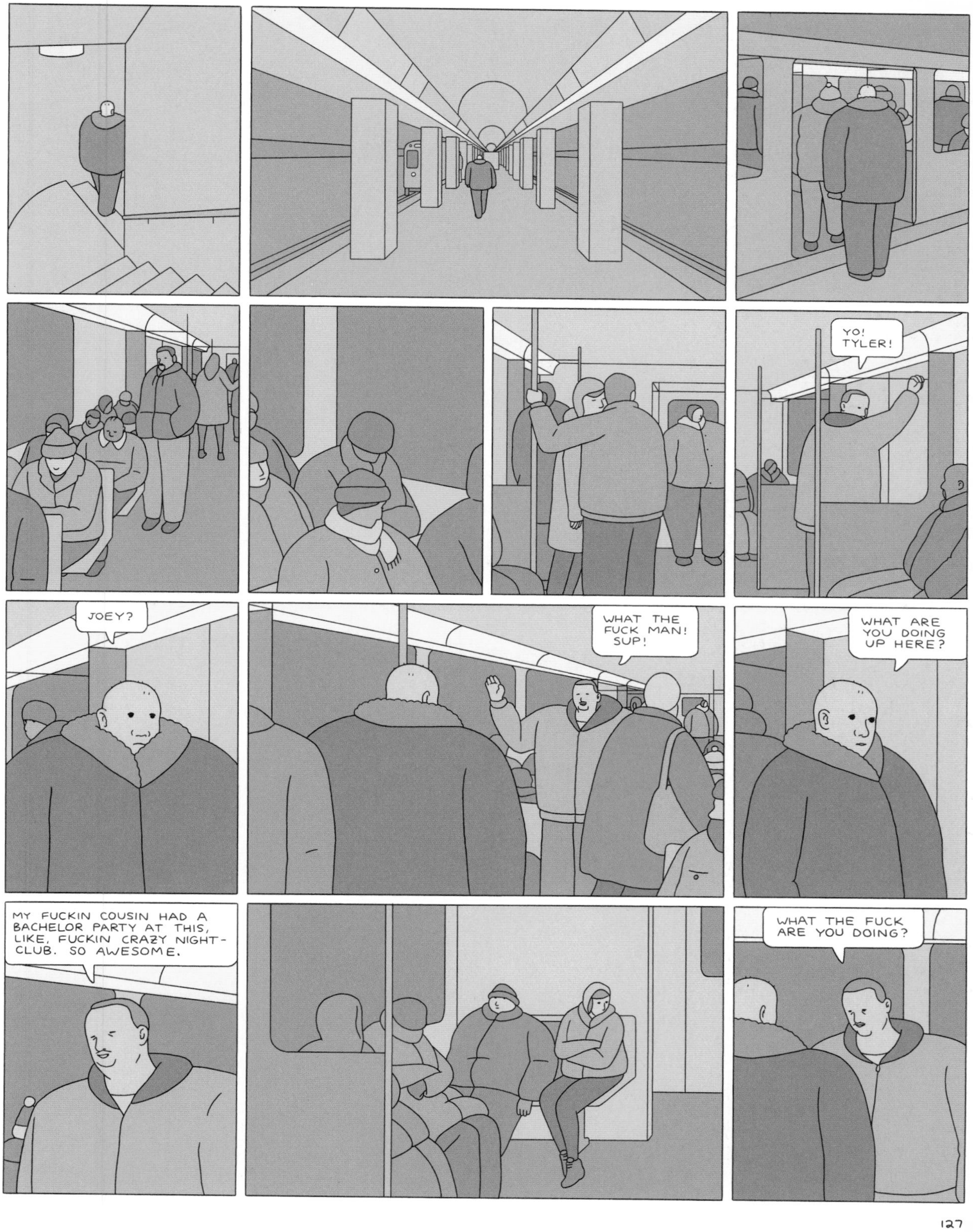
YO! TYLER!
JOEY?
WHAT THE FUCK MAN! SUP!
WHAT ARE YOU DOING UP HERE?
MY FUCKIN COUSIN HAD A BACHELOR PARTY AT THIS, LIKE, FUCKIN CRAZY NIGHT-CLUB. SO AWESOME.
WHAT THE FUCK ARE YOU DOING?

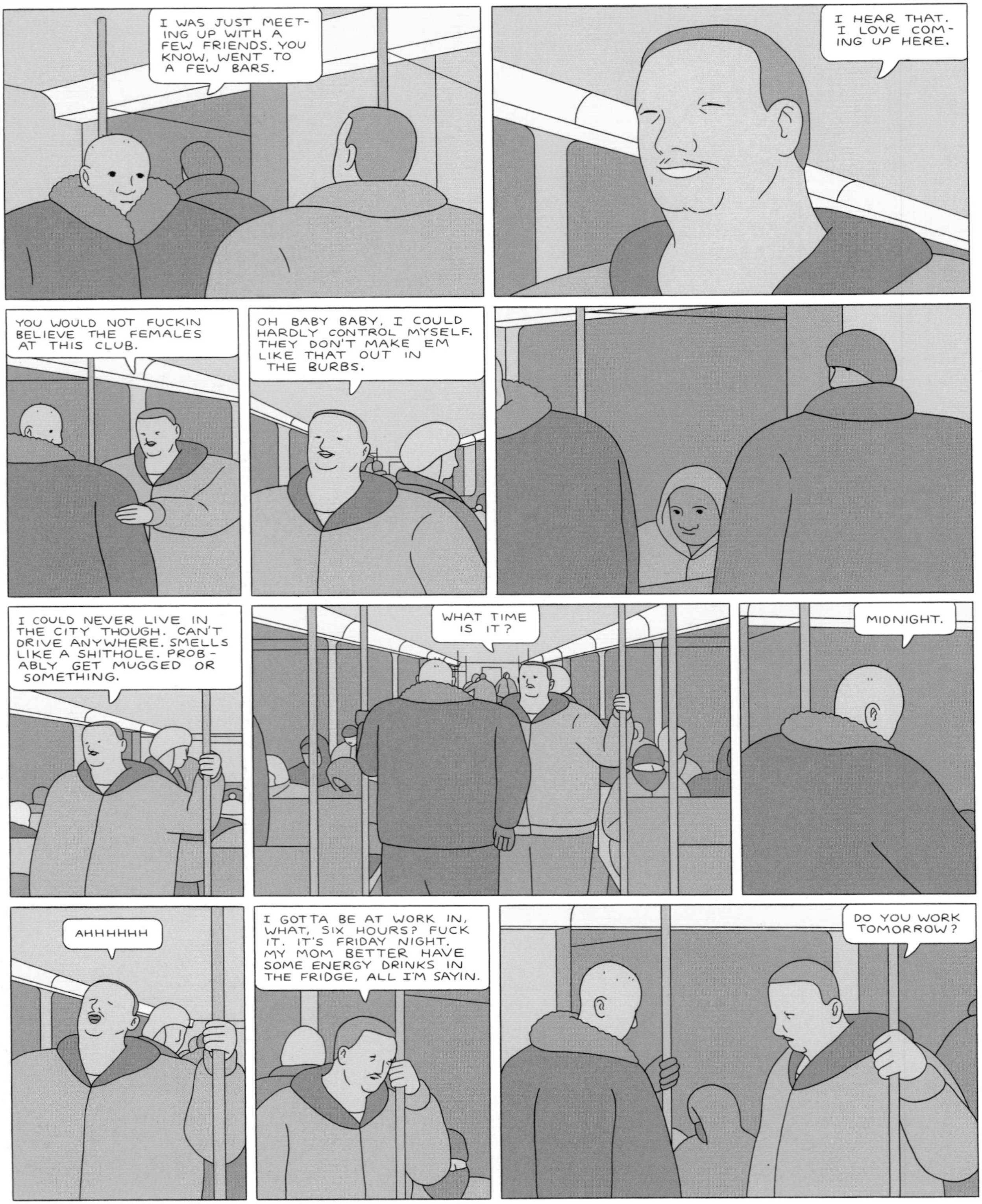

I WAS JUST MEETING UP WITH A FEW FRIENDS. YOU KNOW, WENT TO A FEW BARS.
I HEAR THAT. I LOVE COMING UP HERE.
YOU WOULD NOT FUCKIN BELIEVE THE FEMALES AT THIS CLUB.
OH BABY BABY, I COULD HARDLY CONTROL MYSELF. THEY DON'T MAKE EM LIKE THAT OUT IN THE BURBS.
I COULD NEVER LIVE IN THE CITY THOUGH. CAN'T DRIVE ANYWHERE. SMELLS LIKE A SHITHOLE. PROBABLY GET MUGGED OR SOMETHING.
WHAT TIME IS IT?
MIDNIGHT.
AHHHHHH
I GOTTA BE AT WORK IN, WHAT, SIX HOURS? FUCK IT. IT'S FRIDAY NIGHT. MY MOM BETTER HAVE SOME ENERGY DRINKS IN THE FRIDGE, ALL I'M SAYIN.
DO YOU WORK TOMORROW?

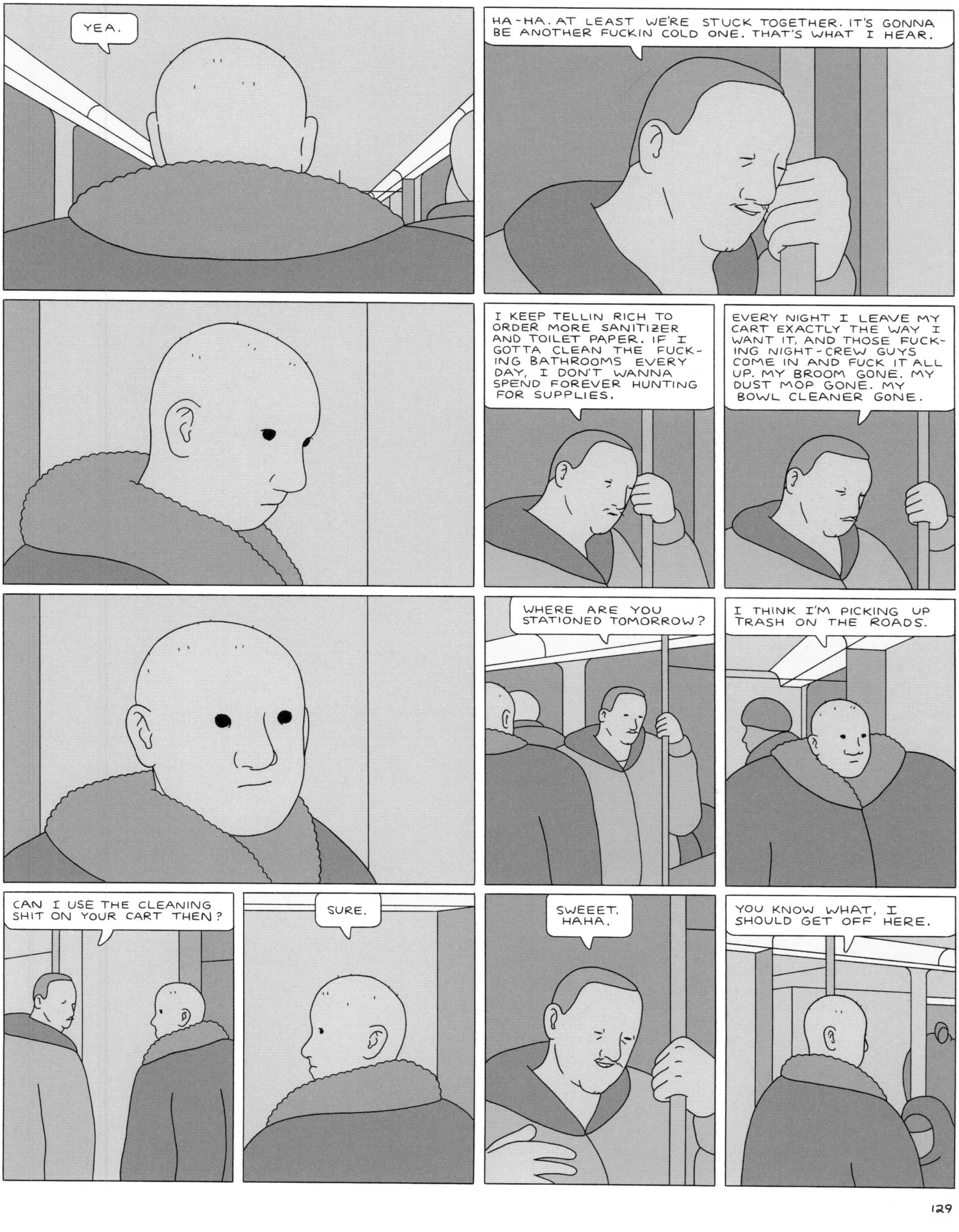
YEA.
HA-HA. AT LEAST WE'RE STUCK TOGETHER. IT'S GONNA BE ANOTHER FUCKIN COLD ONE. THAT'S WHAT I HEAR.
I KEEP TELLIN RICH TO ORDER MORE SANITIZER AND TOILET PAPER. IF I GOTTA CLEAN THE FUCKING BATHROOMS EVERY DAY, I DON'T WANNA SPEND FOREVER HUNTING FOR SUPPLIES.
EVERY NIGHT I LEAVE MY CART EXACTLY THE WAY I WANT IT, AND THOSE FUCKING NIGHT-CREW GUYS COME IN AND FUCK IT ALL UP. MY BROOM GONE. MY DUST MOP GONE. MY BOWL CLEANER GONE.
WHERE ARE YOU STATIONED TOMORROW?
I THINK I'M PICKING UP TRASH ON THE ROADS.
CAN I USE THE CLEANING SHIT ON YOUR CART THEN?
SURE.
SWEEET. HAHA.
YOU KNOW WHAT, I SHOULD GET OFF HERE.

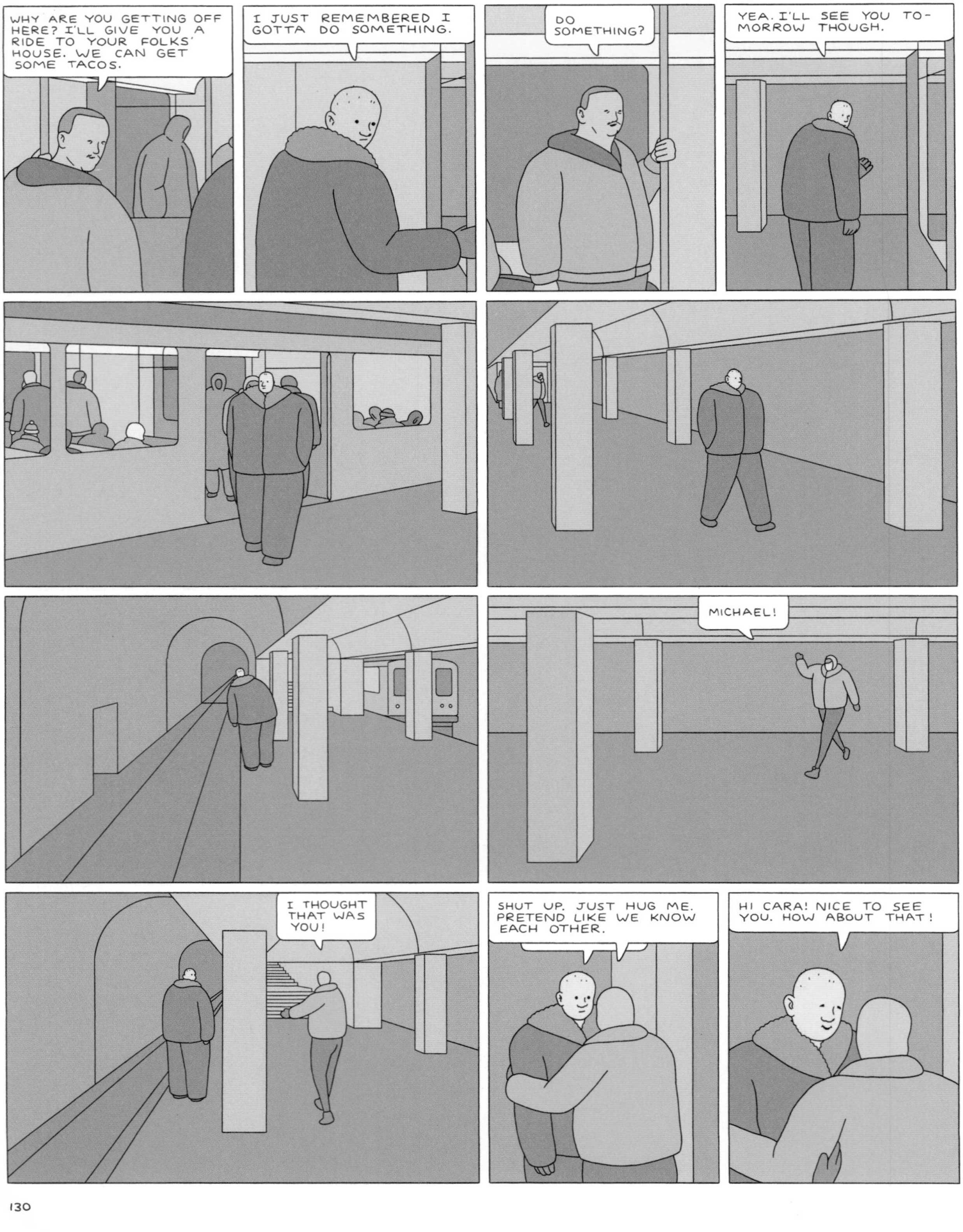
WHY ARE YOU GETTING OFF HERE? I'LL GIVE YOU A RIDE TO YOUR FOLKS' HOUSE. WE CAN GET SOME TACOS.
I JUST REMEMBERED I GOTTA DO SOMETHING.
DO SOMETHING?
YEA. I'LL SEE YOU TO-MORROW THOUGH.
MICHAEL!
I THOUGHT THAT WAS YOU!
SHUT UP. JUST HUG ME. PRETEND LIKE WE KNOW EACH OTHER.
HI CARA! NICE TO SEE YOU. HOW ABOUT THAT!

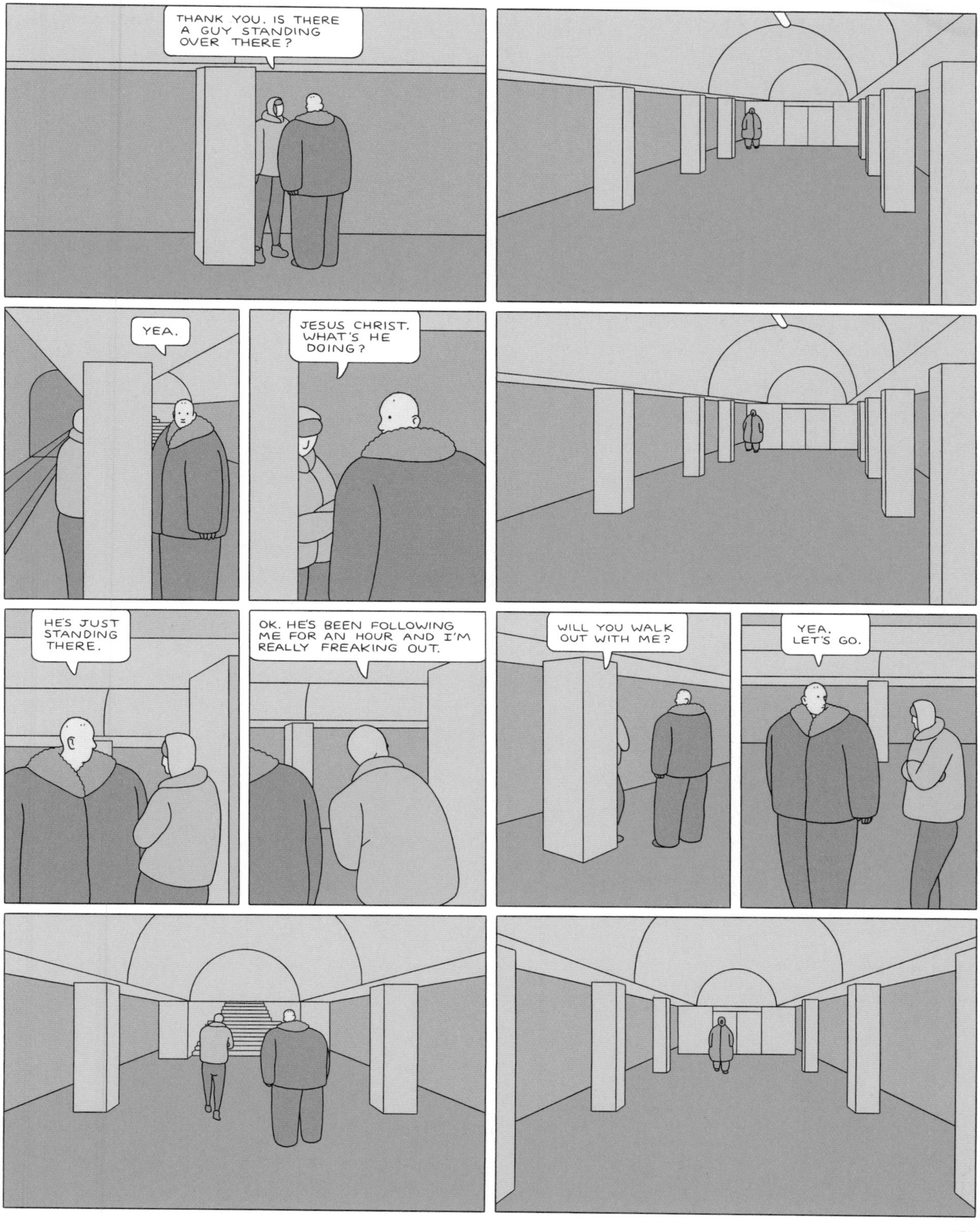
THANK YOU. IS THERE A GUY STANDING OVER THERE?
YEA.
JESUS CHRIST. WHAT'S HE DOING?
HE'S JUST STANDING THERE.
OK. HE'S BEEN FOLLOWING ME FOR AN HOUR AND I'M REALLY FREAKING OUT.
WILL YOU WALK OUT WITH ME?
YEA. LET'S GO.

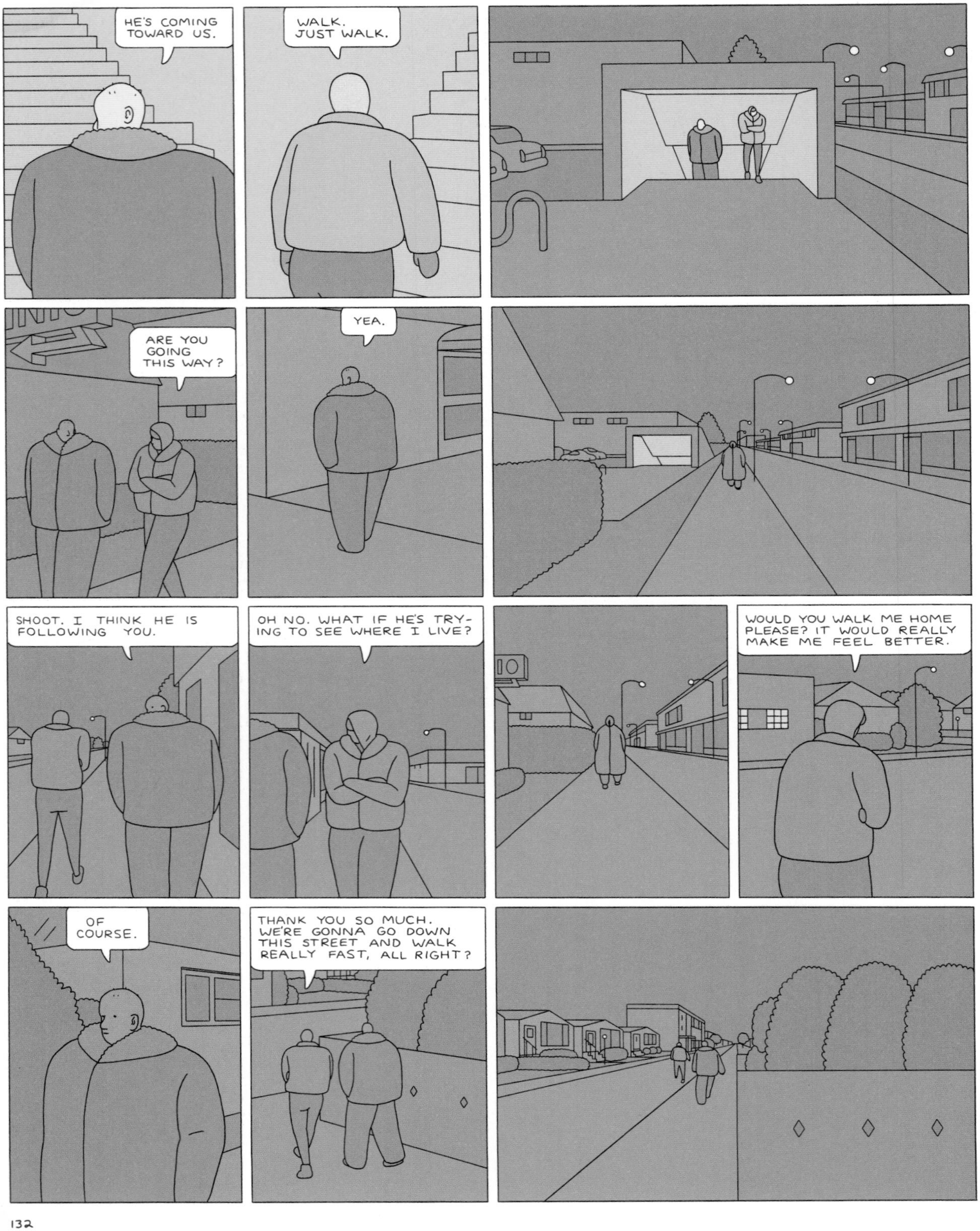
HE'S COMING TOWARD US.
WALK. JUST WALK.
ARE YOU GOING THIS WAY?
YEA.
SHOOT. I THINK HE IS FOLLOWING YOU.
OH NO. WHAT IF HE'S TRY-ING TO SEE WHERE I LIVE?
WOULD YOU WALK ME HOME PLEASE? IT WOULD REALLY MAKE ME FEEL BETTER.
OF COURSE.
THANK YOU SO MUCH. WE'RE GONNA GO DOWN THIS STREET AND WALK REALLY FAST, ALL RIGHT?

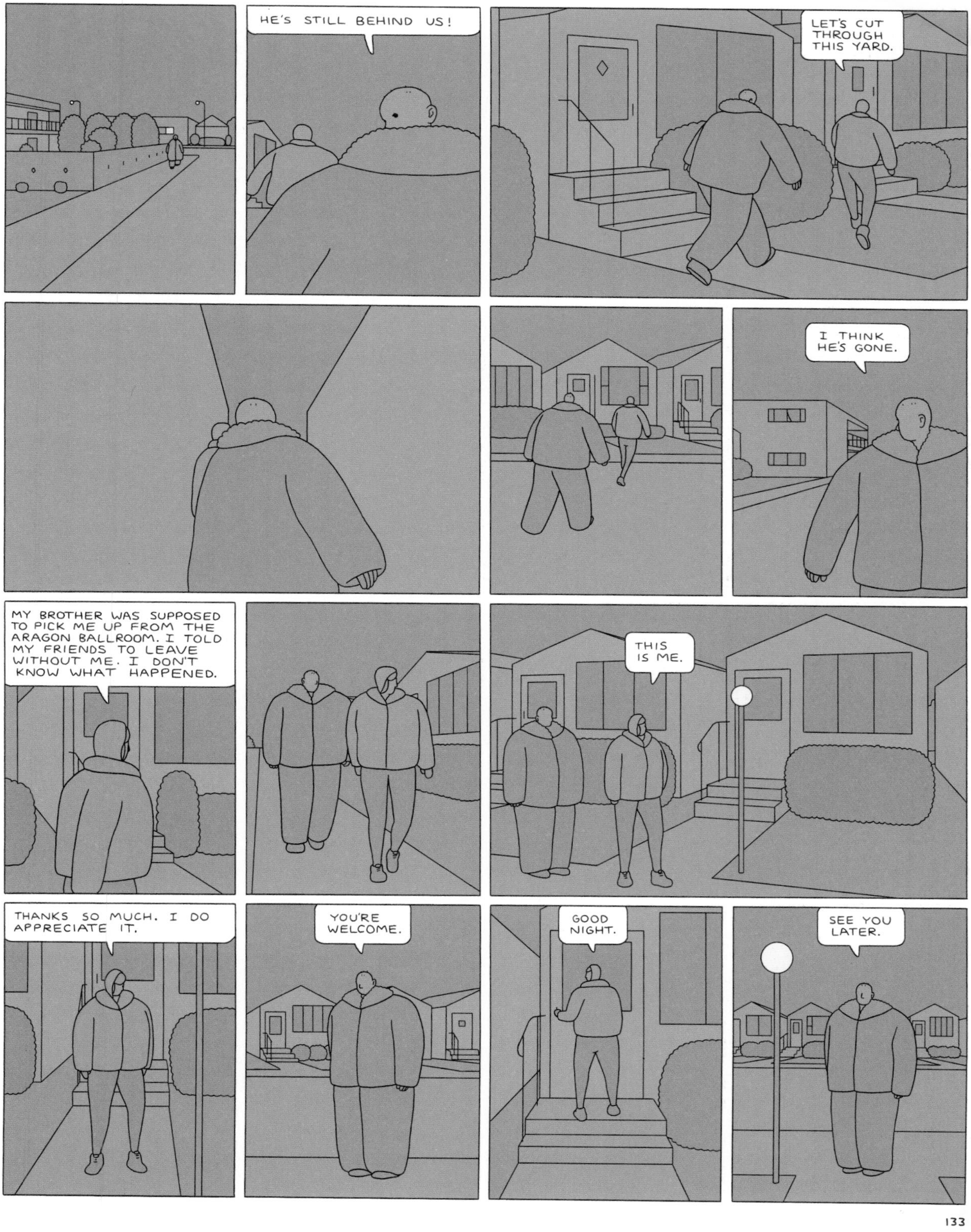
HE'S STILL BEHIND US!
LET'S CUT THROUGH THIS YARD.
I THINK HE'S GONE.
MY BROTHER WAS SUPPOSED TO PICK ME UP FROM THE ARAGON BALLROOM. I TOLD MY FRIENDS TO LEAVE WITHOUT ME. I DON'T KNOW WHAT HAPPENED.
THIS IS ME.
THANKS SO MUCH. I DO APPRECIATE IT.
YOU'RE WELCOME.
GOOD NIGHT.
SEE YOU LATER.

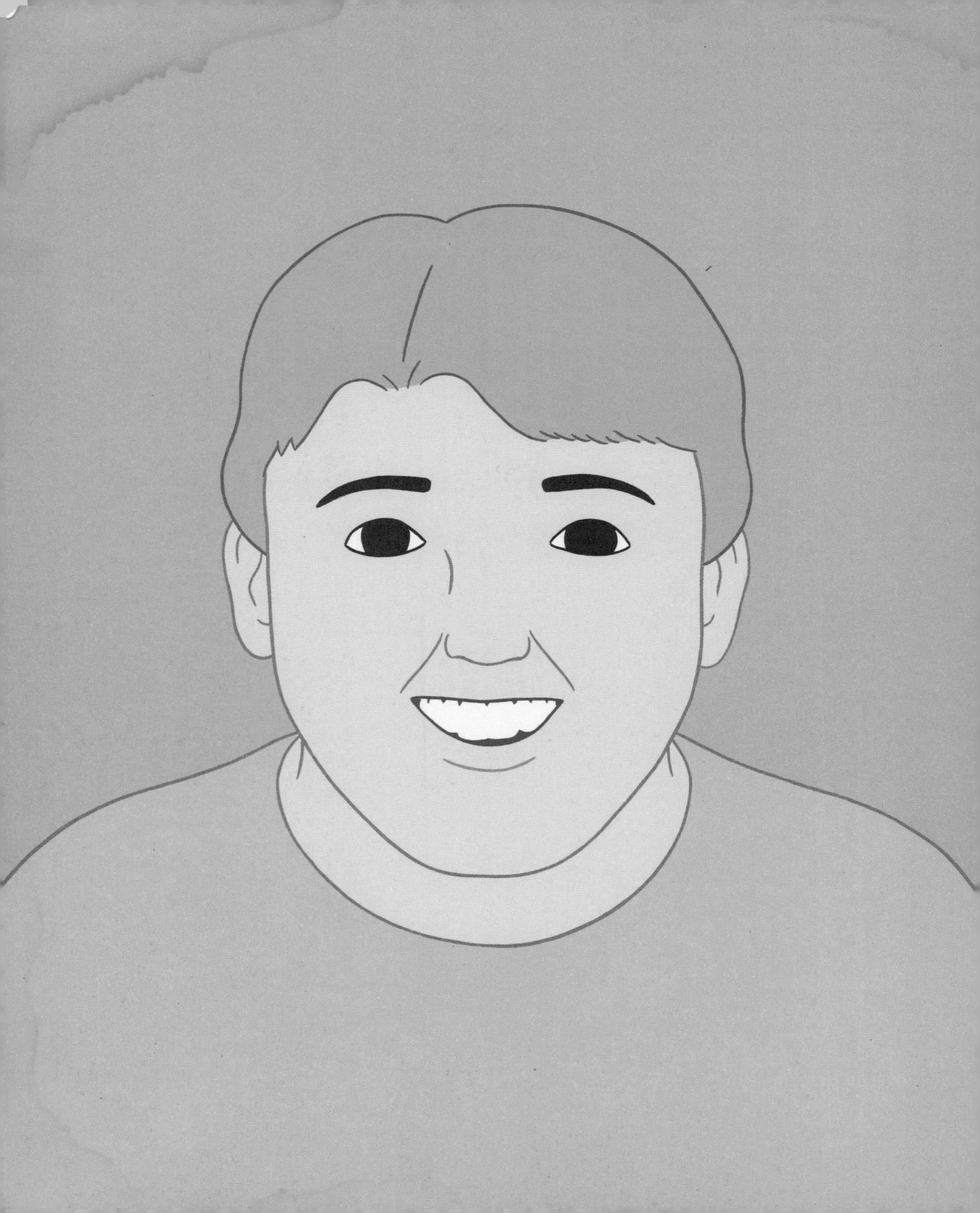